ITALIAN RENAISSANCE ARCHITECTURE

ÉDITIONS
PLACE DES
VICTOIRES

KÖNEMANN

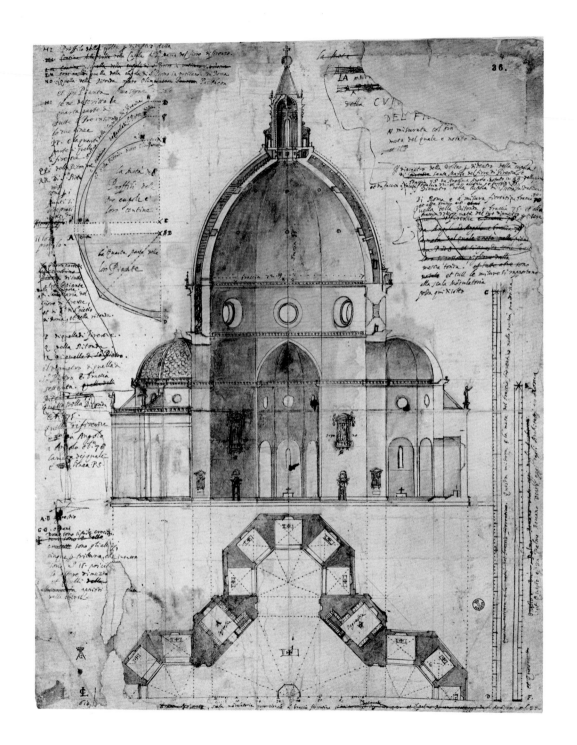

36.

MARCO BUSSAGLI

ITALIAN RENAISSANCE ARCHITECTURE

L'ARCHITECTURE DE LA RENAISSANCE ITALIENNE
ARCHITEKTUR DER RENAISSANCE IN ITALIEN
LA ARQUITECTURA ITALIANA DEL RENACIMIENTO
ARCHITETTURA ITALIANA DEL RINASCIMENTO
ARQUITETURA ITALIANA DO RENASCIMENTO
DE ITALIAANSE RENAISSANCE-ARCHITECTUUR

P. 2

Ludovico Cardi (Cigoli)

Santa Maria del Fiore, Firenze

First publication © 2012
Magnus Edizioni Srl, Udine, Italy

KÖNEMANN

© 2018 koenemann.com GmbH
www.koenemann.com

ÉDITIONS
PLACE DES
VICTOIRES

© Éditions Place des Victoires
6, rue du Mail – 75002 Paris
www.victoires.com
ISBN: 978-2-8099-1658-4

Concept, Project Management: koenemann.com GmbH

Translations: Textcase, NL

Layout: Oliver Hessmann

ISBN: 978-3-7419-2227-5

Printed in China by Shenzhen Hua Xin Colour-printing & Platemaking Co., Ltd

panteon

Raffaello

Pantheon, Roma

FRIULI-VENEZIA GIULIA

Udine • • Cividale del Friuli
• Palmanova

LOMBARDIA

VENETO

Lugo di Vicenza
Maser
Fanzolo di Vedelago
Piombino Dese
San Pietro in Cariano
Vicenza
Verona
Venezia
Milano
Mira
Lonigo
Pontecasale di Candiana
Mantova
Battaglia Terme
Pavia
Pojana Maggiore
Fratta Polesine
Parma
Ferrara

EMILIA-ROMAGNA

Bologna

Rimini
San Leo
Poggio a Caiano
Senigallia
Artimino
Firenze
Urbino
Pisa
Giogoli
Mondavio

TOSCANA

MARCHE

Montepulciano
Pienza
UMBRIA
Todi

Caprarola
L'Aquila

ABRUZZO
Roma

LAZIO

CAMPANIA

Napoli

SICILIA

Palermo

Contents Sommaire Inhalt Índice Indice Índice Inhoud

Italian Renaissance Architecture

The development of Italian Renaissance architecture was one of the most relevant cultural phenomena of the 15th and 16th centuries, not only for the environment that gave birth to it and for centuries followed its course, but also for the reverberations it caused outside of Italy and in the epochs that followed. In fact, it became the reference model for most European courts, which were inspired as much by the decorative elements (take for example France's palace at Fontainebleau or Scotland's Stirling Castle) as by the architectonic system and stylistic conventions. Italian Renaissance architecture was in fact nothing more than a new iteration of Greco-roman architectonic precepts adapted to new structures such as churches, hospitals, and palaces; although it was also used in forms already present in the ancient world such as theatres and villas, now reconsidered in light of different historical and social needs.

This extraordinary flowering, theorised and implemented by people of absolute genius such as Filippo Brunelleschi and Leon Battista Alberti (to limit ourselves to the most prominent figures), encompasses masterpieces such as the dome of Santa Maria del Fiore in Florence or that of Saint Peter's in Rome, as well as perfectly harmonious structures such as Maser's Villa Barbaro, Vicenza's Basilica and Venice's Biblioteca Marciana. These masterpieces became benchmarks for later periods, as much for the emergence of new styles, such as the Neoclassical, as for the design of religious buildings (St. Paul's Cathedral in London) or institutions (the Capitol in Washington D.C.), the domes of which are derived directly from that designed by Michelangelo for St. Peter's in Rome. One need only look at the development of that peculiar cultural phenomenon known as "Palladianism" that was of interest, first of all, to the Anglo-Saxon civilizations of the 17th and 18th centuries—by which is meant not solely that of Great Britain but also its counterpart in the United States—to immediately realise the importance of the role played by Italian Renaissance architecture in the world. A unique artistic period that lasted for almost two centuries, from the early 1400s through the end of the 1500s, two points in time perfectly reflected in the figures of Brunelleschi and Buontalenti.

Donato Bramante

Tempietto di San Pietro in Montorio, Roma

Giuliano da S. Gallo   Archit: Fiorent:

10

L'Architecture italienne de la Renaissance

L e développement de l'architecture Renaissance en Italie a été l'un des phénomènes culturels les plus importants aux XVᵉ et XVIᵉ siècles, non seulement pour le pays dans lequel elle est née et pour les siècles qui l'ont vue s'épanouir, mais aussi pour les échos multiples qu'elle a fait naître, bien au-delà des frontières de l'Italie et au cours des époques qui ont suivi. La Renaissance italienne est en effet devenue le modèle de référence pour un grand nombre de cours européennes qui s'en inspirèrent aussi bien pour la décoration (pensons par exemple au palais royal de Fontainebleau, en France, ou au château de Stirling, en Écosse) que pour l'architecture et les codes stylistiques. L'architecture Renaissance italienne n'est en fait rien d'autre qu'une nouvelle élaboration des principes architecturaux gréco-romains, adaptés à des édifices nouveaux comme les églises, les palais ou les hôpitaux, mais aussi à des monuments déjà présents dans le monde antique, comme les théâtres ou les villas, repensés à la lumière d'exigences historiques et sociales différentes.

Cet épanouissement extraordinaire, conceptualisé et réalisé par de purs génies comme Filippo Brunelleschi ou Leon Battista Alberti (pour ne s'en tenir qu'aux plus illustres) aligne des chefs-d'œuvre absolus comme la coupole de Santa Maria del Fiore à Florence ou celle de Saint-Pierre de Rome ; ou bien des édifices civils d'une harmonie parfaite comme la Villa Barbaro à Maser, la Basilique de Vicence ou la Bibliothèque Marciana à Venise. Tous vont devenir des points de référence pour les époques suivantes, autant pour la naissance de nouveaux styles (comme le néo-classicisme) que pour la conception de monuments religieux (la cathédrale Saint-Paul, à Londres) ou d'édifices civils (le Capitole, à Washington) dont les coupoles dérivent directement de celle de Saint-Pierre de Rome créée par Michel-Ange. Si l'on pense par ailleurs au phénomène particulier connu sous le nom de « palladianisme » qui affecte avant tout la culture anglo-saxonne des XVIIᵉ et XVIIIᵉ siècles, non seulement en Grande-Bretagne mais aussi aux États-Unis, on se rendra immédiatement compte de l'importance du rôle joué par l'architecture Renaissance italienne dans le monde. Cette période artistique unique va durer presque deux siècles, du début du XVᵉ à la fin du XVIᵉ, marqués par les figures de Brunelleschi et de Buontalenti.

Architektur der Renaissance in Italien

D ie Entwicklung der italienischen Architektur der Renaissance bedeutete eines der wichtigsten kulturellen Phänomene des 15. und 16. Jahrhunderts – nicht nur für die Umgebung, die sie hervorbrachte und jahrhundertelang ihrem Kurs folgte, sondern auch für das Echo, das sie außerhalb Italiens und in den folgenden Epochen auslöste. Genau genommen wurde sie zum Referenzmodell der meisten europäischen Höfe, die von den dekorativen Elementen (beispielsweise das Schloss im französischen Fontainebleau oder das schottische Stirling Castle) wie vom architektonischen System und den stilistischen Konventionen gleichermaßen inspiriert wurden. Die Architektur der italienischen Renaissance war eigentlich nicht mehr als eine Wiederholung der griechisch-römischen Prinzipien, die an neue Strukturen wie Kirchen, Krankenhäuser und Schlösser adaptiert wurden. Obwohl sie auch in bereits in der Antike bekannten Formen wie Theatern und Villen eingesetzt wurde, wurde sie jetzt im Lichte veränderter historischer und sozialer Bedürfnisse wieder aufgenommen.

Diese außergewöhnliche Blütezeit, die von Personen absoluten Genies wie Filippo Brunelleschi und Leon Battista Alberti (um uns auf die prominentesten Figuren zu beschränken) theoretisiert und umgesetzt wurde, umfasst Meisterwerke wie die Kathedrale von Santa Maria del Fiore in Florenz oder den Petersdom in Rom, und auch die perfekt harmonischen Strukturen wie in der Villa Barbaro in Maser, der Basilika von Vicenza und der Biblioteca Marciana von Venedig. Diese Meisterwerke wurden zu Maßstäben für spätere Epochen, ebenso wie für die Entstehung neuer Stile wie der Neoklassik, aber auch für das Design religiöser Gebäude (St. Paul's Cathedral in London) oder Institutionen (Kapitol in Washington D.C.), deren Kuppeln direkt von den von Michelangelo für den Petersdom in Rom entworfenen abgeleitet sind. Es genügt schon, die Entstehung des einzigartigen kulturellen Phänomens mit dem Namen „Palladianismus" zu betrachten, da dieses allen voran für die angelsächsischen Zivilisationen des 17. und 18. Jahrhunderts interessant war – womit nicht nur Großbritannien gemeint ist, sondern auch dessen Pendant in den Vereinigten Staaten – um die Wichtigkeit der Rolle der italienischen Architektur der Renaissance in der Welt zu bemerken. Eine einzigartige künstlerische Periode, die für beinahe zwei Jahrhunderte bestand: vom frühen 15. Jahrhundert bis zum Ende des 16. Jahrhunderts. Zwei Zeitpunkte in der Geschichte, die in den Figuren Brunelleschi und Buontalenti perfekt widergespiegelt werden.

Giuliano da Sangallo

Chiesa di San Lorenzo, Firenze

Michelangelo

Porta Pia, Roma

La arquitectura italiana del Renacimiento

El desarrollo de la arquitectura del Renacimiento italiano fue uno de los fenómenos culturales más importantes de los siglos XV y XVI, no sólo por el ambiente donde surgió y por los siglos que perduró, sino por la repercusión que tuvo incluso fuera de Italia y en las épocas sucesivas. De hecho, se convirtió en el modelo de referencia para la mayoría de las cortes europeas. Se inspiraron en el Renacimiento para la decoración (por ejemplo, el palacio de Fontainebleau, Francia, o el castillo de Stirling, Escocia) e incluso para el diseño arquitectónico y el código estilístico. La arquitectura del Renacimiento italiano no fue más que una nueva elaboración de los modelos arquitectónicos greco-romanos adaptados a nuevos edificios como iglesias, hospitales y palacios, e incluso a tipologías ya presentes en el mundo antiguo, como teatros y palacetes, en la actualidad renovados por las diferentes exigencias sociales e históricas.

Este extraordinario florecimiento, teorizado y protagonizado por personajes con una genialidad excepcional como Filippo Brunelleschi y Leon Battista Alberti (sólo por nombrar algunos de los personajes de mayor relevancia), incluye obras de arte como la cúpula de Santa Maria del Fiore en Florencia o de San Pedro en Roma, o incluso edificios de gran armonía como Villa Barbaro en Maser o la Basílica de Vicenza y la Biblioteca Marciana de Venecia, que se convirtieron en puntos de referencia de las épocas sucesivas, tanto por el nacimiento de nuevos estilos como el neoclásico, como por el diseño de edificios religiosos (la catedral de San Pablo en Londres) o de instituciones (el Capitolio de Washington) cuyas cúpulas derivan directamente de la de San Pedro, diseñada por Miguel Ángel. Posteriormente, se desarrolló un particular fenómeno cultural denominado "Palladianismo" y que interesó, sobre todo, a la civilización anglosajona de los siglos XVII y XVIII, no sólo a Gran Bretaña en sentido estricto sino también a su correspondencia en Estados Unidos, e inmediatamente se supo la importancia del papel que jugó la arquitectura del Renacimiento italiano en todo el mundo. Un período artístico irrepetible que duró alrededor de dos siglos, desde principios del año 1400 hasta finales de 1500: dos épocas marcadas por las figuras de Brunelleschi y Buontalenti.

Architettura italiana del Rinascimento

Lo sviluppo dell'architettura rinascimentale italiana fu uno dei fenomeni culturali più rilevanti del XV e XVI secolo, non solo per l'ambiente nel quale nacque e per i secoli che ne videro il percorso, ma anche per gli echi che ne derivarono, anche al di fuori del territorio italiano e nelle epoche successive. Essa, infatti, divenne il modello di riferimento per gran parte delle corti europee che a essa s'ispirarono tanto per la decorazione (si pensi, per esempio, alla reggia di Fontainebleau in Francia oppure al castello di Stirling in Scozia) quanto per l'impianto architettonico e per il codice stilistico. L'architettura rinascimentale italiana, infatti, altro non fu che una nuova elaborazione dei precetti architettonici greco-romani adattati a nuovi edifici come le chiese, gli ospedali e i palazzi, ma anche a tipologie già presenti nel mondo antico, come i teatri e le ville, adesso ripensati alla luce delle diverse esigenze sociali e storiche.

Questa straordinaria fioritura, teorizzata ed attuata da personaggi di assoluta genialità come Filippo Brunelleschi e Leon Battista Alberti (tanto per limitarci ai nomi di maggior spicco), annovera capolavori come la cupola di Santa Maria del Fiore a Firenze o di San Pietro a Roma, oppure edifici di assoluta armonia come Villa Barbaro a Maser, o la Basilica di Vicenza e la Biblioteca Marciana a Venezia, che divennero punti di riferimento per le epoche successive, tanto per la nascita di nuovi stili come quello neoclassico, quanto per la progettazione di edifici religiosi (la cattedrale di Saint Paul a Londra) o delle istituzioni (il Campidoglio di Washington) le cui cupole derivano direttamente da quella di San Pietro a Roma, disegnata da Michelangelo. Si pensi, poi allo sviluppo di quel particolare fenomeno culturale che va sotto il nome di "Palladianesimo" e che interessò, prima di tutto, la civiltà anglosassone del XVII e del XVIII secolo, intendendo per tale non solo la Gran Bretagna in senso stretto ma pure il suo corrispettivo statunitense, e ci si renderà immediatamente conto dell'importanza del ruolo avuto dalla architettura rinascimentale italiana nel mondo. Un periodo artistico irripetibile durato quasi due secoli, dai primi del '400 alla fine del '500: due termini temporali che trovano un preciso riscontro nelle figure di Brunelleschi e del Buontalenti.

Andrea Palladio

Tempietto

Arquitetura italiana do Renascimento

O desenvolvimento da arquitetura renascentista italiana foi um dos fenómenos culturais de maior relevância dos séculos XV e XVI, não apenas pela atmosfera na qual nasceu e pelos séculos que assistiram ao seu percurso, mas também pelos ecos que dela reverberaram, também para lá do território italiano e nas épocas que se sucederam. Aquela, de facto, tornou-se o modelo de referência para uma grande parte das cortes europeias que nela se inspiraram, tanto no que se refere à decoração (pensemos, por exemplo, no palácio de Fontainebleau em França ou no castelo de Stirling na Escócia) como no que respeita à estrutura arquitetónica e ao código estilístico. Na verdade, a arquitetura renascentista italiana não foi mais que uma reelaboração dos preceitos arquitetónicos greco-romanos, adaptados não só a novos edifícios, como igrejas, hospitais e palácios, mas também a tipologias já presentes no mundo antigo, como os teatros e as vilas, então repensadas à luz de diferentes exigências sociais e históricas.

Este extraordinário florescimento, teorizado e realizado por figuras de uma genialidade absoluta, como Filippo Brunelleschi e Leon Battista Alberti (para nos limitarmos aos nomes de maior relevo), conta com obras-primas como a cúpula de Santa Maria del Fiore em Florença ou a de São Pedro em Roma, e com edifícios de uma harmonia absoluta, como vila Barbaro em Maser ou a Basílica de Vicenza e a Biblioteca Marciana em Veneza, que se tornaram pontos de referência para as épocas que se seguiram, tanto no nascimento de novos estilos, como o neoclássico, como no traçado de edifícios religiosos (a Catedral de São Paulo em Londres) ou de Instituições (o Capitólio em Washington), cujas cúpulas se inspiram diretamente na de São Pedro, em Roma, projetada por Michelangelo. Pensemos, também, no desenvolvimento daquele fenómeno cultural específico que surge sob o nome de "Palladianismo", e que suscitou a atenção, sobretudo, da civilização anglo-saxónica dos séculos XVII e XVIII, significando isto não apenas a Grã-Bretanha em sentido estrito mas também a sua contraparte norte-americana, e dar-nos-emos imediatamente conta da importância do papel desempenhado pela arquitetura renascentista italiana no mundo. Um período artístico irrepetível que durou quase dois séculos, do início dos anos 1400 ao final dos anos 1500: dois limites temporais que encontram uma confirmação rigorosa nas figuras de Brunelleschi e de Buontalenti.

Italiaanse renaissance-architectuur

De opkomst van de Italiaanse renaissance-architectuur is een van de belangrijkste culturele fenomenen uit de 15e en 16e eeuw. Niet alleen door waar het plaatsvond en wanneer het zich afspeelde, maar ook door de navolging die het kreeg; ook buiten Italië en in latere tijden. De Italiaanse renaissance-architectuur kreeg een voorbeeldfunctie voor een groot deel van de Europese hoven, die zich zowel lieten inspireren door de decoraties (denk bijvoorbeeld aan Château de Fontainebleau in Frankrijk of aan Stirling Castle in Schotland), als door de architectonische structuur en stijlcode. De Italiaanse renaissance-architectuur was in feite niets anders dan een moderne bewerking van Grieks-Romeinse architectonische regels, die werden toegepast op zowel nieuwe gebouwen zoals kerken, ziekenhuizen en palazzo's, als op gebouwen die er al waren in de antieke wereld, zoals theaters en villa's, en waar inmiddels, in het licht van de veranderde maatschappelijke en geschiedkundige eisen, anders tegenaan werd gekeken.

Uit deze uitzonderlijke bloeitijd, getheoretiseerd en gerealiseerd door absolute genieën als Filippo Brunelleschi en Leon Battista Alberti (om ons maar even te beperken tot de meest vooraanstaande namen), stammen meesterwerken als de koepel van de Santa Maria del Fiore in Florence en de Sint-Pieter in Rome, en gebouwen van volstrekte harmonie zoals Villa Barbaro in Maser, de basiliek van Vicenza en de Marciana-bibliotheek in Venetië. In de daaropvolgende eeuwen werden die het referentiepunt voor zowel opkomende nieuwe stijlen zoals het neoclassicisme, als voor het ontwerp van religieuze gebouwen (St. Paul's Cathedral in Londen) en staatsgebouwen (het Capitool in Washington), waarvan de koepels rechtstreekse kopieën zijn van de door Michelangelo ontworpen koepel van de Sint-Pieter in Rome. Denk ook aan de opkomst van dat bijzondere culturele fenomeen genaamd 'palladianisme', dat vooral de Angelsaksische cultuur van de 17e en 18e eeuw beïnvloedde; niet uitsluitend die van Groot-Brittannië, maar ook die van de Verenigde Staten, en het wordt meteen duidelijk hoe belangrijk de rol van de Italiaanse renaissance-architectuur in de wereld is geweest. Een unieke artistieke periode die bijna twee eeuwen duurde, van begin 1400 tot eind 16e eeuw; twee tijdsgrenzen die nauwkeurig worden afgebakend door de twee personen Brunelleschi en Buontalenti.

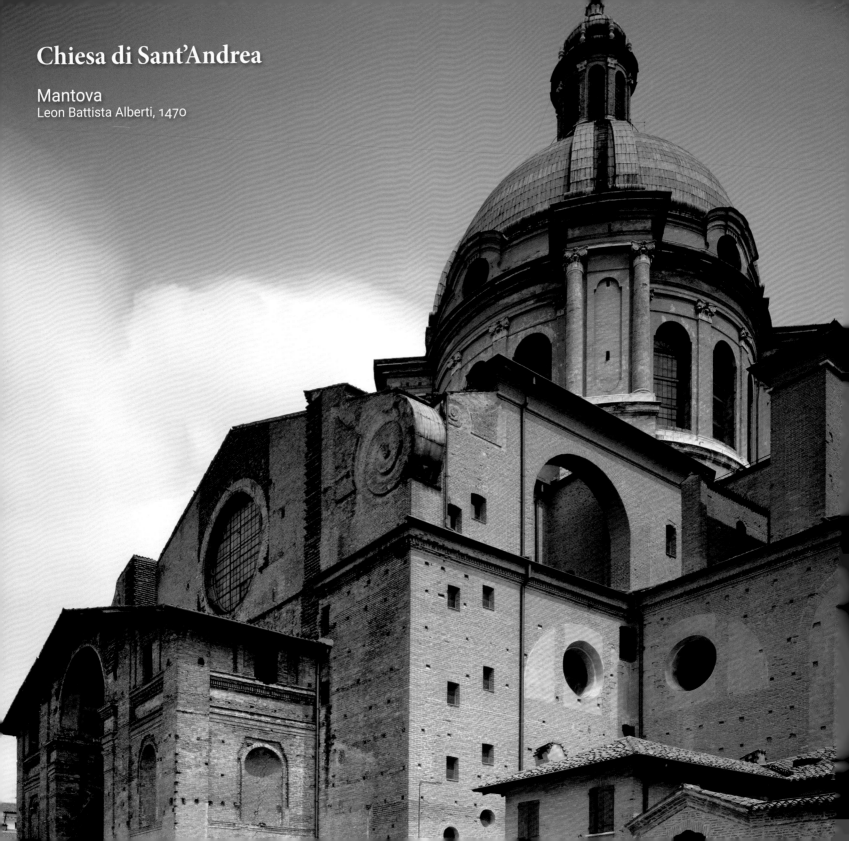

Chiesa di Sant'Andrea

Mantova
Leon Battista Alberti, 1470

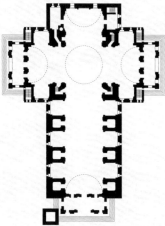

The church is one of the greatest expressions of Renaissance religious architecture. The façade features an impressive (triumphal) arch crowned by a solemn pediment.

Cette église est l'une des expressions majeures de l'architecture sacrée de la Renaissance. La façade s'inspire du monde classique et se présente comme un imposant arc de triomphe, couronné par un fronton solennel.

Sie weist alle typischen Stilelemente der religiösen Architektur der Renaissance auf. Die Fassade präsentiert sich mit einem imposanten (Triumph-)Bogen, gekrönt von einem erhabenen Dreiecksgiebel.

Es una de las máximas expresiones de la arquitectura religiosa renacentista. La fachada presenta un imponente arco (triunfal), coronado por un solemne frontón.

È una delle massime espressioni dell'architettura religiosa rinascimentale. La facciata si presenta con un imponente arco (trionfale), coronato da un solenne frontone.

É uma das expressões máximas da arquitetura religiosa renascentista. A fachada apresenta um imponente arco (triunfal) coroado por um solene frontão.

Dit is een van de sterke staaltjes religieuze architectuur uit de Renaissance. De voorgevel bevat een indrukwekkende (triomf)boog, die bekroond wordt door een statig fronton.

Palazzo Te

Mantova
Giulio Romano, 1524–1534

In 1524 Giulio Romano, Raphael's most talented apprentice, arrived at the court of Federico Gonzaga at Mantua, with the task of redesigning the whole existing complex.

En 1524, Giulio Romano, le meilleur élève de Raphaël – arrive à la cour des Gonzague, à Mantoue, avec la charge de remanier la totalité de l'ensemble existant.

1524 ging Giulio Romano, der beste Schüler von Raffaello, an den Hof von Federico Gonzaga in Mantua, mit dem Auftrag, den ganzen Komplex neu zu entwerfen.

En 1524, Giulio Romano, el mejor discípulo de Rafael, se une a la corte de Federico II Gonzaga en Mantua con el cometido de volver a diseñar el complejo existente completamente.

Nel 1524 Giulio Romano, il migliore allievo di Raffaello, approda alla corte di Federico II Gonzaga a Mantova con l'incarico di riprogettare l'intero complesso esistente.

Em 1524, Giulio Romano e o melhor dos discípulos de Raffaello, apresenta-se na corte dos Gonzaga, em Mântua, com o encargo de projetar novamente todo o complexo já existente.

In 1524 kwam Giulio Romano, de beste leerling van Rafaël, naar het hof van Federico Gonzaga in Mantua met de opdracht om het hele gebouw opnieuw te ontwerpen.

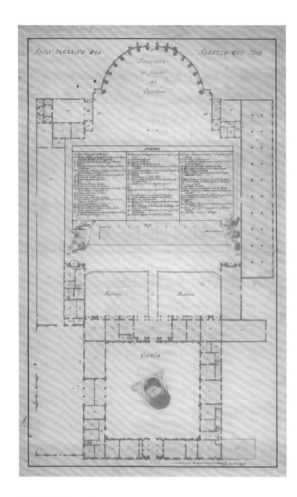

Giambattista Marconi, 1774.

Plan of the ground floor.

Plan du rez-de-chaussée.

Grundriss Erdgeschoss.

Planta baja.

Pianta del pianoterra.

Planta do piso térreo.

Plattegrond van de
benedenverdieping.

The Chamber of the Winds,
the large Renaissance fireplace.

Das Zimmer der Winde mit
dem großen Renaissance-
Kamin.

Chambre des Vents : la grande
cheminée Renaissance.

Sala de los Vientos. La gran
chimenea renacentista.

Camera dei Venti. Il grande
camino rinascimentale.

Sala dos Ventos. A grande
lareira renascentista.

Kamer van de Winden, de
grote renaissancistische
schouw.

Courtyard of the Secret Garden Apartment. An opening leads to the grotto room.

Cour intérieure de l'appartement du Jardin secret, invisible de l'extérieur. Une ouverture mène à l'espace de la grotte.

Innenhof des Geheimgartens. Eine Öffnung führt in das Innere der Grotte.

Patio del Apartamento del Jardín Secreto. Una abertura conduce a la gruta.

Cortile dell'Appartamento del Giardino Segreto. Un'apertura conduce al vano della grotta.

Pátio interior do Apartamento do Jardim Secreto. Uma abertura conduz ao vão da gruta.

Binnenplaats van het Appartement van de Geheime Tuin. Open toegang naar de 'grot'-ruimte.

The dramatic exedra at the end of the vast courtyard.

Une grande cour termine la scénographie de l'exèdre.

Die eindrucksvolle Exedra schließt den weiten Hof ab.

La escenográfica exedra que cierra el amplio patio.

La scenografica esedra che conclude il vasto cortile.

A êxedra magnífica que encerra o amplo pátio.

De uitgestrekte binnenplaats wordt begrensd door een indrukwekkende exedra.

The entryway portal, western façade.

Le portail d'entrée, façade ouest.

El portal de entrada, fachada oeste.

O portal de acesso, fachada oeste.

Das Eingangsportal, Westfassade.

Il portale d'ingresso, facciata ovest.

Toegangspoort, oostelijke gevel.

Palazzo Ducale

Mantova
Giulio Romano, 1531

The illustrious Wedding Room, frescoed by Andrea Mantegna between 1465 and 1474.

La célébrissime Chambre des Époux, décorée de fresques par Andrea Mantegna entre 1465 et 1474.

La célebre Habitación de los novios, con frescos de Andrea Mantegna, realizados entre 1465 y 1474.

O celebérrimo Quarto dos Esposos, decorado com frescos de Andrea Mantegna entre 1465 e 1474.

Das berühmte Hochzeitszimmer mit Fresken von Andrea Mantegna aus den Jahren 1465 bis 1474.

La celeberrima Camera degli Sposi, affrescata da Andrea Mantegna tra il 1465 e il 1474.

De beroemde Kamer van het Bruidspaar, door Andrea Mantegna beschilderd met fresco's tussen 1465 en 1474.

Exposition Gallery. Up until the last years of the 16th century, it housed part of the rich painting collection.

Galerie d'apparat. Jusqu'à la fin du Cinquecento, elle accueillait une partie de la très riche collection de tableaux.

Galleria della Mostra. Bis Ende des 16. Jahrhunderts beherbergte die Galerie eine Sammlung der wertvollsten Gemälde.

Galería de la Muestra. Hasta finales del siglo XVI albergó parte de la rica colección de cuadros.

Galleria della Mostra. Fino agli ultimi anni del Cinquecento ospitava parte della ricchissima quadreria.

Galeria da Exposição. Até aos últimos anos do século XVI reunia uma parte da riquíssima colecção de quadros.

Galerij van de Tentoonstelling. Tot eind 16e eeuw bevond zich hier een deel van de enorme schilderijencollectie.

The Marble Gallery, built in 1572 for the duke Guglielmo Gonzaga.

Galerie des Marbres, construite en 1572 pour le duc Guillaume Gonzague.

Die Galleria dei Marmi wurde 1572 für den Herzog Guglielmo Gonzaga erbaut.

Galería del Mármol, construida en 1572 para el duque Guillermo Gonzaga.

Galleria dei Marmi, costruita nel 1572 per il duca Guglielmo Gonzaga.

Galeria dos Mármores, construída em 1572 para o duque Guglielmo Gonzaga.

De Marmeren Galerij, gebouwd in 1572 voor de hertog Guglielmo Gonzaga.

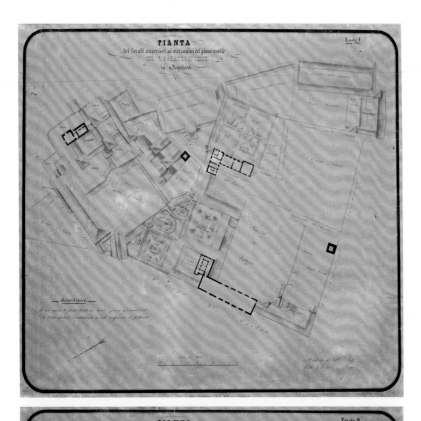

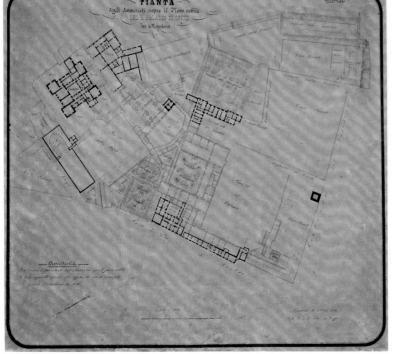

Façade of La Rustica. The building is the result of numerous consolidations of various buildings built between the 12th and 17th centuries. With Isabella d'Este, wife of Francesco II of Gonzaga, it hosted the finest European courts of the day.

Façade de La Rustica. Le palais résulte de la réunion de divers bâtiments construits entre le XIIe et le XVIIe siècle. Avec Isabelle d'Este, épouse de François II Gonzague, il accueillit la cour européenne la plus raffinée de l'époque.

Facciata della Rustica. Il palazzo è l'esito di una serie di accorpamenti di vari edifici costruiti tra il XII e il XVII secolo. Con Isabella d'Este, sposa di Francesco II Gonzaga, ospitò la più raffinata corte europea dell'epoca.

Fassade der La Rustica. Der Palast ist das Ergebnis einer Zusammensetzung verschiedener Gebäude, die zwischen dem 12. und 17. Jahrhundert erbaut wurden. Mit Isabella d'Este, Gemahlin von Francesco II Gonzaga, beherbergte er die damals vornehmste Gesellschaft Europas.

Fachada da Rústica. O palácio é o resultado de uma série de incorporações de vários edifícios construídos entre os séculos XII e XVII. Com Isabella d'Este, esposa de Francesco II Gonzaga, acolheu a fina flor da corte europeia da época.

Fachada de "La Rustica". El palacio es el resultado de la fusión de varios edificios construidos entre los siglos XII y XVII. Con Isabel de Este, mujer de Francisco II Gonzaga, este palacio albergó la corte europea más refinada de la época.

Voorgevel van La Rustica. Dit palazzo is het resultaat van het samenvoegen van meerdere gebouwen die gebouwd zijn tussen de 12e en 17e eeuw. Met Isabella d'Este, echtgenote van Francesco II Gonzaga, huisde hier in die tijd het meest verfijnde hof van Europa.

Chiesa di San Eustorgio
Cappella Portinari

Milano
1462–1468

Wall frescoes by Vincenzo Foppa illustrate the life of St. Peter Martyr.

Sur les murs, des fresques de Vincenzo Foppa illustrent la vie de saint Pierre Martyr.

Die von Vincenzo Foppa mit Fresken geschmückten Wände bebildern das Leben von Petrus Martyr.

En las paredes se encuentran frescos de Vincenzo Foppa que ilustran la vida de San Piedro Mártir.

Alle pareti affreschi di Vincenzo Foppa illustrano la vita di S. Pietro Martire.

Nas paredes, frescos de Vincenzo Foppa ilustram a vida de S. Pedro Mártir.

Fresco's aan de wanden van Vincenzo Foppa illustreren het leven van de heilige Petrus de Martelaar.

It is among the first and most beautiful works of the Milanese Renaissance. Once believed to be by Michelozzo, it appears rather to be Lombard work, influenced by strong references to Brunelleschi.

C'est l'une des premières et des plus belles œuvres de la Renaissance à Milan. Naguère attribuée à Michelozzo, elle apparaît plutôt aujourd'hui de facture lombarde, avec de fortes influences de Brunelleschi.

Das Gebäude gehört zu den ersten und eindrucksvollsten Werken der Renaissancezeit in Mailand. Bereits Michelozzo zugeschrieben, scheint es jedoch aus lombardischen Händen zu stammen, mit starken Einflüssen von Brunelleschi.

Está entre las primeras y de las más bellas obras del Renacimiento de Milán. Aunque la obra se atribuya a Michelozzo, resalta la mano lombarda con fuertes notas de Brunelleschi.

È tra le prime e più belle opere del Rinascimento a Milano. Già attribuita a Michelozzo, appare invece di mano lombarda influenzata da forti richiami a Brunelleschi.

Conta-se entre as primeiras e mais belas obras do Renascimento em Milão. Anteriormente atribuída a Michelozzo, parece contudo de estilo lombardo fortemente influenciado por Brunelleschi.

Dit is een van de eerste en mooiste renaissancistische bouwwerken in Milaan. Hoewel toegeschreven aan Michelozzo, lijkt hij een Lombardische stempel te hebben met sterke invloeden van Brunelleschi.

The shape of the church is linked to the illusionistic perspective of the faux presbytery with three bays conceived by Bramante to address the lack of adequate space behind it.

La célébrité de cette église est liée au trompe-l'œil du faux presbyterium conçu par Bramante pour remédier au manque d'espace nécessaire pour le chœur.

Bekannt ist die Kirche für ihre illusionistische Perspektivmalerei. Statt eine Erweiterung zu bauen, bemalte Bramante die Stelle einfach mit einem täuschend echten Gemälde.

La fama de la iglesia está ligada al ilusionismo visual del presbiterio falso realizado por Bramante para suplir la falta de un espacio adecuado.

La fama della chiesa è legata all'illusionismo prospettico del finto presbiterio a tre campate, concepito da Bramante per ovviare alla mancanza di spazio adeguato nella via retrostante.

A fama da igreja está associada ao ilusionismo perspectivo do presbitério simulado, concebido por Bramante para compensar a falta de um espaço adequado para o coro.

Deze kerk is vooral beroemd vanwege de optische illusie van het valse priesterkoor, dat bedacht is door Bramante om het gebrek aan een dergelijke ruimte te compenseren.

Chiesa di Santa Maria delle Grazie

Milano
Guiniforte Solari, 1466–1490
Donato Bramante, c. 1496–1499

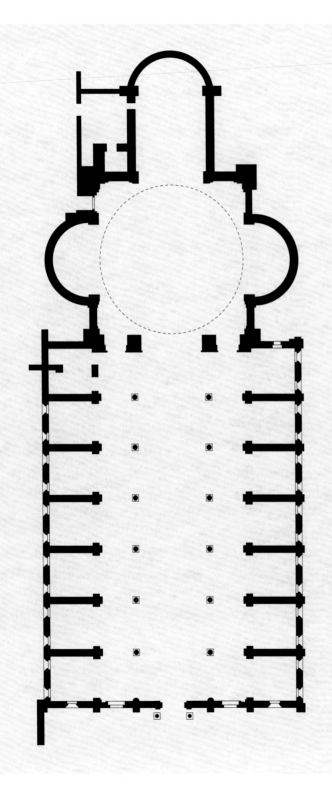

Built between 1466 and 1490, the church was soon enlarged with the tribune in 1492. A new sacristy and the adjoining cloister were added in 1498.

Édifiée entre 1466 et 1490, l'église a été rapidement agrandie de sa tribune. Une nouvelle sacristie et un cloître adjacent ont été ajoutés en 1498.

Die Kirche wurde zwischen 1466 und 1490 erbaut und 1492 mit der Empore erweitert. Eine neue Sakristei mit angrenzendem Kreuzgang wurde 1498 angebaut.

Construida entre 1466 y 1490, fue ampliada posteriormente en 1492 con una tribuna. La nueva sacristía y el claustro contiguo se añadieron en 1498.

Edificata tra il 1466 e il 1490, ben presto venne ampliata con la tribuna nel 1492. Una nuova sagrestia e attiguo chiostro vennero aggiunti nel 1498.

Edificada entre 1466 e 1490, foi rapidamente ampliada com a tribuna em 1492. Uma nova sacristia e um claustro adjacente foram acrescentados em 1498.

De kerk werd gebouwd tussen 1466 en 1490. In 1492 werd zij uitgebreid met een tribune. In 1498 werden een nieuwe sacristie en aangrenzende kloostergang toegevoegd.

The square cloister, attributed to Bramante, features arches with the terracotta soffits typical of the Lombard Renaissance.

Le cloître carré, attribué à Bramante, montre les arcatures à boudins de terre cuite qui sont typiques de la Renaissance lombarde.

Der quadratische Kreuzgang wird Bramante zugeschrieben und weist einen Bogenrücken aus Tonfliesen auf, typisches Merkmal der lombardischen Renaissance.

El claustro cuadrado que se atribuye a Bramante muestra los arcos con dinteles en barro cocido, típico del Renacimiento lombardo.

Il chiostro quadrato, attribuito a Bramante, mostra gli archi con ghiere in cotto, tipici del rinascimento lombardo.

O claustro quadrangular, atribuído a Bramante, apresenta arcos com arquivoltas de terracota, típicos do Renascimento lombardo.

De aan Bramante toegeschreven vierkante kloostergang heeft bogen met betegelde archivolten; kenmerkend voor de Lombardische Renaissance.

In the refectory is the fresco *The Last Supper* by
Leonardo da Vinci, painted between 1495 and 1498
at the request of Ludovico il Moro.

An der Wand des Speisesaals prangt
Das Abendmahl von Leonardo da Vinci, das
zwischen 1495 und 1498 auf Wunsch von Ludovico
il Moro gemalt wurde.

Dans le réfectoire trône *La Cène* de Léonard de
Vinci, peinte entre 1495 et 1498, sur commande de
Ludovic le More.

Nel refettorio campeggia l'*Ultima Cena* di
Leonardo da Vinci, dipinto tra il 1495 e il 1498 per
desiderio di Ludovico il Moro.

En el refectorio se encuentra *La última cena* de
Leonardo da Vinci, realizado entre 1495 y 1498 por
encargo de Ludovico il Moro.

No refeitório impera *A Última Ceia,* de Leonardo
da Vinci, pintado entre 1495 e 1498 a pedido de
Ludovico il Moro.

In de refter *Het Laatste Avondmaal* van Leonardo
da Vinci, geschilderd tussen 1495 en 1498 in
opdracht van Ludovico il Moro.

Palazzo Marino

Milano
Galeazzo Alessi, 1557–1563

The main courtyard, with a ground floor portico and first floor loggia, is enriched by exuberant sculptural decorations.

La grande cour, entourée d'un portique au rez-de-chaussée et d'une galerie au premier étage, est enrichie d'une décoration plastique exubérante.

Der große Innenhof mit Portikus im Erd- und die Loggia im ersten Obergeschoss sind mit überschwänglichen plastischen Verzierungen geschmückt.

El patio principal, caracterizado por un pórtico en la planta baja y una galería en el primer piso, está enriquecido por extraordinarias esculturas.

Il cortile maggiore, porticato al piano terra e loggiato al piano superiore, è arricchito da una esuberante decorazione plastica.

O pátio principal, com um pórtico no piso térreo e uma loggia no primeiro andar, é enriquecido por esculturas extraordinárias.

De grote binnenplaats, met een zuilengalerij onder en een loggia boven, is uitbundig en beeldend versierd.

Castello Sforzesco

Milano
Filarete, 1452
Bartolomeo Gadio, 1455
Vincenzo Seregni, 1550

The nucleus of the castle is from the second half of the 14th century, but its true definition as a military fortress began in the mid-15th century at the behest of Francesco Sforza and continued throughout the 16th century.

Le premier noyau du château date de la seconde moitié du xive siècle, mais sa véritable vocation de forteresse militaire ne commence à se concrétiser qu'au milieu du siècle suivant, par la volonté de Francesco Sforza. Elle se renforcera tout au long du xvie siècle.

Der Grundstein für den Bau des Schlosses wurde in der zweiten Hälfte des 14. Jahrhunderts gelegt. Doch die eigentlichen Arbeiten an der Verteidigungsburg begannen erst ab Mitte des 15. Jahrhunderts im Auftrag von Francesco Sforza und nahmen das ganze 16. Jahrhundert.

El primer núcleo del castillo data de la segunda mitad del siglo XIV, aunque su verdadera definición como fortaleza militar comienza a partir de mitad del siglo XV por voluntad de Francisco Sforza y continuará durante todo el siglo XVI.

Il primo nucleo del castello è della seconda metà del Trecento, ma la vera definizione come fortezza militare si realizza a cominciare dalla metà del Quattrocento per volere di Francesco Sforza e proseguirà per tutto il Cinquecento.

O primeiro núcleo do castelo é da segunda metade do século XIV, mas a verdadeira definição como fortaleza militar apenas começa a ser realizada a partir de meados do século XV, por vontade de Francesco Sforza, prosseguindo durante todo o século XVI.

Het eerste deel van het kasteel dateert uit de tweede helft van de 14e eeuw, maar de daadwerkelijke uitbreiding tot vesting, in opdracht van Francesco Forza, begon midden 15e eeuw en duurde de gehele 16e eeuw.

The Clock Tower, erected by Filarete starting in 1452.

La tour de l'Horloge est édifiée par Filarete à partir de 1452.

Der Uhrturm des Architekten Filarete, ab 1452 erbaut.

La Torre del Reloj, construida por Filarete a partir de 1452.

Torre dell'Orologio, innalzata dal Filarete a partire dal 1452.

A Torre do Relógio, erigida por Filarete a partir de 1452.

De Klokkentoren, gebouwd door Filarete vanaf 1452.

La Certosa

Pavia
Giovanni Solari, 1428–1462
Guiniforte Solari, 1453–1462
Cristoforo Lombardo, 1540–1560

The monastic complex was built at the request of Gian Galeazzo Visconti. The church's façade is a masterpiece of Lombard architecture, Renaissance and Mannerist.

Le complexe monastique a été construit sur ordre de Gian Galeazzo Visconti. La façade est un chef-d'œuvre de l'architecture lombarde Renaissance et maniériste.

Der Klosterkomplex wurde auf Anordnung von Gian Galeazzo Visconti erbaut. Die Kirchenfassade ist ein Meisterwerk der lombardischen und manieristischen Architektur der Renaissance.

El complejo monástico se construyó a petición de Gian Galeazzo Visconti. La fachada de la iglesia es una obra de arte de la arquitectura lombarda renacentista y manierista.

Il complesso monastico venne edificato per volontà di Gian Galeazzo Visconti. La facciata della chiesa è un capolavoro dell'architettura lombarda rinascimentale.

O complexo monástico foi edificado a pedido de Gian Galeazzo Visconti. A fachada da igreja é uma obra-prima da arquitetura lombarda renascentista e maneirista.

Dit kloostergebouw werd gebouwd in opdracht van Gian Galeazzo Visconti. De voorgevel van de kerk is een meesterwerk uit de renaissancistische en maniëristische Lombardische architectuur.

49

The great cloister girdled by a portico of 122 arches.

Le grand cloître est entouré d'un portique de 122 arcades.

Der große Kreuzgang, bestehend aus einem Säulengang aus 122 Bögen.

El claustro grande cercado por un porticado de 122 arcadas.

Il chiostro grande cinto da un porticato di 122 arcate.

O grande claustro cercado por um pórtico de 122 arcos.

De grote kloostergang bestaande uit een galerij met 122 bogen.

Villa Foscari "La Malcontenta"

Mira
Andrea Palladio, 1559

The south-facing view is characterised by a luminous expanse of windows from which the large thermal window stands out.

Die Südfassade ist gekennzeichnet durch eine helle Fensterstruktur, die von einem großen Thermenfenster dominiert wird.

La façade méridionale est caractérisée par son fenêtrage lumineux où domine la grande verrière centrale.

Il prospetto verso mezzogiorno, caratterizzato da una luminosa finestratura in cui spicca la grande finestra termale.

La fachada hacia el sur, caracterizada por un ventanaje luminoso donde resalta la gran ventana termal.

A fachada meridional, caracterizada por uma luminosa fenestragem na qual sobressai a grande janela termal.

De voorzijde rond het middaguur, met het kenmerkende heldere vensterwerk waarin het grote diocletiaanse raam opvalt.

NICOLAVS ET ALOYSIVS FOSCARI FRATRES FEDERICI FILII

A

B

Overlooking the Brenta River, this villa built around 1560 for brothers Nicolò and Alvise Foscari, sits on an elevated base to protect it from flooding. The double staircase of the main façade leads to the solemn pronaos, reminiscent of the Pantheon of ancient Rome.

Édifiée vers 1560 pour les frères Nicolò et Alvise Foscari, la villa se dresse sur un podium élevé qui la protège des inondations de la Brenta coulant à ses pieds. L'escalier à double rampe de la façade principale mène au pronaos solennel rappelant le Panthéon de la Rome antique.

Construida alrededor de 1560 para los hermanos Nicolò y Alvise Foscari, la villa está alzada en lo alto de un zócalo que le protege de los desbordamientos del río Brenta al que se asoma. La escalera de dos rampas de la fachada principal conduce al solemne pronao que recuerda al Panteón de la antigua Roma.

Construída por volta de 1560 para os irmãos Nicolò e Alvise Foscari, a villa assenta numa base alta que a protege das cheias do rio Brenta, para o qual está virada. A escadaria a dois lances da fachada principal conduz ao solene pronau, que recorda o Panteão da Roma Antiga.

Die Villa wurde um 1560 für die Gebrüder Nicolò und Alvise Foscari auf einem hohen Sockel erbaut, der sie vor dem Hochwasser des vorbeifließenden Flusses Brenta schützen sollte. Zwei Treppenläufe mit Podest an der Hauptfassade führen zur erhabenen Säulenvorhalle, die an das Pantheon in Rom erinnert.

Costruita attorno al 1560 per i fratelli Nicolò e Alvise Foscari, la villa poggia su un alto zoccolo che la protegge dalle piene del fiume Brenta, su cui si affaccia. La scalinata a due rampe della facciata principale conduce al solenne pronao che ricorda il Pantheon dell'antica Roma.

Rond 1560 gebouwd voor de twee broers Nicolò en Alvise Foscari. De villa rust op een hoog basement, dat bescherming biedt tegen overstromingen van de naastgelegen rivier de Brenta. De grote trap van twee geledingen aan de hoofdgevel leidt naar het plechtige voorhof, dat doet denken aan het Pantheon uit het antieke Rome.

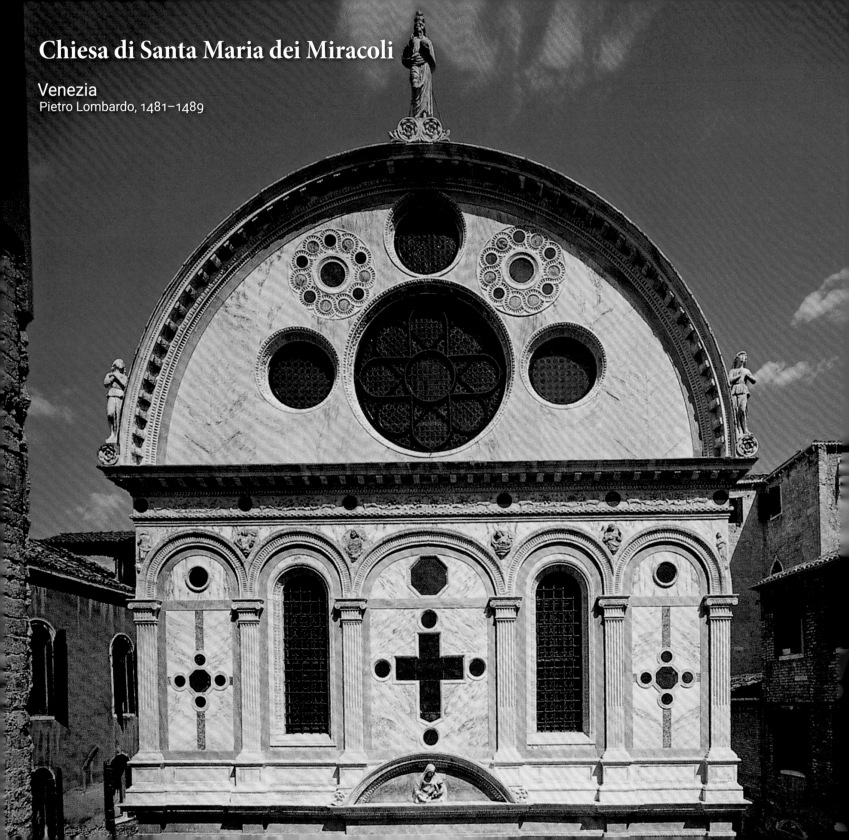

Chiesa di Santa Maria dei Miracoli

Venezia
Pietro Lombardo, 1481–1489

The façade is clad with panels of coloured marble, creating a surprising chromatic effect.

La façade est revêtue de plaques de marbre diversement colorées, qui donnent une polychromie surprenante.

Die Gebäudefassade mit polychromen Marmorplatten besticht durch einen erstaunlichen Farbeffekt.

La fachada está revestida con placas de mármol de diferentes colores que crean un sorprendente efecto cromático.

La facciata è rivestita da lastre marmoree di varie colorazioni, con un sorprendente effetto cromatico.

A fachada é revestida com lajes de mármore de várias cores, cujo efeito cromático é surpreendente.

De voorgevel is bedekt met marmeren tegels in verschillende kleuren, wat een schitterend effect geeft.

Palazzo Loredan Vendramin Calergi

Venezia
Mauro Codussi, 1502–1504

The palazzo's luxurious interior reflects the prestige of the house of Loredan and its economic fortunes.

Les intérieurs somptueux reflètent le prestige de la famille Loredan et sa prospérité économique.

Die prunkvollen Innenräume des Palastes spiegeln das Ansehen und das Vermögen der Loredan-Dynastie wider.

Los fastuosos interiores del palacio reflejan el prestigio de la casa Loredan y sus grandes fortunas económicas.

Gli interni sfarzosi del palazzo riflettono il prestigio della casata Loredan e le sue fortune economiche.

Os interiores suntuosos do palácio refletem o prestígio da família Loredan e a sua prosperidade econômica.

De prachtige binnenkant van het palazzo weerspiegelt het aanzien van het Loredan-geslacht en hun financiële rijkdom.

Palazzo Corner della Ca' Granda

Venezia
Jacopo Sansovino, 1533 - post 1550

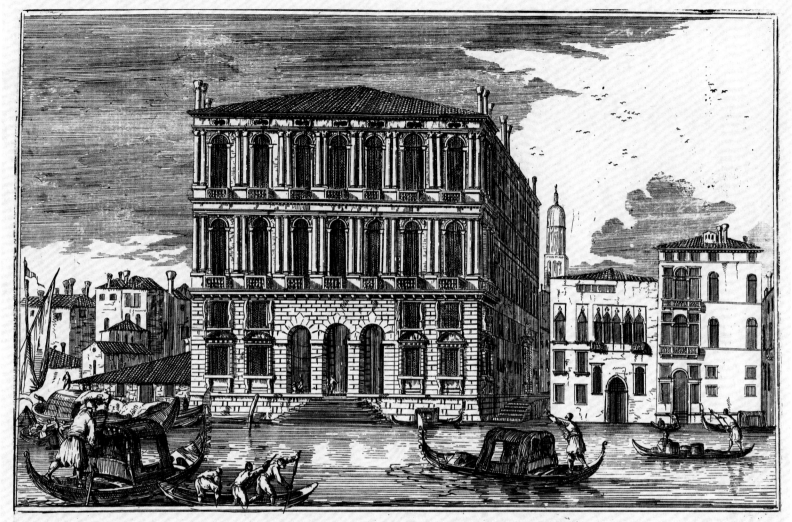

PALAZZO CORNARO A S. MAVRITIO
Architettura di Vicenzo Scamozzio

Luca Carleuarij del: et inc:

65

The palazzo of the influential Corner (or Cornaro) family, was designed by Jacopo Sansovino around 1533 and not—as was erroneously reported in Luca Carlevarij's engraving—by Vincenzo Scamozzi, who only completed the third order around 1580.

Le palais de la puissante famille Corner (ou Cornaro) a été conçu par Jacopo Sansovino vers 1533 et non, comme il est mentionné sur la gravure de Luca Carlevarij, par Vincenzo Scamozzi qui se contenta d'en achever le troisième étage vers 1580.

Der Palast der einflussreichen Familie Corner (oder Cornaro) wurde von Jacopo Sansovino um 1533 entworfen und nicht von Vincenzo Scamozzi, wie eine irrtümliche Inschrift von Luca Carlevarij zeigt, der nur die dritte Säulenordnung um 1580 fertigstellte.

El palacio de la influyente familia Corner (o Cornaro) fue diseñado por Jacopo Sansovino alrededor de 1533 y no como se indica erróneamente en el grabado de Luca Carlevarijs, de la mano de Vincenzo Scamozzi, que solamente completó el tercer orden alrededor de 1580.

Il palazzo della potente famiglia Corner fu progettato da Jacopo Sansovino attorno al 1533 e non (come erroneamente riportato nell'incisione di Luca Carlevarijs) da Vincenzo Scamozzi, che ne completa soltanto il terzo ordine intorno al 1580.

O palácio da influente família Corner (ou Cornaro) foi projetado por Jacopo Sansovino cerca de 1533 - e não, como erradamente é indicado na gravura de Luca Carlevarij, por Vincenzo Scamozzi, que dele apenas completou o terceiro piso por volta de 1580.

Het palazzo van de invloedrijke Corner (of Cornaro)-familie werd rond 1533 ontworpen door Jacopo Sansovino en niet, zoals fout vermeld staat in de gravure van Luca Carlevarij, door Vincenzo Scamozzi, die rond 1580 slechts de derde verdieping voltooide.

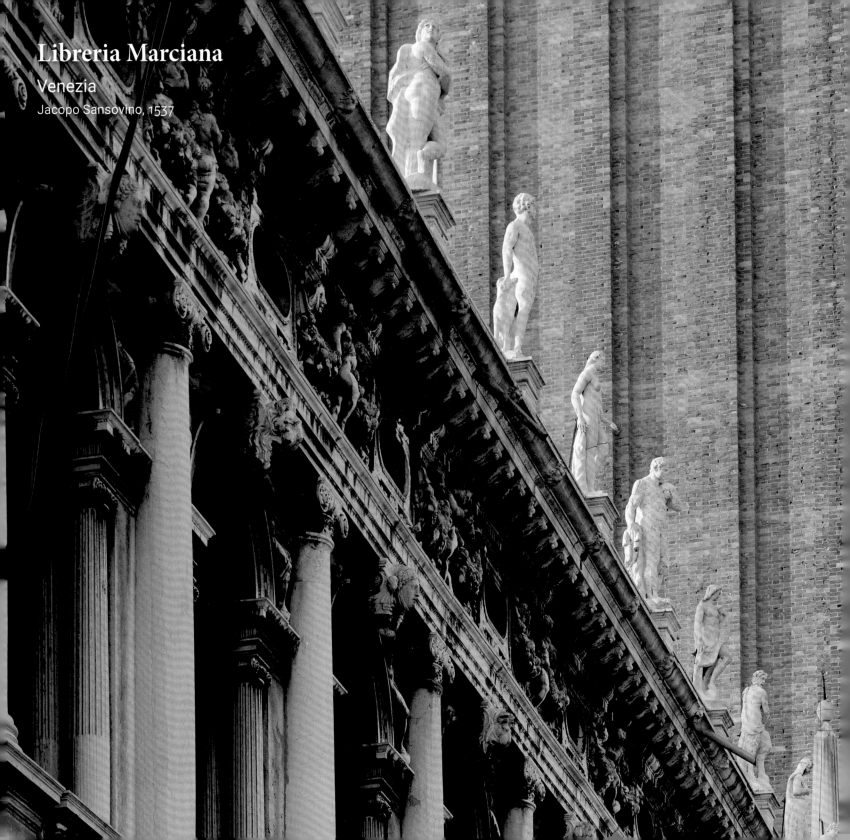

Libreria Marciana

Venezia

Jacopo Sansovino, 1537

Its construction was assigned to Jacopo Sansovino who planned it in 1537. Unfinished when the great Florentine architect died, it was completed by Vincenzo Scamozzi between 1583 and 1588.

Der Bau wurde Jacopo Sansovino anvertraut, der die Pläne um 1537 entwarf. Nach dem Tod des herausragenden florentinischen Architekten wurde der Bau von Vincenzo Scamozza zwischen 1583 und 1588 vollendet.

La construction fut confiée à Jacopo Sansovino, qui la conçut en 1537. Inachevée à la mort du grand architecte florentin, elle fut complétée par Vincenzo Scamozzi entre 1583 et 1588.

La construcción fue asignada a Jacopo Sansovino, que la diseñó en 1537. Estando incompleta, Vincenzo Scamozzi la completó entre 1583 y 1588 tras la muerte del gran arquitecto florentino.

L'incarico di costruirla fu affidato al Sansovino che la progettò nel 1537. Incompiuta alla morte del grande architetto fiorentino, fu completata da Vincenzo Scamozzi tra il 1583 e il 1588.

A sua construção foi confiada a Jacopo Sansovino, que a projetou em 1537. Ainda por concluir à morte do grande arquiteto florentino, veio a ser terminada por Vincenzo Scamozzi entre 1583 e 1588.

Jacopo Sansovino kreeg opdracht voor de bouw en ontwierp het gebouw in 1537. Na de dood van de grote Florentijnse architect, werd het gebouw tussen 1538 en 1588 voltooid door Vincenzo Scamozzi.

The entryway portal and spacious hall of the library.

Le portail d'entrée et la grande salle de la bibliothèque.

Das Eingangsportal und der große Saal der Bibliothek.

El portal de acceso y el gran salón de la librería.

Il portale d'ingresso e l'ampio salone della Libreria.

O portal de entrada e o amplo salão da biblioteca.

De toegangsdeur en de grote bibliotheek.

VEDVTA DELLA PIAZZA DI S. MARCO
Verſo il Canale

Luca Carleuarijs del. et inc.

47

Luca Carlevarijs, 1703.

View of the Marcian Library with the Doge's Palace.

Vue sur la Bibliothèque Marciana et le palais ducal.

Sicht auf die Bibliothek Marciana mit dem Palazzo Ducale.

Vista de la Librería Marciana y del Palacio ducal.

Veduta della Libreria Marciana con il palazzo ducale.

Vista da Biblioteca Marciana e do palácio ducal.

Tekening van de Marciana-bibliotheek met het hertogelijk paleis.

Monastero di San Giorgio Maggiore

Venezia
Fondato nel 982

Ingressus in Urbem uenienti e Clodia, cum insula S Georgij maioris ad dexteram a longe Platea minor D: marci, cum proxima ripa Illijricorum.

Nich! Marieschi dellet incif

Michele Marieschi, 1741

Engraving

Gravure

Stich

Grabado

Incisione

Gravura

Gravure

VENETO   67

The monks' choir in the apse.

Le chœur des moines dans l'abside.

Der Mönchschor in der Apsis.

El coro de los monjes en el ábside.

Il coro dei monaci nell'abside.

O coro dos monges na abside.

Het monnikenkoor in de apsis.

Within the ancient Benedictine monastery, Palladio was called upon to design one of his masterpieces, the church of San Giorgio Maggiore, 1565–1566.

Im antiken Benediktinerkloster wurde Palladio mit der Planung der Kirche San Giorgio Maggiore (1565–1566) beauftragt, ein weiteres seiner Meisterwerke.

Palladio est appelé à créer dans l'ancien monastère bénédictin, un de ses chefs-d'œuvre, l'église de San Giorgio Maggiore, 1565–1566.

En el antiguo monasterio benedictino Palladio fue el encargado de diseñar una de sus obras de arte: la iglesia de San Giorgio Maggiore, 1565–1566.

Nell'antico monastero benedettino Palladio viene chiamato a progettare uno dei suoi capolavori: la chiesa di San Giorgio Maggiore, 1565–1566.

Palladio é chamado a projetar uma das suas obras-primas no antigo mosteiro beneditino, a Basílica de São Jorge Maior, 1565–1566.

Palladio kreeg opdracht van het antieke benedictijnenklooster voor een van zijn grootste meesterwerken: de San Giorgio Maggiore-kerk, 1565–1566.

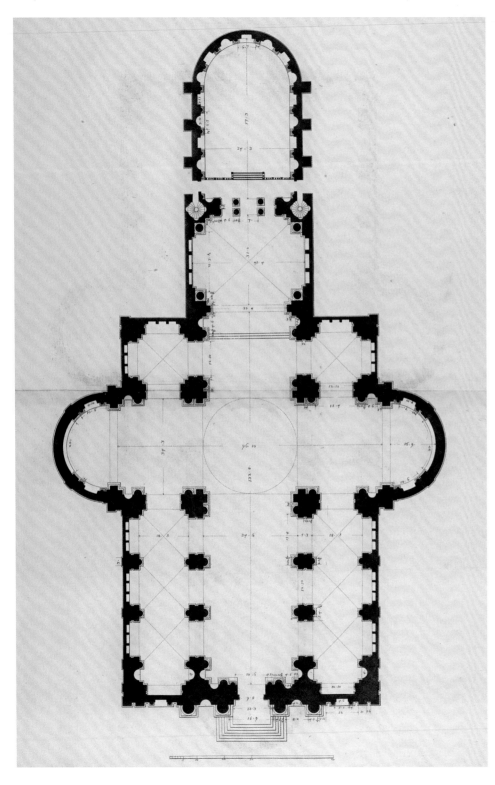

Floorplan.

Plan de l'édifice.

Gebäudegrundriss.

Planta del edificio.

Pianta dell'edificio.

Planta do edifício.

Plattegrond van het gebouw.

The vestibule with twin, red-marble washbasins before the great hall of the refectory.

Le vestibule, avec ses vasques jumelles en marbre rouge, précède la grande salle du réfectoire.

Das Vestibül mit einem Zwillings-Brunnenbecken aus rotem Marmor vor dem großen Refektorium.

El vestíbulo con los dos lavamanos gemelos de mármol rojo precede la gran aula del refectorio.

Il vestibolo con i due lavamani gemelli di marmo rosso precede la grande aula del refettorio.

O vestíbulo, com as duas pias gémeas em mármore vermelho, antecede a grande sala do refeitório.

De hal met de twee identieke wasbakken van roze marmer die aan de grote zaal van de refter voorafgaat.

The first grand portal leading into the vestibule.

Le premier portail, grandiose, mène au vestibule.

Das mächtige Portal, das in das Vestibül führt.

El primer gran portal que conduce al vestíbulo.

Il primo grandioso portale che introduce al vestibolo.

O primeiro grandioso portal que dá acesso ao vestíbulo.

De eerste schitterende deur die naar de hal leidt.

Chiesa del Redentore

Venezia
Andrea Palladio, 1577

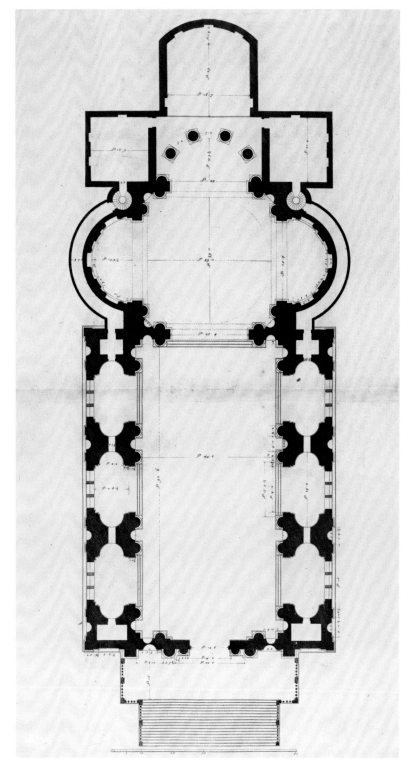

Plan of the church.

Plan de l'église.

Grundriss der Kirche.

Planta de la iglesia.

Pianta della chiesa.

Planta da igreja.

Plattegrond van de kerk.

Elevation with the wide staircase rising from the banks. On behalf of the Senate, Palladio designed this votive church, Il Redentore, in 1577 in the aftermath of a terrible plague that had decimated Venice.

Vue du grand escalier montant du quai. En 1577, le Sénat commande à Palladio de réaliser l'église votive Il Redentore, au lendemain de la terrible épidémie de peste qui vient de ravager Venise.

Frontseite mit breiter Freitreppe, die vom Ufer bis zur Kirche führt. Kurz nach Ausbruch der Pest in ganz Venedig entwarf Palladio 1577 im Auftrag des Senats die Votivkirche Il Redentore.

Prospetto della Chiesa del Redentore alla Giudecca de' Padri Capuccini

Giuseppe Valeriani del.

Per Domenico Lousia in Venetia

La fachada con la gran escalera que inicia desde la orilla. Por encargo del senado, Palladio diseñó la iglesia votiva del Redentor en el año 1577, en la época sucesiva a la terrible peste que golpeó Venecia.

Il prospetto con l'ampia scalea che sale dalla riva. Per incarico del Senato, Palladio progetta la chiesa votiva del Redentore nel 1577, all'indomani della terribile pestilenza che aveva sconvolto Venezia.

A fachada, com a ampla escadaria que sobe da margem. O Senado encarrega Palladio da concepção da Igreja votiva do Redentor em 1577, após a terrível peste que assolara Veneza.

De voorzijde met de brede trap die omhoogloopt vanaf het water. In opdracht van de senaat ontwierp Palladio in 1577 deze kerk gewijd aan de Verlosser, vlak nadat de verschrikkelijke pestepidemie in Venetië had huisgehouden.

Interior of the church. The presbytery ends, behind the main altar, in a semi-circular colonnade.

Intérieur de l'église. Le presbyterium est fermé, derrière le grand autel, par une colonnade en hémicycle.

Das Innere der Kirche. Der Chorraum wird hinter dem Hochaltar durch eine halbrunde Säulenstellung abgeschlossen.

El interior de la iglesia. El presbiterio, detrás del altar mayor, se concluye con una hilera de columnas en hemiciclo.

L'interno della chiesa. Il presbiterio è concluso dietro l'altar maggiore da un colonnato a emiciclo.

O interior da igreja. Por trás do altar-mor, o presbitério é terminado por uma colunata em hemiciclo.

Interieur van de kerk. Het priesterkoor wordt achter het hoofdaltaar afgesloten door een hemicyclische zuilenrij.

Chiesa di San Francesco della Vigna

Venezia
Jacopo Sansovino, 1534
Andrea Palladio, 1564–1565

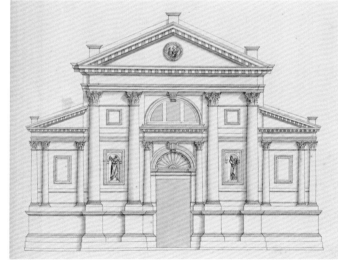

The history of its construction places in comparison, thirty years later, two of the greatest architects of the Renaissance: Jacopo Sansovino, who was responsible for the construction of the building in 1534 and Andrea Palladio who, in 1564–1565 redesigned the façade.

Die Bauweise zeigt, im Abstand von 30 Jahren, den Vergleich zweier der bedeutendsten Architekten der Renaissance: Jacopo Sansovino, der das Gebäude um 1534 errichtete, und Andrea Palladio, der von 1564 bis 1565 die Neugestaltung der Fassade übernahm.

Les vicissitudes de la construction rapprochent, à trente ans de distance, deux des plus grands architectes de la Renaissance : Jacopo Sansovino à qui l'on doit la construction de l'édifice en 1534 et Andrea Palladio qui en redessine la façade en 1564–1565.

Le vicende costruttive mettono a confronto, a distanza di trent'anni, due dei più grandi architetti del Rinascimento: Jacopo Sansovino, a cui si deve la costruzione dell'edificio (1534), e Andrea Palladio, che nel 1564–1565 ne ridisegna la facciata.

Los elementos de construcción, en una distancia de treinta años, comparan dos de los arquitectos más importantes del Renacimiento: Jacopo Sansovino, quien realizó la construcción del edificio en 1534, y Andrea Palladio, que en los años 1564 y 1565 volvió a diseñar la fachada.

As vicissitudes da construção colocam em confronto, com uma distância de trinta anos, dois dos maiores arquitetos do Renascimento: Jacopo Sansovino, a quem se deve a construção do edifício em 1534, e Andrea Palladio que, em 1564–1565, redesenha a sua fachada.

Het bouwproces brengt, met dertig jaar ertussen, twee van de grootste architecten uit de renaissance bij elkaar: Jacopo Sansovino, die opdracht kreeg voor de bouw van de kerk in 1534 en Andrea Palladio, die in 1564–1565 de voorgevel opnieuw ontwierp.

Arsenale

Venezia
Bartolomeo Bon, 1460

Veduta esteriore delle porte dell' Arsenale, in Venezia.

The landward entryway to the vast military complex is marked by Bartolomeo Bon's grand portal.

L'accès terrestre au vaste complexe militaire est signalé par le grand portail de Bartolomeo Bon.

Der landseitige Eingang zum imposanten Marinearsenal erfolgt durch das grandiose Portal von Bartolomeo Bon.

La entrada por tierra al inmenso complejo militar se caracteriza por el grandioso portal de Bartolomeo Bon.

L'ingresso di terra al vastissimo complesso militare è segnato dal grandioso portale di Bartolomeo Bon.

A entrada por terra para o vastíssimo complexo militar é marcada pelo grandioso portal de Bartolomeo Bon.

De landingang van het uitgestrekte militaire complex bestaat uit een prachtige poort van Bartolomeo Bon.

Magni Armamentarij Veneziarum portæ duæ; artificibus altera, altera nauibus duplex aditus

Entryway to the Arsenal, land and water portals, engraving, 18th century.

Les portes terrestre et maritime à l'entrée de l'Arsenal, gravure, XVIIIᵉ siècle.

Die Eingangsportale zu Wasser und zu Land, Stich, 18. Jahrhundert.

Las puertas de agua y de tierra, grabado, siglo XVIII.

Entrata dell'Arsenale, le porte di acqua e di terra, incisione, Settecento.

Entrada do Arsenale: as portas em terra e por água, gravura, Setecento.

Toegangsportalen over water en over land, gravure, 18e eeuw.

Gian Maria Maffioletti

Perspective view of the Arsenale, 1798

Vue en perspective de l'Arsenal, 1798.

Das Arsenal aus der Vogelperspektive, 1798.

Vista en perspectiva del Arsenal, 1798.

Vedute prospettiche dell'Arsenale, 1798.

Vista perspectiva do Arsenale, 1798.

Perspectivische tekening van het Arsenaal, 1798.

Villa Barbaro

Maser
Andrea Palladio, c. 1560

This villa, also known as "the harmonious" for the perfect integration of the building with the surrounding landscape, was commissioned from Palladio around 1560 for the brothers Daniele and Marcantonio Barbaro.

Dank der perfekten Einbettung in die umliegende Natur wird sie auch „Villa der Harmonie" genannt. Sie wurde 1560 im Auftrag der Gebrüder Daniele und Marcantonio Barbaro von Palladio entworfen.

Cette villa, réputée pour l'extraordinaire harmonie avec laquelle l'édifice se fond dans la nature environnante, a été commandée à Palladio vers 1560 par les frères Daniele et Marcantonio Barbaro.

La villa, también denominada "villa de la armonía" por la perfecta introducción del edificio en la naturaleza que lo rodea, fue encargada a Palladio alrededor del año 1560 por los hermanos Daniele y Marcantonio Barbaro.

La villa, detta anche "dell'armonia" per il perfetto inserimento dell'edificio nella natura circostante, fu commissionata a Palladio verso il 1560 dai fratelli Daniele e Marcantonio Barbaro.

A villa, também chamada "da harmonia" pela perfeita integração do edifício na natureza circundante, foi encomendada a Palladio por volta de 1560 pelos irmãos Daniele e Marcantonio Barbaro.

De opdracht voor deze villa, die ook wel 'in harmonie' wordt genoemd omdat het gebouw volledig opgaat in de omringende natuur, kreeg Palladio rond 1560 van de broers Daniele en Marcantonio Barbaro.

LA SOTTOPOSTA fabrica è à Mafera Villa vicina ad Afolo Caftello del Triuigiano, di Monfignor Reuerendifsimo Eletto di Aquileia, e del Magnifico Signor Marc'Antonio fratelli de' Barbari. Quella parte della fabrica, che efce alquanto in fuori; ha due ordini di ftanze, il piano di quelle di fopra è à pari del piano del cortile di dietro, oue è tagliata nel monte rincontro alla cafa vna fontana con infiniti ornamenti di ftucco, e di pittura. Fa quefta fonte vn laghetto, che ferue per pefchiera: da quefto luogo partitafi l'acqua fcorre nella cucina, & dapoi irrigati i giardini, che fono dalla deftra, e finiftra parte della ftrada, la quale pian piano afcendendo conduce alla fabrica; fa due pefchiere co i loro beueratori fopra la ftrada commune: d'onde partitafi; adacqua il Bruolo, ilquale è grandifsimo, e pieno di frutti eccellentifsimi, e di diuerfe feluaticine. La facciata della cafa del padrone hà quattro colonne di ordine Ionico: il capitello di quelle de gli angoli fa fronte da due parti: i quai capitelli come fi facciano; porrò nel libro de i Tempij. Dall'vna, e l'altra parte ui fono loggie, le quali nell'eftremità hanno due colombare, e fotto quelle ui fono luoghi da fare i uini, e le ftalle, e gli altri luoghi per l'vfo di Villa.

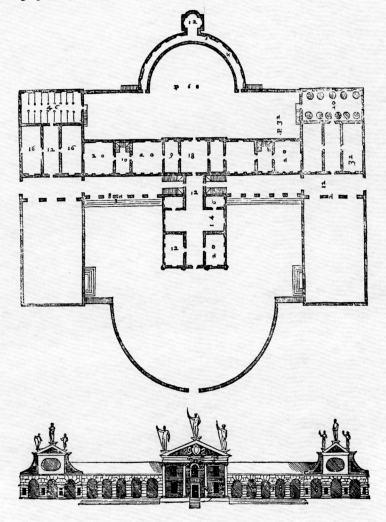

GG 2   LA SEGVENTE

One of the two dovecotes, decorated with recessed statuary, which ends the portico.

Un des deux colombiers, orné de statues dans des niches fermant le portique.

Eine der zwei mit Statuen verzierten Kolumbarien, die den Portikus abschließen.

Uno de los dos columbarios, decorado con estatuas empotradas, que concluye el porticado.

Una delle due colombare, ornata di statue a incasso, che conclude il porticato.

Uma das duas torres-pombal, ornamentada com estátuas e que encerra o pórtico.

Een van de twee duiventillen, versierd met beeldhouwwerken, aan het einde van de zuilengalerij.

Around 1561 Paolo Veronese created one of 16th century Venetian painting's most important pictorial cycles, frescoing five rooms and the cruciform vestibule of the piano nobile.

Vers 1561, Véronèse réalise un des cycles picturaux les plus importants du Cinquecento vénitien en peignant à fresque les cinq salles et le vestibule à voûte d'arêtes de l'étage noble.

Um 1561 schuf Paolo Veronesi einen der bedeutendsten venezianischen Bilderzyklen des 16. Jahrhunderts. Er malte fünf Säle und das Vestibül mit Kreuzgewölbe des Hauptgeschosses mit Fresken aus.

Alrededor del año 1561, Paolo Veronese realizó uno de los ciclos pictóricos más importantes del siglo XVI de Venecia con frescos en cinco salas y el vestíbulo en crucería del piano nobile.

Intorno al 1561, Paolo Veronese realizzò uno dei più significativi cicli pittorici del Cinquecento veneto, affrescando cinque sale e il vestibolo a crociera del piano nobile.

Por volta de 1561, Paolo Veronese produziu um dos mais significativos ciclos pictóricos da era quinhentista véneta, pintando frescos em cinco salas e no vestíbulo com abóbada de aresta do andar nobre.

Rond 1561 maakt Paolo Veronese een van de belangrijkste serie schilderingen uit het Venetië van de 15e eeuw door vijf kamers en de kruisvormige vestibulum van de bel-etage met fresco's te versieren.

The fishpond, fed by a perennial spring, in front of the nymphaeum. It develops around the exedra decorated by Alessandro Vittoria.

Le vivier, en face du nymphée, est alimenté par une source pérenne. Tout autour se développe l'exèdre, avec une décoration d'Alessandro Vittoria.

Der Fischteich vor dem Nymphäum wird mit stetig fließendem Wasser gespeist und ist von einer kunstvoll verzierten Exedra von Alessandro Vittoria gesäumt.

El estanque de peces frente al ninfeo está alimentado por una fuente de agua constante. Alrededor del mismo se desarrolla una exedra con decoración de Alessandro Vittoria.

La peschiera di fronte al ninfeo è alimentata da una fonte perenne. Intorno ad essa si sviluppa l'esedra con decorazioni di Alessandro Vittoria.

O viveiro em frente ao ninfeu é alimentado por uma nascente de água perene. Em seu redor estende-se a êxedra, com uma decoração de Alessandro Vittoria.

De vijver voor het nymfaeum wordt gevoed door een duurzame waterbron. Daaromheen bevindt zich de exedra met versieringen van Alessandro Vittoria.

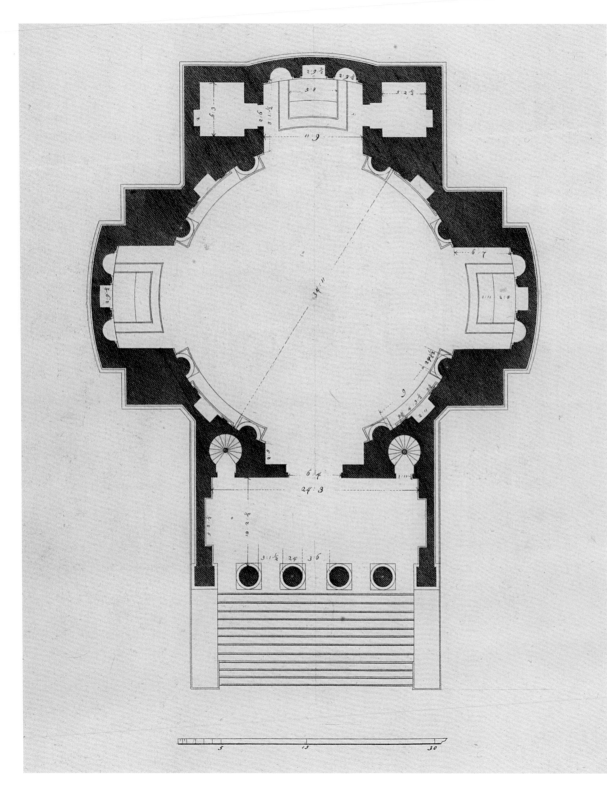

The 'Tempietto' Barbaro, positioned outside the villa, was Palladio's last religious building designed around 1580, a few months before his death.

Le tempietto Barbaro, situé à l'extérieur de la villa, est le dernier édifice religieux signé Palladio qui en dresse les plans vers 1580, quelques mois avant sa mort.

Der Tempietto Barbaro liegt außerhalb der Villa und ist das letzte religiöse Gebäude von Palladio. Er entwarf es um 1580, nur wenige Monate vor seinem Tod.

El templete Barbaro, ubicado fuera de la villa, es el último edificio religioso que diseñó Palladio alrededor del año 1580, pocos meses antes de su fallecimiento.

Il Tempietto Barbaro, situato al di fuori della villa, è l'ultimo edificio religioso di Palladio, che lo progettò attorno al 1580, pochi mesi prima della morte.

O tempietto Barbaro, situado no exterior da villa, é o último edifício religioso projetado por Palladio por volta de 1580, poucos meses antes da sua morte.

Het Barbaro-tempeltje, buiten de villa, is het laatste religieuze bouwwerk van Palladio. Hij ontwierp het rond 1580, een paar maanden voor zijn dood.

A FANZOLO Villa del Triuigiano discosto da Castelfranco tre miglia, è la sottoposta fabrica del Magnifico Signor Leonardo Emo . Le Cantine, i Granari, le Stalle, e gli altri luoghi di Villa sono dall'vna, e l'altra parte della casa dominicale, e nell'estremità loro vi sono due colombare, che
apportano utile al padrone, & ornamento al luogo, e per tutto si può andare al coperto: ilche è vna
delle principal cose, che si ricercano ad vna casa di Villa, come è stato auertito di sopra . Dietro à
questa fabrica è vn giardino quadro di ottanta campi Triuigiani: per mezo il quale corre vn fiumicel
lo, che rende il sito molto bello, e diletteuole . È stata ornata di pitture da M. Battista Venetiano.

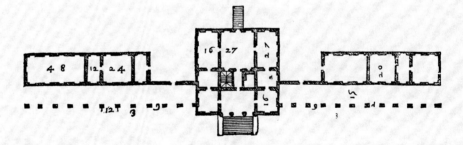

In Villa Emo, Palladio again proposed the solution
for aligning the main house with its annexes.

Pour la Villa Emo, Palladio reprend la solution de
l'alignement entre le corps de logis seigneurial et
les bâtiments annexes.

Mit der Villa Emo gelang Palladio eine optimale
Anordnung von Haupt- und Nebengebäuden.

En Villa Emo Palladio vuelve a proponer la
solución de alineación entre el cuerpo principal y
los edificios anexos.

In Villa Emo, Palladio ripropone la soluzione
dell'allineamento tra corpo padronale ed
edifici annessi.

Na villa Emo, Palladio torna a propor a
solução de alinhamento entre corpo principal e
edifícios anexos.

Bij Villa Emo scheidt Palladio het hoofdgebouw
opnieuw van de bijgebouwen.

DE I

Villa Garzoni

Pontecasale di Candiana
Jacopo Sansovino, c. 1550

Jacopo Sansovino designed a building for the Venetian Garzoni family with a façade interrupted by an harmonious double-tiered loggia, preceded by an impressive staircase.

Jacopo Sansovino errichtete das Gebäude für die venezianische Familie Garzoni mit einer Fassade, die durch eine harmonische Loggia mit zwei Säulenordnungen unterbrochen wird und der ein breiter Treppenlauf vorangeht.

Pour la famille vénitienne des Garzoni, Jacopo Sansovino conçoit un édifice dont la façade est scandée par une harmonieuse galerie centrale à double étage, précédée d'un imposant escalier.

Jacopo Sansovino concepì per la famiglia veneziana dei Garzoni un edificio con la facciata interrotta da un armonioso loggiato a due ordini, preceduto da un'imponente scalinata.

Jacopo Sansovino diseñó un edificio para la familia veneciana Garzoni con una fachada interrumpida por una armoniosa arcada de dos órdenes precedida por una imponente escalinata.

Jacopo Sansovino concebeu para a família veneziana Garzoni um edifício de fachada descontinuada por uma harmoniosa galeria de camada dupla, precedida por uma imponente escadaria.

Voor de Venetiaanse Garzoni-familie bedacht Jacopo Sansovino een gebouw waarbij de voorgevel onderbroken wordt door een harmonieuze zuilengalerij van twee lagen, met een imposante trap ervoor.

The fortified palazzo was constructed in just two years for the Serenissima's military commander, Enea Pio degli Obizzi, who is linked to the invention of the 'obice' cannon which takes its name from him.

Die Schlossanlage wurde in nur zwei Jahren vom Söldnerführer der Republik Venedig Pio Enea degli Obizzi erbaut, der durch die Erfindung der Haubitze (Obice) berühmt wurde und ihr den Namen gab.

Le palais fortifié a été construit en deux ans seulement par Enea Pio degli Obizzi, condottiere de la Sérénissime, dont le nom reste lié par ailleurs à un type de bouche à feu (l'obusier, obice en italien) qu'il a mis au point.

Il palazzo fortificato fu costruito in soli due anni dal condottiero della Serenissima Enea Pio degli Obizzi, il cui nome è legato all'invenzione della bocca di fuoco, l'obice, che da lui prende il nome.

El edificio fortificado fue construido en sólo dos años para el comandante militar de la Serenísima, Enea Pio degli Obizzi, famoso por haber inventado el obús, que hace referencia a su nombre.

O palácio fortificado foi construído em apenas dois anos pelo comandante da Sereníssima Enea Pio degli Obizzi, cuja figura está associada à invenção do obus, de quem lhe provém o nome.

Het versterkte palazzo werd in slechts twee jaar tijd gebouwd door de condottiere van de Republiek Venetië Enea Pio degli Obizzi, die in verband wordt gebracht met de uitvinding van een wapen: de houwitser, die naar hem vernoemd is ('obice' in het Italiaans).

Villa Cornaro

Piombino Dese
Jacopo Sansovino, c. 1550

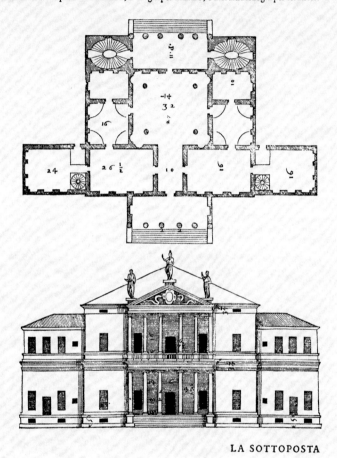

LA FABRICA, che fegue è del Magnifico Signor Giorgio Cornaro in Piombino luogo di Caftel Franco. Il primo ordine delle loggie è Ionico. La Sala è pofta nella parte più a dentro della cafa, accioche fia lontana dal caldo, e dal freddo: le ale oue fi ueggono i nicchi fono larghe la terza parte della fua lunghezza: le colonne rifpondono al diritto delle penultime delle loggie, e fono tanto diftanti tra fe, quanto alte: le ftanze maggiori fono lunghe un quadro, e tre quarti: i uolti fono alti fecondo il primo modo delle altezze de' volti: le mediocri fono quadre il terzo più alte che làrghe; i uolti fono à lunette: fopra i camerini vi fono mezati. Le loggie di fopra fono di ordine Corinthio: le colonne fono la quinta parte più fottili di quelle di fotto. Le ftanze fono in folaro, & hanno fopra alcuni mezati. Da vna parte ui è la cucina, e luoghi per maffare, e dall'altra i luoghi per feruitori.

LA SOTTOPOSTA

The villa was a troubled project and appeared in its final form only in a drawing from around 1613. As in the villa Pisani di Montagnana, it is the central hall with its four freestanding columns that confers prestige.

Die Villa durchlebte schwere Zeiten und nur eine Zeichnung aus ca. 1613 zeigt sie in ihrer vollendeten Form. Wie bei der Villa Pisani in Montagnana, ist es die mittlere Halle mit den vier freistehenden Säulen, die dem Gebäude Prestige verleiht.

La villa a connu bien des vicissitudes et seul un dessin d'environ 1613 la représente dans sa forme définitive. Comme pour la villa Pisani à Montagnana, c'est la grande salle centrale avec ses quatre colonnes libres qui lui confère son prestige.

La villa ebbe vicende travagliate e solo un disegno del 1613 ca. la presenta nella sua forma definitiva. Come per Villa Pisani a Montagnana è il salone centrale con le sue quattro colonne libere a conferirle prestigio.

La villa vivió graves cambios y solo se conserva un dibujo de ca 1613 que representa su estado definitivo. Como en la Villa Pisani, en Montagnana es el salón central con cuatro columnas libres el que le confiere cierto prestigio.

Circunstâncias difíceis envolvem a construção da villa, e só um projeto de cerca de 1613 a apresenta na sua forma definitva. À semelhança de Villa Pisani, em Montagnana, é o salão central com as suas quatro colunas livres a conferir-lhe prestígio.

Na een aantal tragische voorvallen was in 1613 eindelijk het definitieve ontwerp klaar voor deze villa. Net als bij Villa Pisani in Montagnana, is het de grote hoofdzaal met vier vrijstaande zuilen die het gebouw zijn aanzien geeft.

Palazzo Chiericati

Vicenza
Andrea Palladio, 1550

An absolute novelty gives this building its charm: free-standing columns on two levels, the ground floor portico uninterrupted along all of the façade while on the upper floor.

L'apport d'éléments novateurs offre à cet édifice une originalité séduisante : des colonnes libres embrassant deux niveaux, un portique ininterrompu sur toute la façade pour le rez-de-chaussée, mais une solution de continuité au premier étage.

Dieses Gebäude fasziniert durch absolut neue Aspekte: ein offener Säulenvorbau auf zwei Geschossen, ein ununterbrochener Portikus über die ganze Fassade und eine gelungene Kontinuität im Obergeschoss.

Este palacio resalta por rasgos completamente nuevos: columnas libres en dos pisos, pórtico inferior continuo a lo largo de toda la fachada y una solución de continuidad en el piso superior.

Qualcosa di assolutamente nuovo affascina in questo edificio: colonne libere su due piani, portico inferiore ininterrotto per tutta la facciata e una soluzione di continuità al piano superiore.

Algo absolutamente inovador nos fascina neste edifício: colunas livres em dois pisos, um pórtico inferior ininterrupto ao longo de toda a fachada e uma solução de continuidade no piso superior.

Iets volkomen nieuws siert dit gebouw: twee verdiepingen van losstaande zuilen, een ononderbroken zuilengalerij beneden langs de gehele voorkant en eentje met een onderbreking op de bovenste verdieping.

Teatro Olimpico

Vicenza
Andrea Palladio, 1580

View of the front of the stage. Palladio's plan is the Renaissance style reproduction of the ancient Roman theatres. After his death in 1584, the building was continued and completed by Vincenzo Scamozzi.

Vue du front de scène. Le projet de Palladio reprend le modèle des anciens théâtres romains, dans une interprétation Renaissance. Après sa mort, Vincenzo Scamozzi en a repris et achevé en 1584 la construction.

Frontansicht der Bühne. Palladios Entwurf ist eine Rekonstruktion antiker römischer Theater im Stil der Renaissance. Nach seinem Tod wurden die Arbeiten von Vincenzo Scamozzi 1584 weitergeführt und abgeschlossen.

Vista de la parte central del escenario. El proyecto de Palladio es una reproducción de los antiguos teatros romanos en clave renacentista. Tras su fallecimiento, Vincenzo Scamozzi prosiguió con su construcción y la finalizó en 1584.

Veduta del fronte della scena. Il progetto di Palladio è la riproposizione in chiave rinascimentale degli antichi teatri romani. Dopo la sua morte, l'edificio fu proseguito e ultimato nel 1584 da Vincenzo Scamozzi.

Vista do proscénio. O projeto de Palladio é o regresso dos antigos teatros romanos, agora em registo renascentista. Após a sua morte, o edifício foi retomado por Vincenzo Scamozzi que terminou a construção em 1584.

Vooraanzicht van het podium. Het ontwerp van Palladio is een renaissancistische herbewerking van het antieke Romeinse theater. Na zijn dood werd het gebouw verder gebouwd en in 1584 voltooid door Vincenzo Scamozzi.

Details of the front of the stage.

Détails du front de scène.

Details der Frontansicht.

Detalles de la parte central del escenario.

Dettagli del fronte della scena.

Detalhe do proscênio.

Details van de voorkant van het decor.

The decorative statues represent members of the Olympian academy, in ancient Roman attire.

Sie wird von Statuen geschmückt, welche Mitglieder der Olympischen Akademie in römischen Gewändern darstellen.

Les statues qui le décorent représentent les membres de l'Académie olympique, vêtus à la mode des anciens Romains.

En las estatuas que lo decoran están caracterizados los miembros de la Academia Olímpica vestidos de romanos antiguos.

Nelle statue che lo decorano sono raffigurati i membri dell'Accademia Olimpica vestiti da antichi romani.

Nas estátuas que o decoram estão representados os membros da Academia Olimpica, vestidos de antigos romanos.

De beelden die er staan zijn van leden van de Accademia Olimpica gekleed als oude Romeinen.

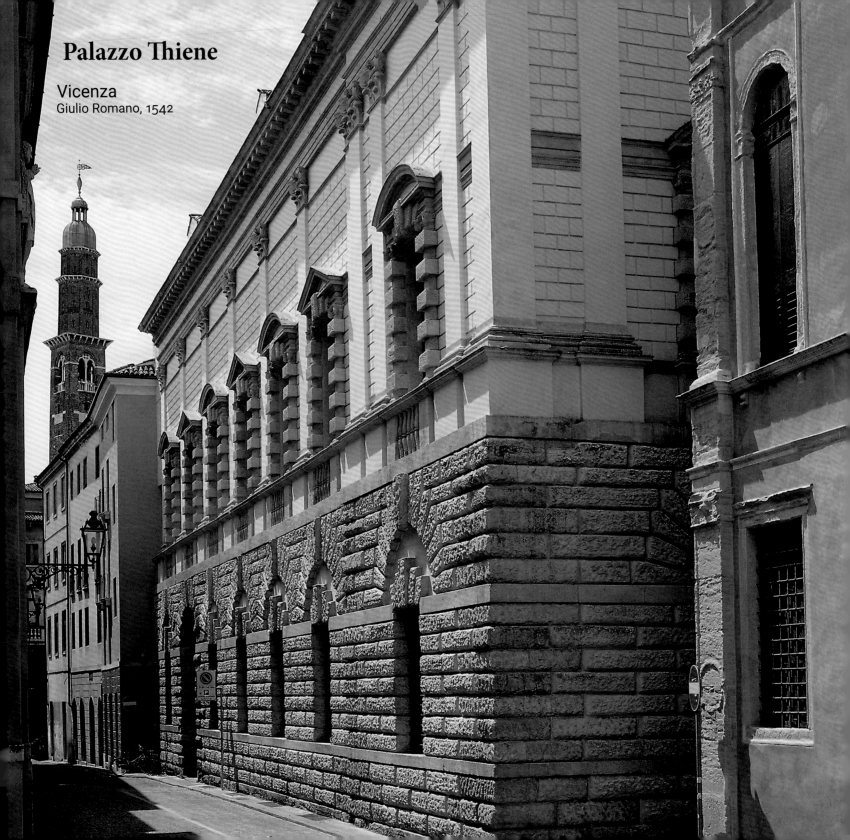

Palazzo Thiene

Vicenza
Giulio Romano, 1542

Giulio Romano, the most famous architect of that period, designed the building around the year 1542 for the influential Thiene family. He was the Gonzaga family's favourite architect, and when he died in 1546, Palladio was assigned the task of implementing the project.

Giulio Romano – le plus illustre de son temps – conçut l'édifice vers 1542 pour la puissante famille Thiene. Mais l'architecte préféré des Gonzague mourut en 1546 et Palladio fut chargé de réaliser le projet.

Giulio Romano, einer der damals bedeutendsten Architekten, entwarf das Gebäude 1542 für die mächtige Familie Thiene. Nach dem Tod des Lieblingsarchitekten der Familie Gonzaga im Jahr 1546 wurde Palladio mit der Ausführung des Projekts beauftragt.

Giulio Romano, el arquitecto más famoso de la época, diseñó el edificio alrededor de 1542 para la poderosa familia Thiene. El arquitecto preferido de los Gonzaga falleció en 1546 y Palladio fue el encargado de finalizar el proyecto.

Giulio Romano, l'architetto più famoso del tempo, disegnò l'edificio attorno al 1542 per la potente famiglia Thiene. L'architetto preferito dei Gonzaga morì nel 1546 e a Palladio spettò il compito di rendere esecutivo il progetto.

Giulio Romano, o mais famoso arquiteto da época, projetou o edifício por volta de 1542 para a poderosa família Thiene. Em 1546, com a morte do arquiteto favorito dos Gonzaga, recai sobre Palladio a tarefa de tornar o projeto exequível.

Giulio Romano, toentertijd een zeer beroemde architect, ontwierp het gebouw rond 1542 voor de machtige familie Thiene. De lievelingsarchitect van de Gonzaga's stierf in 1546 en Palladio kreeg opdracht het ontwerp verder uit te werken.

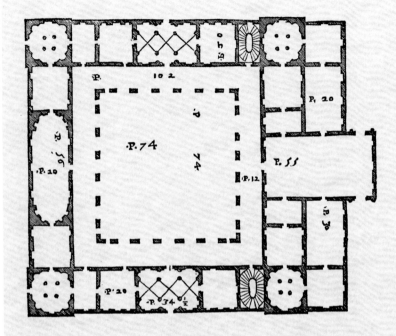

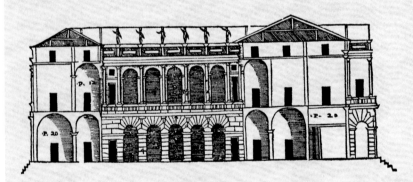

DE I DISEGNI che feguono in forma maggiore; il primo è di parte della facciata; il fecondo di parte del Cortile della forapofta fabrica.

HANNO

In the Quattro Libri, Palladio claims the project as his own, but the square plan style of the palace, with massive ashlar masonry on its façades, is too similar to the Palazzo Te at Mantua to corroborate that affirmation.

Dans ses Quattro Libri, Palladio s'attribue la paternité du projet, mais le style du palais et son plan carré, avec ses blocs de bossages massifs sur les façades, rappellent trop le palais du Te, à Mantoue, pour corroborer cette affirmation.

In Quattro Libri beansprucht Palladio die Urheberschaft des Projekts, doch erinnert der Baustil des Palastes mit quadratischem Grundriss und der Fassade mit massivem Bossenwerk zu sehr an den Palazzo del Te in Mantua, um dieser Behauptung Glauben schenken zu können.

Palladio, en su obra Quattro Libri, se atribuye la paternidad del proyecto aunque el estilo del palacio, de planta cuadrada con revestimientos de bloques de paramento macizos en las fachadas, evoca notablemente al Palacio Te de Mantua.

Palladio nei Quattro Libri dell'Architettura si attribuisce la paternità del progetto, ma lo stile del palazzo a pianta quadrata con i massicci blocchi di bugnato nelle facciate ricorda troppo Palazzo Te a Mantova per avvalorare tale affermazione.

Na sua obra Quattro Libri, Palladio reclama a paternidade do projeto, mas o estilo do palácio, de planta quadrangular e com blocos maciços de bossagem nas fachadas, lembra demasiado o Palazzo Te em Mântua para corroborar tal afirmação.

Palladio beweert in Quattro Libri de bedenker van het ontwerp te zijn, maar de vierkante plattegrond van het palazzo en de gevels met massieve bossages doen te veel denken aan palazzo Te in Mantova om die bewering te staven.

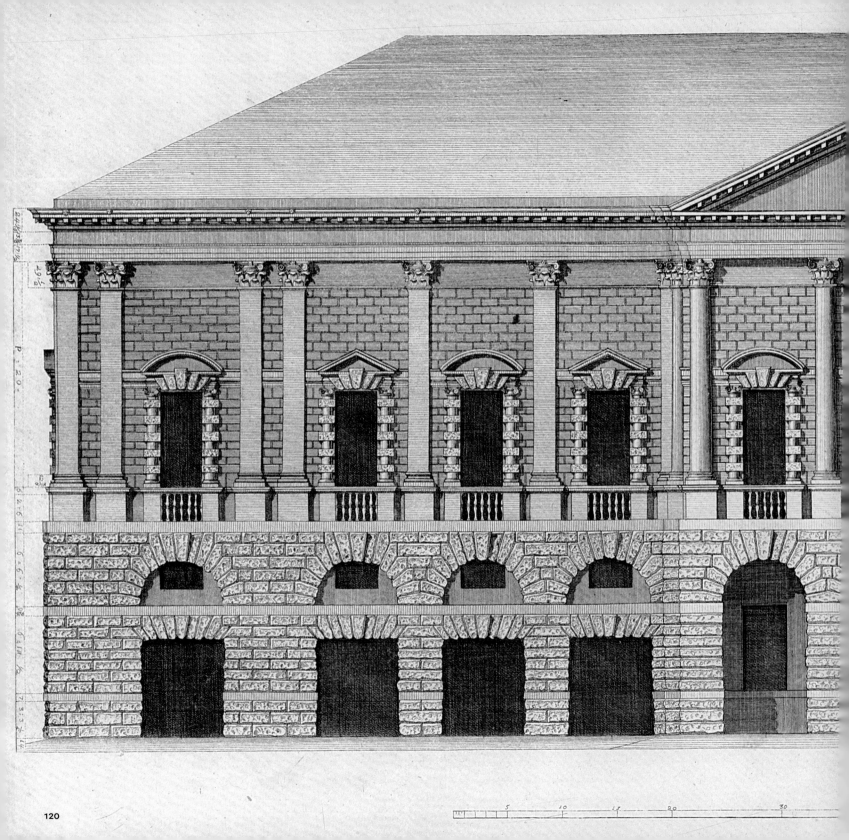

Palazzo della Ragione

Vicenza
Andrea Palladio, 1549

In 1546 the City Council entrusted the reconstruction of the loggias of this ancient palace to the young Andrea Palladio. After countless disputes the project was finally approved in 1549.

En 1546, le Conseil municipal confie au jeune Andrea Palladio la charge de reconstruire les loggias de l'ancien palais public. Après d'innombrables discussions, le projet est définitivement approuvé en 1549.

1546 wurde der junge Andrea Palladio vom Stadtrat beauftragt, die Loggien des antiken Palastes wiederherzustellen. Nach unzähligen Disputen wurde das Projekt 1549 definitiv bewilligt.

En 1546 el Consejo ciudadano le encargó la reconstrucción de las galerías del antiguo palacio al joven Andrea Palladio. Tras numerosas disputas, el proyecto fue aprobado definitivamente en 1549.

Nel 1546 il Consiglio cittadino affida l'incarico di ricostruire le logge dell'antico palazzo al giovane Andrea Palladio. Dopo innumerevoli dispute il progetto è definitivamente approvato nel 1549.

Em 1546 o Conselho municipal confia a tarefa de reconstrução das loggias do antigo palácio ao jovem Andrea Palladio. Após incontáveis disputas, o projeto é definitivamente aprovado em 1549.

In 1546 gaf het stadsbestuur opdracht aan de jonge Andrea Palladio om de loggia's van het antieke paleis opnieuw te ontwerpen. Na talloze debatten werd het project in 1549 eindelijk goedgekeurd.

Doric semi-columns and entablatures in the northeastern corner of the basilica.

Dorische Halbsäulen und Gebälk in der nordöstlichen Ecke der Basilika.

Colonnes engagées et entablements doriques, dans l'angle nord-est de la basilique.

Semicolonne e trabeazione doriche nell'angolo nord orientale della basilica.

Semicolumnas y entablamentos dóricos en la zona nororiental de la basílica.

Meias-colunas e entablamentos dóricos no ângulo nordeste da basílica.

Halfzuilen en Dorische hoofdgestellen in de noordoosthoek van de basiliek.

Villa Almerico Capra "La Rotonda"

Vicenza
Andrea Palladio, 1566

The villa was conceived by Palladio as a commemoration of its owner, Paolo Almerico from Vicenza, who was Apostolic Referendary for popes Pius IV and Pius V. The building is characterised by a Ionic pronaos that recurs on all four sides, and by the dome that evokes that of the Baths of Caracalla.

Die Villa wurde von Palladio für seinen vicentinischen Auftraggeber Paolo Almerico, einen hohen Beamten des Hofstaates von Papst Pius IV. und Pius V., entworfen. Jede Gebäudeseite ist durch einen Pronaos mit ionischen Säulen gekennzeichnet. Die Kuppel erinnert an jene der Caracalla-Thermen.

Palladio a conçu l'édifice comme une glorification de son commanditaire, le Vicentin Paolo Almerico, référendaire apostolique des papes Pie IV et Pie V. L'édifice est caractérisé par un pronaos ionique répété sur les quatre côtés et par sa coupole qui rappelle celle des thermes de Caracalla.

Palladio diseñó la villa como conmemoración de su dueño, el vicentino Paolo Almerico, vicario apostólico de los papas Pío IV y Pío V. El edificio está caracterizado por un pronao jónico que se repite en los cuatro lados y por la cúpula que recuerda a la de Terme di Caracalla.

La villa fu pensata da Palladio come celebrazione del suo committente, il vicentino Paolo Almerico, Referendario Apostolico dei pontefici Pio IV e Pio V. L'edificio è caratterizzato dal pronao ionico che si ripete sui quattro lati e dalla cupola che richiama quella delle Terme di Caracalla.

A villa foi concebida por Palladio como celebração do seu proprietário, Paolo Almerico, de Vicenza, Referendário Apostólico dos papados de Pio IV e Pio V. O edifício caracteriza-se por um pronau jónico repetido nos quatro lados do edifício e pela cúpula que lembra a das termas de Caracalla.

Deze villa ontwierp Palladio in opdracht van de Vicentijnse Paolo Almerico, apostolisch referendaris onder de pausen Pius IV en Pius V. Kenmerkend voor het gebouw zijn het Ionische voorhof aan alle vier de zijden en de koepel die doet denken aan die van de Thermen van Caracalla.

MEMORIÆ PERPETVÆ MANDANS
HÆC DVM SVSTINET AC
ABSTINET

Details of the pronaos and of the ornamental statues.

Détails du pronaos et du décor de statues.

Details des Vorhofs mit schmückenden Skulpturen.

Detalles del pronao y de la decoración de estatuas.

Particolari del pronao e della ornamentazione statuaria.

Pormenor do pronau e da decoração estatuária.

Details van het voorhof en van de statuaire ornamenten.

One of the corridors, which opens onto
the central hall, and the grand dome that
crowns it. The decorations and frescoes are by
Alessandro Maganza.

Un des couloirs d'accès à la grande salle centrale,
avec la coupole grandiose qui la couronne. Les
décors et les fresques sont d'Alessandro Maganza.

Die beeindruckende Kuppel, die einen
der Zugangskorridore zum Hauptsaal
krönt. Verzierungen und Fresken von
Alessandro Maganza.

Uno de los pasillos de acceso al salón central y
la magnífica cúpula que lo corona. Decoración y
frescos de Alessandro Maganza.

Uno dei corridoi di accesso al salone centrale e
la grandiosa cupola che lo corona. Decorazioni e
affreschi di Alessandro Maganza.

Um dos corredores de acesso ao Salão central e a
grandiosa cúpula que o coroa. Decoração e frescos
de Alessandro Maganza.

Een van de gangen naar de centrale zaal en
de beschilderde koepel die haar bekroont.
Versieringen en fresco's van Alessandro Maganza.

Villa Piovene

Lonedo di Lugo
Andrea Palladio, 1545

The villa is characterised by contrasts between the Palladian style, in particular the pronaos marked by six Ionic columns holding up the tympanum, and the entrance portal's baroque diversions.

La villa se distingue par l'opposition entre le plan palladien, spécialement dans le pronaos rythmé par les six colonnes ioniques qui soutiennent le tympan, et l'animation toute baroque du grand portail d'entrée.

Die Villa ist gekennzeichnet durch den Kontrast von palladianischen Elementen, wie dem Pronaos mit sechs ionischen Säulen, die das Tympanon stützen, und barocken Elementen am Eingangsportal.

La villa resalta por el contraste entre el proyecto de estilo palladiano, en particular el pronao caracterizado por seis columnas jónicas que soportan el tímpano, y la decoración barroca del portal de acceso.

La villa si connota per il contrasto tra l'impianto palladiano, specie nel pronao scandito da sei colonne ioniche che sostengono il timpano, e l'animazione barocca del portale d'accesso.

O edifício caracteriza-se pelo contraste entre a estrutura palladiana, em especial no pronau delimitado por seis colunas jónicas que sustentam o tímpano, e a animação barroca do portão de entrada.

Opvallend aan de villa is het contrast in de palladiaanse opbouw, vooral wat betreft het voorhof met zes Ionische zuilen die het timpaan ondersteunen, en de drukke, barokke toegangsdeur.

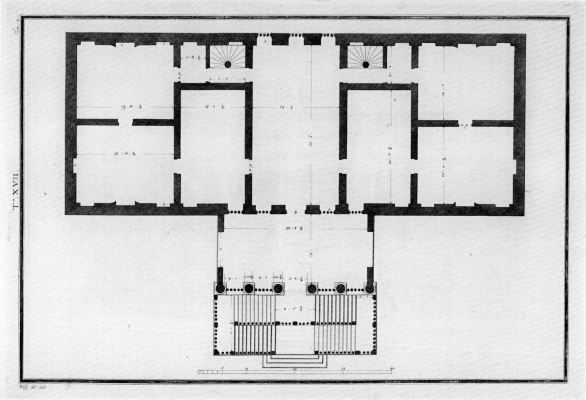

Villa Pojana

Pojana Maggiore
Andrea Palladio, 1548–1549

58   LIBRO

IN POGLIANA Villa del Vicentino è la fottopofta fabrica del Caualier Pogliana : le fue ftanze fono ftate ornate di pitture,e ftucchi bellifsimi da Meffer Bernardino India, & Meffer Anfelmo Canera pittori Veronefi, e da Meffer Bartolomeo Rodolfi Scultore Veronefe : le ftanze grandi fono lunghe vn quadro,e due terzi,e fono in uolto : le quadre hanno le lunette ne gli angoli : fopra i camerini ui fono mezati : la altezza della Sala è la metà più della larghezza , e uiene ad effere al pari dell'altezza della loggia : la fala è inuolata à fafcia, e la loggia à crociera : fopra tutti quefti luoghi è il Granaro,e fotto le Cantine, e la cucina : percioche il piano delle ftanze fi alza cinque piedi da terra : Da vn lato ha il cortile,& altri luoghi per le cofe di Villa, dall'altro vn giardino,che corrifponde a detto Cortile, e nella parte di dietro il Bruolo,& una Pefchiera, di modo che quefto gentil'huomo, come quello che è magnifico,e di nobilifsimo animo,non ha mancato di fare tutti quegli ornamenti, & tutte quelle commodità che fono pofsibili per rendere quefto fuo luogo bello , diletteuole , & commodo .

Bonifacio Pojana commissioned the building from Palladio. The façade recalls Bramantesque elements with its Serlian double-soffit that surrounds five oculi and its broken tympanum.

L'édifice a été commandé à Palladio par Bonifacio Pojana. La façade renvoie à des éléments inspirés de Bramante, avec la serlienne à double bordure contenant cinq oculi, et avec le fronton brisé.

Das Gebäude wurde im Auftrag von Bonifacio Pojana von Palladino entworfen. Elemente von Bramante tauchen im Tympanon auf, das von einer Serliana mit doppeltem Bogenrücken durchbrochen wird und fünf Oculi umschliesst.

Bonifacio Pojana encargó este proyecto a Palladio. La fachada evoca elementos bramantescos en la serliana de doble dintel con cinco óculos, y en el tímpano dividido.

Fu commissionata a Palladio da Bonifacio Pojana. La facciata richiama elementi bramanteschi nella serliana a doppia ghiera, che racchiude cinque oculi, e nel timpano spezzato.

Foi encomendada a Palladio por Bonifacio Pojana. A fachada apresenta elementos que remetem para Bramante, com a serliana em duplo arco que contém cinco óculos redondos e o tímpano quebrado.

Palladio kreeg de ontwerpopdracht van Bonifacio Pojana. Bramantische elementen in de voorgevel zijn de serliana met twee archivolten en vijf vensters en het onderbroken timpaan.

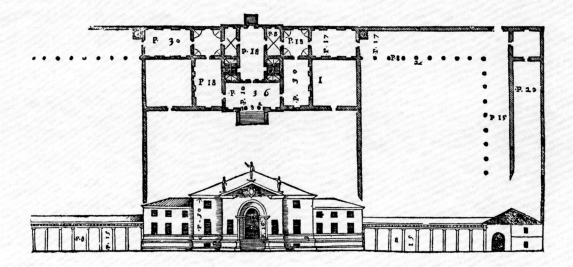

The bellicose family origins of the owner are revealed by the interior decorations, especially in the Emperor's Hall.

Les origines guerrières du commanditaire se manifestent dans la décoration intérieure, en particulier dans la salle des Empereurs.

Die kriegerische Familiengeschichte des Auftraggebers wird in der Innendekoration widergespiegelt, vor allem im Kaisersaal.

El pasado militar del comitente está reflejado en la decoración interior, en particular en la Sala de los Emperadores.

La matrice guerriera del committente è rivelata dalla decorazione interna, specie nella Sala degli Imperatori.

As origens guerreiras do proprietário revelam-se na decoração interior, sobretudo na Sala dos Imperadores.

Het oorlogsverleden van de opdrachtgever spreekt uit de decoraties binnen, vooral die in de Zaal van de Keizers.

La Rocca Pisana

Lonigo
Vincenzo Scamozzi, 1576

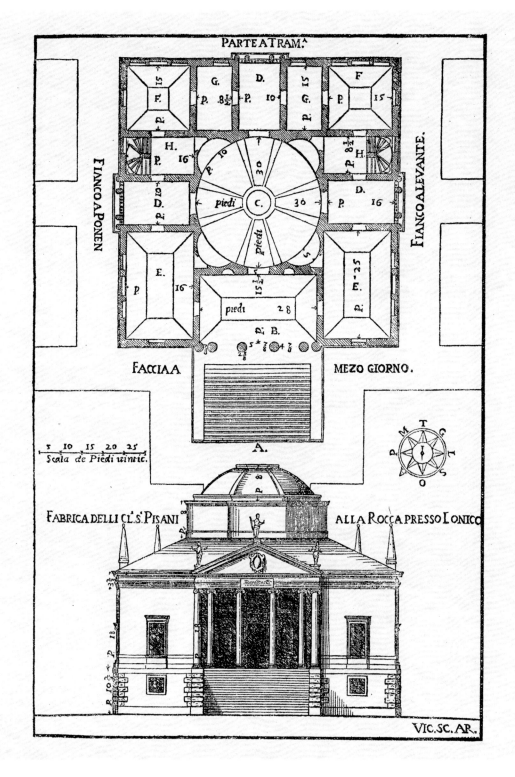

Vincenzo Scamozzi built the villa for the Pisani family as a residence of pleasure and relaxation, on a hilltop overlooking the green plains below.

Vincenzo Scamozzi a réalisé cette villa pour la famille Pisani, comme résidence d'agrément et de repos, au sommet d'une colline qui domine la verte plaine environnante.

Vincenzo Scamozzi erbaute die Villa für die Familie Pisani als einen Ort der Zerstreuung und der Erholung dienen. Sie liegt auf einer Anhöhe, inmitten einer grünen Landschaft.

Vincenzo Scamozzi construyó la villa para la familia Pisani como residencia de placer y de descanso sobre la cumbre de una colina que domina la verde llanura que la rodea.

Vincenzo Scamozzi costruì la villa per la famiglia Pisani come dimora di piacere e di riposo sulla sommità di un colle che domina la verde pianura sottostante.

Vincenzo Scamozzi construiu a villa para a família Pisani como residência de lazer e repouso, no alto de uma colina que domina a verde planície que se estende abaixo.

Vincenzo Scamozzi ontwierp deze villa voor de familie Pisani als rust- en ontspanningsoord op de top van een heuvel die de omringende groene vlakte domineert.

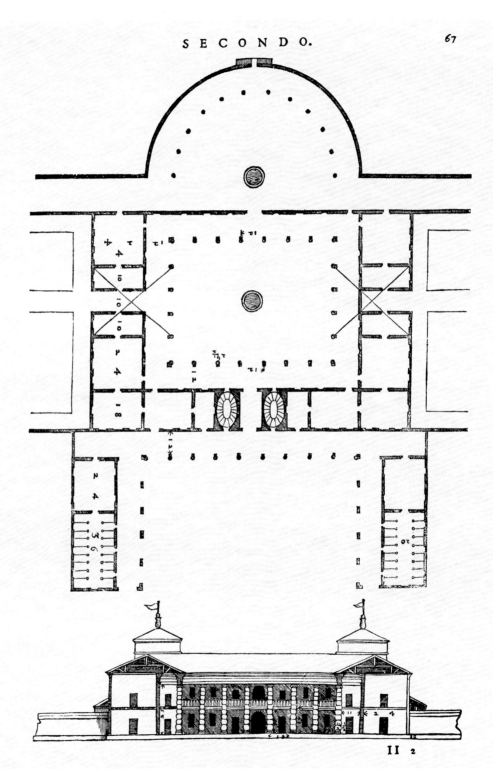

Palladio designed this building for the Serego family, one of the areas dominant feudal families since 1381. The materials and structure of this massive building refer to this aspect of the family.

Palladio a conçu cet édifice pour les Serego, une famille féodale qui dominait ce territoire depuis 1381. La construction massive rappelle cette puissance, dans ses matériaux comme dans ses structures.

Palladio entwarf dieses Gebäude für die feudale Familie Serego, die nach 1381 über die Region herrschte. Die massive Konstruktion unterstreicht diesen Aspekt zusätzlich in den Materialien und Strukturen.

Palladio diseñó este edificio para los Serego, una familia feudal que dominaba el territorio desde 1381. Este aspecto se refleja claramente en los materiales y la estructura de esta grandiosa construcción.

Palladio progettò questo edificio per i Serego, una famiglia feudale dominante nel territorio fin dal 1381. La massiccia costruzione richiama questo aspetto nei materiali e nelle strutture.

Palladio projetou este edifício para os Serego, uma família feudal que dominou o território desde 1381. A construção maciça remete para esta dominação, tanto nos materiais como nas estruturas.

Palladio ontwierp dit gebouw voor de Serego's, een feodale familie die tot 1381 de heerschappij over het gebied had. De materialen en de structuur van het massieve gebouw weerspiegelen dit aspect.

100

Loggia del Consiglio

Verona
Fra' Giocondo, 1476–1493

Villa Badoer

Fratta Polesine
Andrea Palladio, 1556

A stately staircase leads to the elegant Ionic loggia of the main house.

Eine edle Freitreppe führt zur eleganten, ionischen Loggia des Hauptgebäudes.

Un grand escalier noble conduit à l'élégante galerie ionique de la maison de maître.

Una imponente escalera conduce a la elegante galería jónica de la casa principal.

Una nobile scalea conduce all'elegante loggia ionica della casa dominicale.

Uma nobre escadaria conduz à elegante loggia jónica do edifício principal.

Een monumentale trap leidt naar de elegante Ionische loggia van het hoofdgebouw.

LA SEGVENTE fabrica è del Magnifico Signor Francefco Badoero nel Polefine ad vn luo
go detto la Frata, in vn fito alquanto rileuato, e bagnata da un ramo dell'Adige, oue era anticamente vn Caftello di Salinguerra da Efte cognato di Ezzelino da Romano.   Fa bafa à tutta la fabrica
vn piedeftilo alto cinque piedi: a quefta altezza è il pauimento delle ftanze: lequali tutte fono in folaro, e fono ftate ornate di Grottefche di belliffima inuentione dal Giallo Fiorentino.   Di fopra
hanno il granaro, e di fotto la cucina, le cantine, & altri luoghi alla commodità pertinenti: Le colonne delle Loggie della cafa del padrone fono Ioniche: La Cornice come corona circonda tutta la cafa.   Il frontefpicio fopra loggie fa vna belliffima vifta: perche rende la parte di mezo più eminente de i fianchi.   Difcendendo poi al piano fi ritrouano luoghi da Fattore, Gaftaldo, ftalle, & altri alla
Villa conueneuoli.

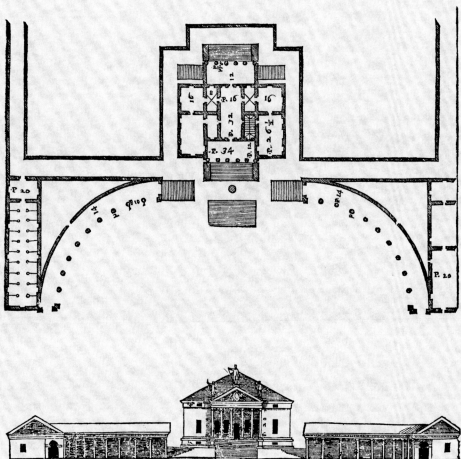

IL MAGNIFICO

The villa, built on reclamation land, is not only a functional farmhouse but also rises like an ancient temple over the flat land.

Construite dans une zone de mise en valeur et parfaitement fonctionnelle sur le plan de l'exploitation agricole, cette villa a pourtant l'allure d'un temple antique dressé dans une plaine.

Das Gebäude wurde auf einer trockengelegten Zone als landwirtschaftlicher Betrieb errichtet und ragt wie ein antiker Tempel aus der Ebene hervor.

La villa, construida sobre un terreno fértil, no es sólo una granja funcional, sino que se eleva como un templo antiguo sobre el llano territorio.

Costruita in una zona di bonifica, questa villa benché funzionale alla conduzione agricola s'innalza come un antico tempio sul piatto territorio.

Construída numa zona de drenagem e ainda que adequada à exploração agrícola, esta villa ergue-se como um templo antigo sobre as terras planas.

Deze villa, gebouwd op drooggelegd land, heeft allereerst een agrarische functie, maar op het vlakke terrein verheft ze zich als een antieke tempel.

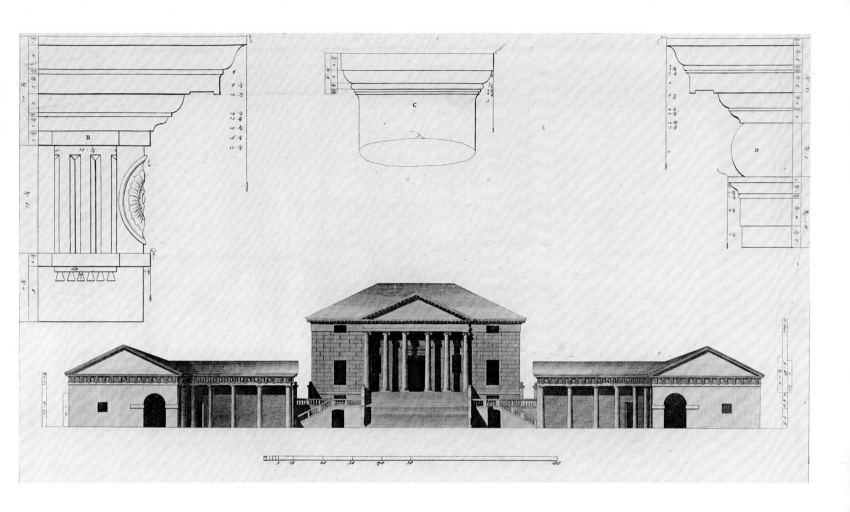

The main house is completed by two curved, exedra porticos.

Das Hauptgebäude wird durch zwei gebogene Portiken in Form einer Exedra vervollständigt.

Le corps de logis seigneurial est complété par deux communs incurvés en exèdre.

Il corpo padronale è completato da due barchesse curvate a esedra.

La casa principal está integrada por dos alas curvadas con forma de exedra.

O corpo principal é acrescido de duas alpendradas curvas em êxedra.

Palazzo Antonini

Udine
Andrea Palladio, 1556

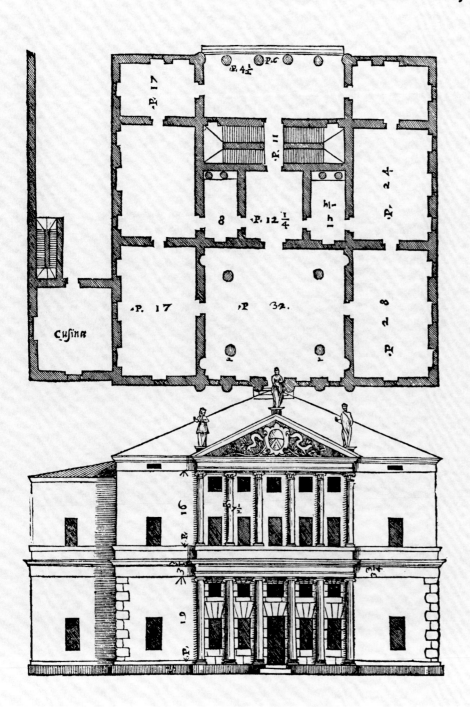

The building's dual role of city palace and suburban villa is clearly visible in its façades: on the front façade, massive ashlar masonry confers an official appearance to the building; on the rear façade, the two-tiered loggia that opens onto the garden pertains to the owner's private sphere.

La double fonction de palais de ville et de villa suburbaine est manifeste dans les façades : à l'avant, des bossages massifs confèrent un caractère officiel à l'édifice ; à l'arrière, la double galerie qui s'ouvre sur le jardin délimite la sphère privée du commanditaire.

Die Doppelfunktion als Stadt- und Landhaus ist in der Fassade gut ersichtlich; das massive Bossenwerk vorne verleiht dem Gebäude einen strengen Charakter, der hintere Teil mit Garten wird durch eine doppelte Loggia abgeschlossen und gewährleistete so die Privatsphäre des Auftraggebers.

La doble función de palacio urbano y de villa suburbana está resaltada en las fachadas. En la parte anterior, el revestimiento de paramento macizo le otorga un aspecto de oficialidad al edificio; en la parte posterior, la doble galería, que se asoma al jardín, sirve como lugar privado del comitente.

La duplice funzione di palazzo cittadino e di villa suburbana è evidente nelle facciate: anteriormente un massiccio bugnato conferisce carattere di ufficialità all'edificio; posteriormente la doppia loggia che si apre sul giardino è in funzione della sfera privata del committente.

A dupla função de palácio citadino e villa suburbana é evidente nas fachadas: na parte anterior, uma bossagem maciça confere um caráter oficial ao edifício; na parte posterior, a loggia dupla que se abre para o jardim serve a esfera privada do proprietário.

De dubbele functie van stadspaleis en landelijke villa blijkt uit de buitenkant: aan de voorzijde geeft een grote bossage het gebouw iets statigs; aan de achterzijde heeft de dubbele loggia, die uitkijkt op de tuin, vooral een privéfunctie.

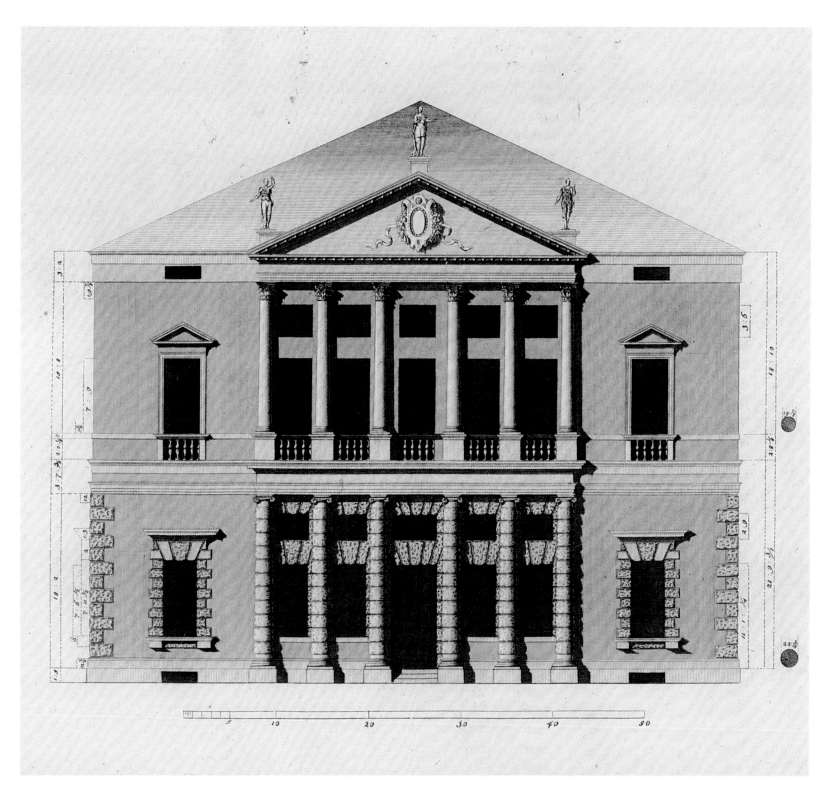

Palazzo Pretorio

Cividale del Friuli
Andrea Palladio, 1565

Designed by Palladio as a residence for the Venetian Provveditori.

Das Gebäude wurde von Palladio als Wohnsitz für die venezianischen Aufsichtsbeamten entworfen.

L'édifice a été conçu par Palladio, comme résidence des Provéditeurs de Venise.

Progettato da Palladio come residenza dei Provveditori Veneti.

Fue diseñado por Palladio como residencia de los Proveedores venezianos.

Projetado por Palladio como residência dos Provedores vénetos.

Ontworpen door Palladio als onderkomen voor Venetiaanse gouverneurs.

Fortezza di Palma

Palmanova
Giulio Savorgnan, Vincenzo Scamozzi, 1598

REALLE FORTEZZA DI PALMA

Scalla di Piedcento aventi per i Profilio.

Scalla di Passi venti per la Piantu.

Anonymous

The Palma Fortress, drawing, 1710.

La Forteresse di Palma, dessin, 1710.

Festung von Palma, Zeichnung, 1710.

Fortaleza di Palma, diseño, 1710.

Fortezza di Palma, disegno, 1710.

A Fortaleza de Palma, desenho, 1710.

Het Palma-fort, tekening, 1710.

Vincenzo Maria Coronelli

The Palma Fortress, engraving, 1708. The military fortifications were built at the end of the 16th century at the behest of the Venetian state.

La Forteresse di Palma, gravure, 1708. Les fortifications ont été construites à la fin du XVIe siècle, sur décision de l'État vénitien.

Festung von Palma, Stich, 1708. Die militärische Befestigungsanlage wurde Ende des 16. Jahrhunderts auf Anordnung der Republik Venedig erbaut.

Fortaleza di Palma, grabado, 1708. Las fortificaciones militares fueron construidas a finales del siglo XVI a instancias del estado de Venecia.

Fortezza di Palma, disegno, 1708. Le fortificazioni militari furono edificate alla fine del Cinquecento per volontà dello Stato veneziano.

A Fortaleza de Palma, gravura, 1708. As fortificações militares foram edificadas no final do século XVI por vontade do Estado de Veneza.

De vesting van Palma, gravure, 1708. Deze militaire vesting werd aan het eind van de 16e eeuw gebouwd in opdracht van de Venetiaanse Staat.

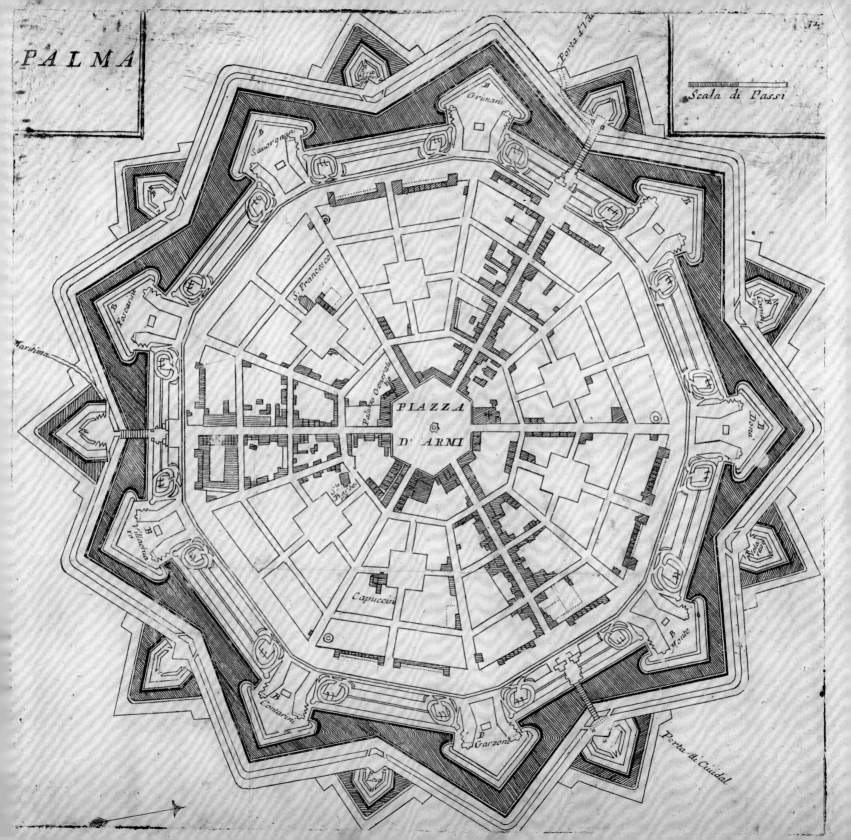

PALMA

Scala di Passi

PIAZZA
D'ARMI

Palazzo dei Diamanti

Ferrara
Biagio Rossetti, 1493

Amongst the most important palazzi of the Italian Renaissance. Built for Sigismondo d'Este from a design by Biagio Rossetti. The diamond-cut, ashlar masonry cladding is its most original feature. The four candelabras and the decorative entrance portal are splendid.

Dieses Gebäude gehört zu den bedeutendsten Palästen der italienischen Renaissance. Es wurde von Biagio Rossetti im Auftrag von Sigismondo d'Este entworfen. Die Fassade mit Bossenwerk und Diamantquadern aus Marmor hat dem Palast den Namen gegeben. Mit vier wunderbar gearbeiteten Kandelabern und Verzierungen am Portal.

Ce palais, l'un des édifices les plus importants de la Renaissance italienne, a été réalisé pour Sigismondo d'Este sur les plans de Biaggio Rossetti. Le revêtement de bossages taillés en pointe de diamant en constitue l'aspect le plus original. Les quatre candélabres et les ornements du portail sont remarquables.

Está clasificado como uno de los edificios más importantes del Renacimiento italiano. Fue realizado por Biagio Rossetti por encargo de Segismundo de Este. El revestimiento de paramento con cortes en forma de punta de diamante es el elemento más original. Aspectos extraordinarios: los cuatro candelabros y la decoración del portal.

È tra i più importanti palazzi del Rinascimento italiano. Realizzato per Sigismondo d'Este su progetto di Biagio Rossetti. Il rivestimento in bugnato tagliato a punte di diamante ne costituisce l'aspetto più originale. Splendide le quattro candelabre e le decorazioni del portale.

Conta-se entre os mais importantes palácios do Renascimento italiano. Foi realizado por Sigismondo d'Este, com projeto de Biagio Rossetti. O revestimento em bossagem talhada a ponta de diamante constitui o seu aspeto mais original. Os quatro candelabros e as decorações do pórtico são esplêndidos.

Een van de opvallendste palazzo's uit de Italiaanse renaissance. Gebouwd voor Sigismondo d'Este naar een ontwerp van Biagio Rossetti. De bossage rondom met diamantreliëf vormt het origineelste aspect. De vier kandelaars en de versieringen op de deur zijn prachtig.

Chiesa di Santa Maria della Steccata

Parma
1521–1539

The magnificent Church established the assertion of Renaissance architecture in Parma. Attribution of the project is uncertain: from Bramante to Sangallo the Younger. Working drawings: Bernardino Zaccagni.

Cette magnifique église marque l'affirmation de l'architecture Renaissance à Parme. La paternité du projet est incertaine – de Bramante à Sangallo le Jeune. Dessins d'exécution : Bernardino Zaccagni.

Die prächtige Kirche ist ein Zeugnis der Renaissance-Architektur in Parma. Unklar ist, ob der Entwurf von Bramante oder Sangallo il Giovane stammt. Entwurfszeichnungen: Bernardino Zaccagni.

La magnífica iglesia ratifica el asentamiento de la arquitectura renacentista en Parma. La atribución del proyecto es incierta, se duda entre Bramante o Sangallo el Joven. Diseño ejecutivo: Bernardino Zaccagni.

La splendida chiesa sancisce l'affermazione dell'architettura rinascimentale a Parma. Incerta l'attribuzione progettuale: da Bramante a Sangallo il Giovane. Disegni esecutivi: Bernardino Zaccagni.

A esplêndida igreja corrobora a afirmação da arquitectura renascentista em Parma. É incerta a atribuição do projeto: de Bramante a Sangallo, o Jovem. Projeto executivo: Bernardino Zaccagni.

Deze prachtige kerk is een prima voorbeeld van renaissance-architectuur in Parma. Het is niet zeker wie hem ontworpen heeft: Bramante of Sangallo de Jongere. Werktekeningen: Bernardino Zaccagni.

Basilica di San Petronio

Bologna
Domenico Aimo da Varignana, 1538
Jacopo Barozzi da Vignola, 1543–1548

Although incomplete, the façade's covering of Istrian stone with the insertion of panels of red marble from Verona is a perfect example of Renaissance architecture in Bologna. Especially noteworthy is the central portal by Jacopo della Quercia.

Quoique inachevé, le revêtement de la façade en pierre d'Istrie, avec insertion de panneaux en marbre rouge de Vérone, est un heureux exemple de l'architecture Renaissance à Bologne. On remarquera le portail central, signé Jacopo della Quercia.

Obwohl die Fassade aus istrischem Stein und Platten aus rotem Veroneser Marmor bis heute unvollendet ist, gilt die Kirche als gelungenes Beispiel der Renaissance-Architektur in Bologna. Nennenswert ist auch das Hauptportal von Jacopo della Quercia.

El revestimiento en piedra de Istria de la fachada incompleta con la introducción de entrepaños de mármol rojo de Verona es un claro ejemplo de la arquitectura renacentista en Bolonia. Cabe resaltar el portal central realizado por Jacopo della Quercia.

Benché incompiuto, il rivestimento della facciata in pietra d'Istria con l'inserimento di specchiature in marmo rosso di Verona è un felice esempio dell'architettura rinascimentale a Bologna. Notevole il portale di mezzo di Jacopo della Quercia.

Embora incompleto, o revestimento da fachada em pedra de Ístria com molduras em mármore vermelho de Verona é um exemplo feliz da arquitetura renascentista em Bolonha. Notável o portal de entrada, por Jacopo della Quercia.

Hoewel de kerk niet is voltooid, is de bedekking van de gevel met Istrische steen en ingevoegd rood marmer uit Verona een prachtig voorbeeld van renaissance-architectuur in Bologna. De opvallende toegangsdeur is een ontwerp van Jacopo della Quercia.

Andrea Palladio

Design for the façade, 1571-1572.

Projet pour la façade, 1571-1572.

Fassadenentwurf, 1571-1572.

Proyecto de fachada, 1571-1572.

Progetto di facciata, 1571-1572.

Projeto de fachada, 1571-1572.

Ontwerp voor de voorgevel, 1571-1572.

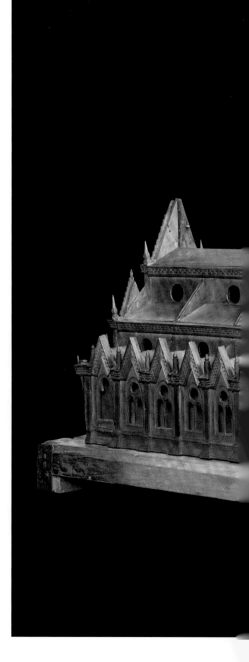

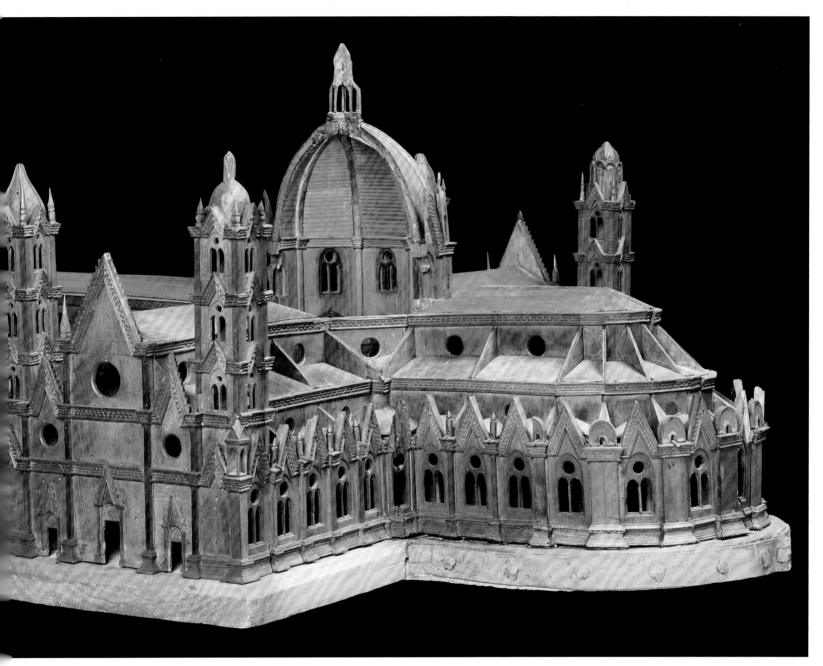

Wooden model for the completion of San Petronio.

Maquette pour l'achèvement de San Petronio.

Entwurf für die Fertigstellung von San Petronio.

Modelo de madera para la finalización de San Petronio.

Modello ligneo per il completamento di San Petronio.

Modelo em madeira para a conclusão de São Petrónio.

Houten model voor de voltooiing van de San Petronio.

Tempio Malatestiano

Rimini
Leon Battista Alberti, 1450

Leon Battista Alberti's project is inspired by the great models of classical Rome. The façade, uncompleted in the upper part, rests on a high base, decorated by a frieze that also runs along the sides. Malatestian symbols, such as the rose with four petals, alternate with the monogram of Sigismondo.

Leon Battista Alberti inspiriert sich für das Projekt an der klassisch-römischen Architektur. Das Gebäude blieb im oberen Teil unvollendet und ruht auf einem hohen, mit einem Band gekrönten Sockel mit alternierenden malatestianischen Wappenelementen, der vierblättrigen Rose und dem Monogramm von Sigismondo.

Le projet d'Alberti s'inspire des grands modèles de l'art romain classique. La façade – restée inachevée dans sa partie supérieure – s'élève sur un puissant podium décoré d'une frise qui règne aussi sur les côtés. Sur cette frise alternent les symboles malatestiens comme la rose à quatre pétales et le monogramme de Sigismondo.

Il progetto di Leon Battista Alberti si ispira ai grandi modelli della classicità romana. La facciata, rimasta incompiuta nella parte superiore, poggia su un alto basamento, decorato da un fregio che corre anche lungo i fianchi.

El proyecto de Leon Battista Alberti está inspirado en los grandes modelos de la época romana clásica. La fachada, incompleta en la parte superior, se apoya sobre una base decorado por un friso a lo largo de los laterales y donde se alternan símbolos malatestianos: la rosa de cuatro pétalos y el monograma de Segismundo.

O projeto de Leon Battista Alberti inspira-se nos grandes modelos clássicos romanos. A fachada, que permaneceu inacabada na parte superior, assenta numa base alta, decorada com um friso que se prolonga em ambas as paredes laterais e no qual se alternam os símbolos malatestianos: a rosa de quatro pétalas e o monograma de Sigismundo.

Het ontwerp van Leon Battista Alberti is geïnspireerd op de grote voorbeelden uit de Romeinse oudheid. De voorgevel, waarvan het bovenste deel onvoltooid is, rust op een hoge fundering versierd met een fries die doorloopt langs de zijkanten en waarin de symbolen van de familie Malatesta elkaar afwisselen: de roos met vier blaadjes en het monogram van Sigismondo.

The temple interior is formed by one huge nave with wooden roof trusses.

Das Innere des Tempels besteht aus einem einzigen breiten Schiff und wird von einer Decke mit hölzernem Dachstuhl überspannt.

L'intérieur du sanctuaire est constitué d'une nef unique dotée d'un plafond en bois à chevrons.

L'interno del tempio è formato da un'unica vasta navata con soffitto ligneo a capriate.

El interior del templo está formado por una única nave amplia con techo de madera con cerchas.

O interior do templo é formado por uma única e extensa nave, com teto de asnas de madeira.

De binnenkant van de tempel bestaat uit één breed middenschip met een plafond met houten spanten.

One of the three lateral chapels, contemporary to Sigismondo, elaborately decorated and enclosed by marble balustrades.

Une des trois chapelles latérales contemporaines de Sigismondo, fermées par des balustres en marbre et richement décorées.

Eine der drei Seitenkapellen stammt vom zeitgenössischen Sigismondo und wird durch reich verzierte Balustraden aus Marmor abgeschlossen.

Una de las tres capillas laterales, de la misma época de Segismundo, rodeada por balaustradas en mármol y profusamente decoradas.

Una delle tre cappelle laterali, coeve a Sigismondo, chiuse da balaustre in marmo e riccamente decorate.

Uma das três capelas laterais, contemporâneas de Sigismondo, cercadas por balaustradas em mármore e ricamente decoradas.

Een van de drie zijkapellen, uit de tijd van Sigismondo, omsloten door rijk versierde, marmeren balustraden.

Rocca di San Leo

San Leo
Francesco di Giorgio Martini, 1479

Contested since the 14th century between the Malatesta and Montefeltro families, who alternated in its possession, it was rebuilt by Federico da Montefeltro in light of the new and crucial importance of artillery.

Disputée à partir du XIVᵉ siècle par les Malatesta et les Montefeltro qui l'occupèrent tour à tour, la forteresse a été restructurée par Frédéric III de Montefeltro, en tenant compte de la nouvelle et décisive importance de l'artillerie.

Seit dem 14. Jahrhundert Schauplatz zahlreicher Auseinandersetzungen zwischen den Familien Malatesta und Montefeltro, ließ Federico da Montefeltro die Festung im Lichte der gewachsenen Bedeutung der Artillerie umbauen.

Disputada desde el siglo XIV por los Malatesta y los Montefeltro, Federico da Montefeltro ordenó su reconstrucción en vistas de la nueva y decisiva importancia de la artillería.

Contesa fin dal secolo XIV fra i Malatesta e i Montefeltro che si alternavano nel suo possesso, fu fatta riedificare da Federico da Montefeltro alla luce della nuova e decisiva importanza dell'artiglieria.

Disputada desde o século XIV entre os Malatesta e os Montefeltro, que se alternavam na sua posse, foi mandada reedificar por Federico da Montefeltro, à luz da nova e decisiva importância da artilharia.

Nadat de Malatesta's en de Montefeltro's elkaar vanaf de 15e eeuw het bezit van het fort hadden betwist, werd het, gezien het toenmalige belang van een fort, herbouwd door Federico da Montefeltro.

Villa Medicea "Ambra"

Poggio a Caiano
Giuliano da Sangallo, 1485

Giuliano da Sangallo prepared the project for Lorenzo the Magnificent. Some further modifications partly changed its original look. Among these, the curved double staircase, originally straight, and the 18th-century gable.

Giuliano da Sangallo prépara le projet pour Laurent le Magnifique. Certaines modifications en ont altéré depuis l'aspect d'origine – entre autres l'escalier à double rampe incurvée (à l'origine droit) et les combles du XVIIIᵉ siècle.

Giuliano da Sangallo bereitete das Projekt für Lorenzo Il Magnifico vor. Einige Abänderungen veränderten Teile des ursprünglichen Aspekts. Zu diesen gehören die zwei gebogenen Treppenläufe mit Podest, die ursprünglich gerade waren, und der Giebel aus dem 18. Jahrhundert.

Giuliano da Sangallo realizó el proyecto para Lorenzo el Magnífico. Algunas modificaciones que se realizaron alteraron parcialmente aspecto original. Entre estas se encuentran la escalinata curvilínea de dos rampas, originariamente rectilínea, y el gablete del siglo XVIII.

Giuliano da Sangallo preparò il progetto per Lorenzo il Magnifico nel 1485. Alcune modificazioni ne alterarono in parte l'aspetto originario. Tra queste la scalinata a due rampe curvilinee, in origine rettilinea, e il fastigio settecentesco.

Giuliano da Sangallo elaborou o projeto para Lourenço, o Magnífico. Algumas modificações alteraram parcialmente o seu aspecto original. Entre estas, a escadaria de dois lances curvilíneos (originalmente retilíneos) e o frontão setecentista.

Giuliano da Sangallo maakte het ontwerp voor Lorenzo il Magnifico. Een aantal wijzigingen veranderde gedeeltelijk het originele aanzicht, waaronder de dubbele gebogen trap, die oorspronkelijk recht was, en de 18e-eeuwse gevelspits.

Salone di Leone X. Frescoes in the lunettes by Pontormo (1520–1525); wall paintings by Andrea del Sarto and Franciabigio (1519–1521) and Alessandro Allori (1578–1582).

Salon de Léon X. Dans les lunettes, fresques de Pontormo (1520–1525) ; sur les murs, fresques d'Andrea del Sarto, de Franciabigio (1519–1521) et d'Alessandro Allori (1578–1582).

Saal von Leo X. Mit Fresken dekorierte Lunetten von Pontormo (1520–1525); an den Wänden Fresken von Andrea del Sarto und Franciabigio (1519–1521) und Alessandro Allori (1578–1582).

Salón de León X. En las bóvedas hay frescos de Pontormo (1520–1525), en la pared de Andrea del Sarto y Franciabigio (1519–1521) y Alessandro Allori (1578–1582).

Salone di Leone X. Nelle lunette, affreschi del Pontormo (1520–1525); alle pareti di Andrea del Sarto e Franciabigio (1519–1521) e Alessandro Allori (1578–1582).

Salão de Leão X. Nas lunetas, frescos de Pontormo (1520–1525) e nas paredes, de Andrea del Sarto e Franciabigio (1519–1521) e Alessandro Allori (1578–1582).

Zaal van Leo X. Op de lunetten fresco's van Pontorno (1520–1525); op de wanden van Andrea del Sarto e Franciabigio (1519–1521) en Alessandro Allori (1578–1582).

Villa Medicea di Artimino

Artimino

Bernardo Buontalenti, 1594–1600

View of the side of the villa and eastern elevation with entrance portal, surmounted by balconies and windows.

Seiten- und Ostansicht der Villa mit Eingangsportal, durchbrochen durch eine Loggia und Fenster.

Vue du côté de la villa et de sa façade est, avec le portail d'entrée surmonté d'un balcon et de fenêtres.

Vista lateral y este de la villa con portal de entrada, atravesado por una logia y ventanas.

Vista laterale ed est della villa con portale d'ingresso, trafitto da una loggia e finestre.

Vista lateral e leste da vila com Portal de entrada, quebrado através de uma loggia e janelas.

Oostelijk uitzicht op de zijkant van de villa en de voorgevel met de toegangsdeur en daarboven ramen en een balkon.

Also known as 'La Ferdinanda', it was created by
Bernardo Buontalenti at the request of Grand
Duke Ferdinando I.

Dite aussi « La Ferdinanda », la villa a été réalisée
pour le compte du grand-duc Ferdinand Iᵉʳ.

Sie ist berühmt als „La Ferdinanda" und war
eine Auftragsarbeit von Großherzog Ferdinand I.
an Buontalenti.

También denominada "La Ferdinanda", fue
realizada por Bernardo Buontalenti por encargo
del Gran Duque Fernando I.

Detta anche "La Ferdinanda", fu realizzata da
Bernardo Buontalenti per incarico del granduca
Ferdinando I.

Também chamada "La Ferdinanda", foi construída
a pedido do grão-duque Fernando I.

Deze villa, ook wel 'La Ferdinanda' genoemd, werd
gebouwd door Bernardo Buontalenti in opdracht
van de groothertog Ferdinando I.

Villa Medicea La Petraia

Firenze
Bernardo Buontalenti, 1576–1589

The inner courtyard was completely frescoed by Cosimo Daddi and Volterrano. In the 19th century the Savoy family, new owners of the villa, decided to cover it with a large skylight, and so transformed the 16th-century courtyard into a ballroom.

La cour intérieure a été entièrement peinte à fresque par Cosimo Daddi et par le Volterrano. Au XIXᵉ siècle, les Savoie – nouveaux propriétaires de la villa – décidèrent de fermer cette cour par une grande verrière, pour la transformer en une grande salle de bal.

Alle Fresken im Innenhof stammen von Cosimo Daddi und Volterrano. Im 19. Jahrhundert beschlossen die Savoyer, neue Eigentümer der Villa, den Hof aus dem 16. Jahrhundert mit einem großen Lichtschacht zu überdachen und ihn in einen Ballsaal umzuwandeln.

Cosimo Daddi y Volterrano realizaron los frescos de todo el patio. En el siglo XIX, los Saboya, los nuevos propietarios de la villa, decidieron cubrirlo con un gran tragaluz transformando de esta forma el patio del siglo XVI en un gran salón de baile.

Il cortile interno venne interamente affrescato da Cosimo Daddi e dal Volterrano. Nell'Ottocento i Savoia, nuovi proprietari della villa, ne decisero la copertura con un grande lucernaio trasformando così il cortile cinquecentesco in un salone da ballo.

O pátio interior foi inteiramente decorado com afrescos por Cosimo Daddi e por Volterrano. No século XIX, os Sabóia, novos proprietários da villa, decidiram cobri-lo com uma grande clarabóia, transformando assim o pátio quinhentista num salão de baile.

De binnenplaats werd geheel met fresco's bedekt door Cosimo Daddi en Volterrano. In de 19e eeuw besloten de Savoia's, de nieuwe eigenaren van de villa, om de 16e-eeuwse binnenplaats af te dekken met een groot dakraam en hem zo te veranderen in een balzaal.

Around 1568, Cardinal Ferdinando de' Medici (son of Cosimo I), wanted to restructure a 14th-century, walled, rural home that belonged to his family. It is doubtful that the project was assigned to Bernardo Buontalenti as has been held up until now; in any event, the work ended in 1589, including organising the Mannerist style garden.

Vers 1568, le cardinal Ferdinand de Médicis (fils de Côme Iᵉʳ) voulut faire remanier à son usage une ferme fortifiée du XIVᵉ siècle, propriété de la famille. Les travaux furent achevés en 1589, y compris l'aménagement maniériste du jardin.

Um 1568 wollte Kardinal Ferdinand (Sohn von Cosimo) ein befestigtes Bauernhaus aus Familienbesitz umstrukturieren. Bis heute ist fraglich, ob der Auftrag an Bernardo Buontalenti vergeben wurde. Jedenfalls waren die Arbeiten 1589 vollendet, inklusive der manieristischen Anordnung des Gartens.

Alrededor del año 1568, el cardenal Fernando, hijo de Cosme I, quiso reconstruir un caserío fortificado del siglo XIV de propiedad de la familia. Hasta ahora se ha asignado la paternidad del proyecto a Bernardo Buontalenti aunque existen dudas al respecto. De todas formas, las obras finalizaron en 1589, incluida la disposición manierista del jardín.

Attorno al 1568 il cardinale Ferdinando (figlio di Cosimo I) volle ristrutturare un casale fortificato trecentesco di proprietà della famiglia. Nel 1589 i lavori erano conclusi, compresa la sistemazione manierista del giardino.

Por volta de 1568, o cardeal Fernando (filho de Cosme I) quis reconstruir uma propriedade de família, um edifício fortificado trecentista. Em 1589 os trabalhos estavam já terminados, incluindo a composição maneirista do jardim.

Rond 1568 wilde kardinaal Ferdinando (zoon van Cosimo I) een 14e-eeuws versterkt plattelandshuis van de familie renoveren. Het is niet zeker of de opdracht werd toegewezen aan Bernardo Buontalenti, zoals men tot nu toe beweert, maar in elk geval waren de werkzaamheden, inclusief de maniëristische aanleg van de tuin, in 1589 voltooid.

Villa Medicea di Castello

Firenze
Niccolò Tribolo, c. 1540
Bernardo Buontalenti, 1576

Owned by the Medici since 1477, the first significant modifications were made by Tribolo on behalf of Duke Cosimo, and then by Buontalenti between 1575 and the end of the century.

Propriété des Médicis depuis 1477, elle subit des transformations importantes, réalisées d'abord par Tribolo sur les instructions du duc Côme, puis par Buontalenti, entre 1575 et la fin du siècle.

Das seit 1477 zum Besitz der Familie Medici gehörende Gebäude wurde signifikanten Veränderungen unterzogen. Zuerst von Tribolo im Auftrag vom Herzog Cosimo, dann von Buontalenti zwischen 1575 und dem Ende des Jahrhunderts.

De propiedad de la familia Medici desde 1477, sufrió modificaciones importantes primero de la mano de Tribolo, por encargo del duque Cosme y, posteriormente, de Buontalenti entre 1576 y finales del siglo.

Già in proprietà dei Medici dal 1477, ebbe significative modificazioni prima ad opera del Tribolo su incarico del duca Cosimo, e poi del Buontalenti tra il 1576 e la fine del secolo.

Propriedade dos Medici desde 1477, sofreu alterações significativas, primeiro por obra de Tribolo encomendada pelo duque Cosme, e depois por Buontalenti, entre 1576 e o final do século.

De villa, al eigendom van de De' Medici's in 1477, onderging talloze aanpassingen; eerst door Tribolo in opdracht van hertog Cosimo en daarna door Buontalenti tussen 1576 en het einde van de eeuw.

Bartolomeo Ammannati, 1559

The giant bronze representing *Winter*.

Géant de bronze représentant *L'Hiver*.

Die mächtige Bronzefigur *L'Inverno*, die den Winter darstellt.

El gigante de bronce que representa *El invierno*.

Il gigante bronzeo che raffigura *Inverno*.

O gigante de bronze que representa *O Inverno*.

De bronzen reus die *De winter* verbeeldt.

The Grotto of the Animals, a fantastic Rocailles setting in which real and imaginary animals sport, work by Bartolomeo Ammannati and others.

La grotte des Animaux – étrange espace de rocailles rempli d'animaux réels et fantastiques – est, entre autres, l'œuvre de Bartolomeo Ammannati.

Die bizarre Welt der Rocaille mit der Tiergrotte, in der sich Tiere und Fabeltiere tummeln. Das Werk stammt von Bartolomeo Ammannati und anderen Künstlern.

La Gruta de los Animales: un ambiente singular con roncailles que acoge animales reales y de fantasía, obra de Bartolomeo Ammannati y otros.

La Grotta degli Animali, bizzarro ambiente a rocailles nel quale si affollano animali reali e fantastici, opera di Bartolomeo Ammannati e altri.

A Gruta dos Animais, singular ambiente de jardim de pedra no qual se misturam animais reais e fantásticos, é obra de Bartolomeo Ammannati e outros.

De Grot van de Dieren, een bizar vertrek vol gebeeldhouwde levensechte en verzonnen dieren, een werk van Bartolomeo Ammannati en anderen.

The stupendous mannerist garden with Tribolo's fountain in the centre.

L'étonnant jardin maniériste, avec au centre la fontaine de Tribolo.

Der Brunnen von Tribolo, inmitten des prächtigen manieristischen Gartens.

El extraordinario jardín de estilo manierista con la fuente de Tribolo en el centro.

Lo stupendo giardino manierista con al centro la fontana del Tribolo.

O magnífico jardim maneirista com a fonte do Tribolo ao centro.

De schitterende maniëristische tuin met in het midden de fontein van Tribolo.

Palazzo Medici Riccardi

Firenze

Michelozzo Michelozzi, 1444

This elegant palace, luxurious inside but with a moderately opulent exterior, was built for Cosimo I the Elder.

Cet élégant palais, aussi riche à l'intérieur que sobre dans son décor extérieur, a été construit pour Côme Ier l'Ancien.

Der elegante Palast mit prunkvollen Innenräumen und schlichter Aussenfassade wurde für Cosimo I il Vecchio erbaut.

Este elegante palacio, rico en su interior y comedido en la fastuosidad del exterior, fue construido para Cosme I el Viejo.

L'elegante palazzo, ricco all'interno quanto misurato nello sfarzo esteriore, fu costruito per Cosimo I il Vecchio.

O elegante palácio, tão opulento no seu interior quanto comedido no luxo exterior, foi construído para Cosme, o Velho.

Dit elegante palazzo, vanbinnen zo rijk versierd en vanbuiten zo sober, werd gebouwd voor Cosimo I de Oudere.

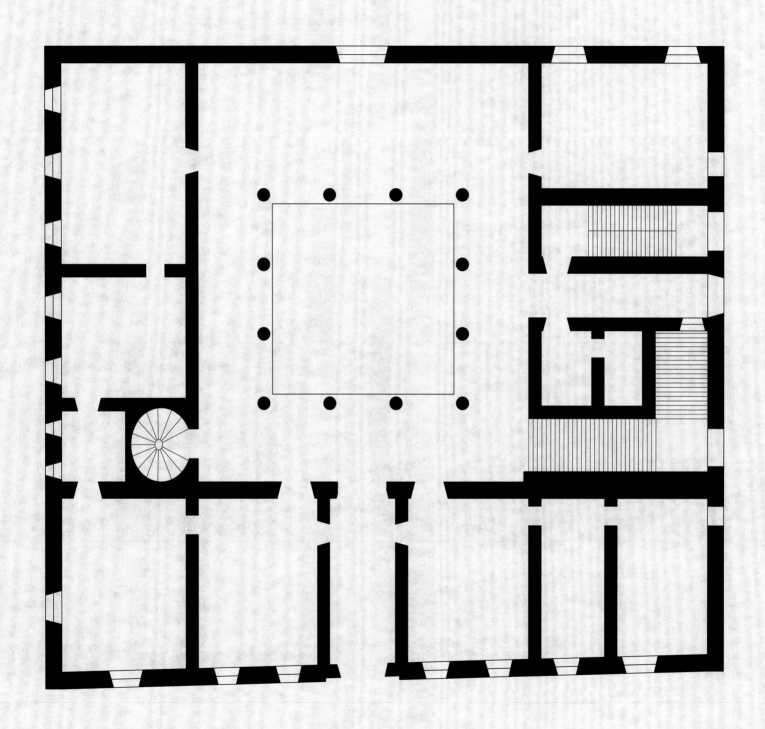

The walled garden adorned with statues.

Le jardin clos, orné de statues.

Der geschlossene, mit Statuen geschmückte Garten.

El jardín cerrado decorado por estatuas.

Il giardino chiuso, ornato di statue.

O jardim interior, ornamentado com estátuas.

De besloten, met beelden versierde tuin.

The Palazzo's Magi chapel. In less than three years, from 1459 to 1461, Benozzo Gozzoli completed the entire fresco cycle.

Die Palastkapelle, Zug der Heiligen Drei Könige. In weniger als drei Jahren, von 1459 bis 1461, vervollständigte Benozzo Gozzoli den gesamten Freskenzyklus.

La chapelle des Mages. Benozzo Gozzoli acheva en moins de trois ans, de 1459 à 1461, le cycle complet des fresques.

La capilla del Palacio, Corteo dei Magi. En menos de tres años, entre 1459 y 1461, Benozzo Gozzoli completó todo el ciclo de frescos.

La cappella di palazzo, Corteo dei Magi. In meno di tre anni, dal 1459 al 1461, Benozzo Gozzoli completò l'intero ciclo di affreschi.

Capela do palácio, Corteo dei Magi. Em menos de três anos, de 1459 a 1461, Benozzo Gozzoli terminou o ciclo completo dos afrescos.

De kapel van het palazzo, Optocht van de koningen. In minder dan drie jaar tijd, van 1459 tot 1461, schilderde Benozzo Gozzoli de hele fresco-reeks.

Palazzo della Signoria

Firenze
Arnolfo di Cambio, Duecento
Michelozzo Michelozzi, 1470
Benedetto e Giuliano da Majano, 1470–1480
Simone del Pollaiolo, 1495
Giorgio Vasari, 1540–1572

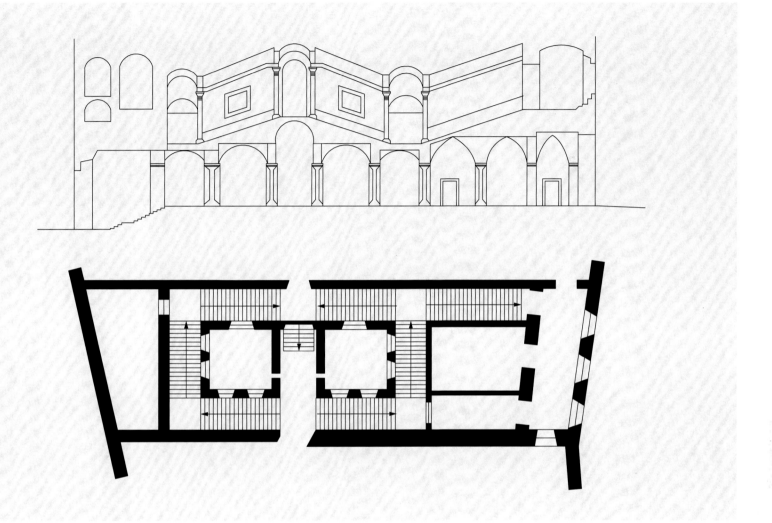

The exterior shell of the palazzo is from the last years of the 13th century, and built according to a project by Arnolfo di Cambio. However, over the centuries a succession of numerous and radical interventions to its interior, especially between the years 1441 and 1572, have actually transformed it into a Renaissance building.

L'enveloppe extérieure du palais, datée des premières années du XIVᵉ siècle, a été conçue par Arnolfo di Cambio. Toutefois, les nombreuses interventions radicales qui se sont succédé au fil des siècles (spécialement entre 1441 et 1572) en ont fait un édifice Renaissance.

Die Ummantelung des Palastes stammt aus dem Ende des 13. Jahrhunderts und beruht auf Plänen von Arnolfo di Cambio. Im Laufe der Jahrhunderte folgten jedoch zahlreiche und radikale Veränderungen im Innern, vor allem zwischen 1441 und 1572, was es de facto zu einem Renaissance-Gebäude macht.

El revestimiento exterior del palacio data de los últimos años del siglo XIII construido sobre una idea de proyecto realizada por Arnolfo di Cambio. Sin embargo, las numerosas y radicales intervenciones de su interior a lo largo de los siglos, especialmente entre 1441 y 1572, lo convierten en un edificio renacentista.

L'involucro esterno del palazzo è degli ultimi anni del Duecento, costruito su un'idea progettuale di Arnolfo di Cambio. Tuttavia i numerosi e radicali interventi succedutisi al suo interno nel corso dei secoli, specie tra il 1441 e il 1572, lo rendono di fatto un edificio rinascimentale.

A parte exterior do palácio é de finais do século XIII e foi concebida por Arnolfo di Cambio. Contudo, as inúmeras e radicais intervenções a que o interior foi sujeito ao longo dos séculos, em especial entre 1441 e 1572, fazem dele um edifício renascentista de fato.

De buitenkant van het paleis werd eind 13e eeuw gebouwd volgens een ontwerp van Arnolfo di Cambio. De talloze radicale ingrepen die in de loop der eeuwen aan de binnenkant zijn uitgevoerd, vooral tussen 1441 en 1572, maken het tot een renaissancegebouw.

Section and plan of Vasari's staircase.

Coupe et plan du grand escalier de Vasari.

Schnitt und Grundriss der vasarianischen Freitreppe.

Sección y planta de la escalinata vasariana.

Sezione e pianta dello scalone vasariano.

Secção e planta da escadaria vasariana.

Doorsnede en plattegrond van de vasariaanse trap.

Giorgio Vasari

Courtyard, 1555–1556.

Cour, 1555–1556.

Patio, 1555–1556.

Pátio, 1555–1556.

Hof, 1555–1556.

Cortile, 1555–1556.

Binnenplaats, 1555–1556.

The Hall of the Five Hundred: the decorated, coffered ceiling is the work of Vasari, 1563–1565.

Der Saal der Fünfhundert. Die dekorierte Kassettendecke ist ein Werk von Vasari, 1563–1565.

Dans la salle des Cinq-Cents, le plafond à caissons décorés est l'œuvre de Vasari, 1563–1565.

Salón de los Quinientos: el techo con casetones decorados es obra de Vasari, 1563–1565.

Il Salone dei Cinquecento: il soffitto a cassettoni decorati è opera del Vasari, 1563–1565.

O Salão dos Quinhentos: o teto com caixotões decorados é obra de Vasari, 1563–1565.

Zaal van de Vijfhonderd. Het versierde cassetteplafond is het werk van Vasari, 1563–1565.

Audience Hall (or of the Two Hundred). Frescoes by Francesco Salviati, 1543–1545.

Salle d'Audience (ou des Deux-Cents). Fresques de Francesco Salviati, 1543–1545.

Der Audienzsaal (oder Saal der Zweihundert). Fresken von Francesco Salviati, 1543–1545.

Sala de la Audiencia (o del Doscientos). Frescos de Francesco Salviati, 1543–1545.

Sala dell'Udienza (o dei Duecento). Affreschi di Francesco Salviati, 1543–1545.

Sala da Audiência (ou dos Duzentos). Afrescos de Francesco Salviati, 1543–1545.

Audiëntiezaal (of Zaal van de Tweehonderd). Fresco's van Francesco Salviati, 1543–1545.

The small study of Francesco I. Decorated by Vasari between 1570 and 1572 for the duke, who was a keen alchemist.

Cabinet de travail de François Iᵉʳ de Médicis, réalisé entre 1570 et 1572 par Vasari pour le grand-duc, alchimiste passionné qui y faisait ses expériences.

Das Studierzimmer von Francesco I. wurde von Vasari zwischen 1570 und 1572 für den Herzog entworfen, der ein leidenschaftlicher Alchimist war.

Estudio de Francisco I realizado por Vasari entre 1570 y 1572 para el duque, apasionado alquimista.

Studiolo di Francesco I. Realizzato dal Vasari tra il 1570 e il 1572 per il duca, appassionato alchimista.

Estúdio de Francisco I de Médicis, realizado entre 1570 e 1572 por Vasari para o duque, um alquimista apaixonado.

Studeervertrek van Francesco I. Tussen 1570 en 1572 door Vasari ontworpen voor de hertog, een zeer fervent alchemist.

Chiesa di Santa Maria Novella

Firenze
Leon Battista Alberti, 1470

Leon Battista Alberti designed the upper façade with the two large volutes for Santa Maria Novella.

L'idée du couronnement de la façade de Santa Maria Novella vient d'Alberti.

Leon Battista Alberti entwarf die Fassade mit den beiden großen Voluten für die Kirche Santa Maria Novella.

La idea del coronamiento de la fachada de S. Maria Novella se atribuye a Leon Battista Alberti.

È di Leon Battista Alberti l'ideazione del coronamento con le due grandi volute per la facciata di Santa Maria Novella.

É de Leon Battista Alberti a concepção do coroamento com as duas grandes volutas para a fachada de Santa Maria Novella.

Het idee voor de kroonlijst op de voorgevel van de Santa Maria Novella is afkomstig van Leon Battista Alberti.

212　　TOSCANA

The use of white and green marble represented a perfect solution for harmonising the two different architectural styles of the façade: Romanesque-Gothic in the lower part up to the entablature and Renaissance above.

L'utilisation de marbres blancs et verts est une solution géniale pour harmoniser les différences entre les styles architecturaux présents dans la façade : roman et gothique pour la partie inférieure jusqu'à l'entablement ; Renaissance dans la partie supérieure.

Die Verwendung von weißem und grünem Marmor erwies sich als geniale Lösung, um die zwei verschiedenen architektonischen Stile der Fassade harmonisch zu verbinden: Der untere Teil bis zum Gebälk ist romanisch-gotisch, der obere Teil stammt aus der Renaissance-Zeit.

El uso de mármol blanco y verde representó una estupenda solución para armonizar los dos estilos de arquitectura diferentes que caracterizan la fachada: románico-gótico en la parte inferior hasta los entablamentos y renacentista en la parte superior.

L'utilizzo di marmi bianchi e verdi rappresentò la geniale soluzione per armonizzare i due differenti stili architettonici presenti nella facciata: romanico-gotico nella parte inferiore fino alla trabeazione; rinascimentale in quella superiore.

A utilização de mármores brancos e verdes constituiu a genial solução para a harmonização dos dois diferentes estilos arquitectónicos presentes na fachada: romano-gótico na parte inferior até ao entablamento; renascentista na parte superior.

Het slimme gebruik van wit en groen marmer brengt evenwicht in de twee verschillende architectonische stijlen in de voorgevel: het onderste deel tot aan het hoofdgestel romaans-gotisch, het bovenste deel renaissancistisch.

Masaccio's *Trinità* reflects the revolution in painting perspective begun by Brunelleschi.

La Trinité de Masaccio introduit dans la peinture la révolution perspective lancée par Brunelleschi.

Mit der *Dreifaltigkeit* gelang es Masaccio, die von Brunelleschi entwickelte Zentralperspektive in der Malerei anzuwenden.

La Trinità de Masaccio representa la revolución de las perspectivas inaugurada por Brunelleschi.

La Trinità di Masaccio recepisce nella pittura la rivoluzione prospettica inaugurata da Brunelleschi.

A Sagrada Trindade de Masaccio introduz na pintura a revolução de perspectiva inaugurada por Brunelleschi.

Het fresco *de Drie-eenheid* van Masaccio voldoet aan de principes van de perspectivische revolutie die door Brunelleschi was ingeleid.

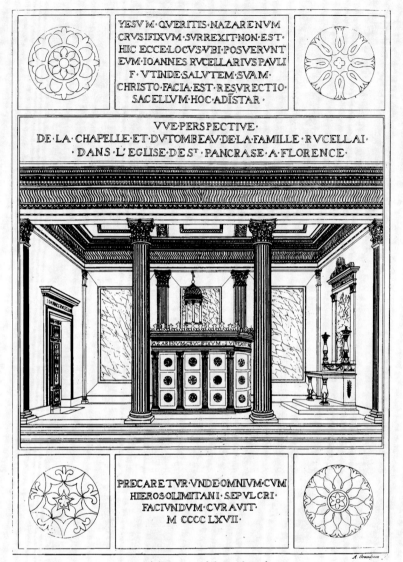

YESVM · QVERITIS · NAZARENVM ·
CRVSIFIXVM · SVRREXIT · NON · EST ·
HIC · ECCE · LOCVS · VBI · POSVERVNT ·
EVM · IOANNES · RVCELLARIVS · PAVLI ·
F · VTINDE · SALVTEM · SVAM ·
CHRISTO · FACIA · EST · RESVRECTIO ·
SACELLVM · HOC · ADISTAR ·

VVE · PERSPECTIVE ·
DE · LA · CHAPELLE · ET · DV · TOMBEAV · DE · LA · FAMILLE · RVCELLAI ·
· DANS · L'EGLISE · DE S^t · PANCRASE · A · FLORENCE ·

PRECARETVR · VNDE · OMNIVM · CVM ·
HIEROSOLIMITANI · SEPVLCRI ·
FACIVNDVM · CVRAVIT ·
M CCCC LXVII

A. Grandjean

Completed in 1467, it appears in rectangular form with a small apse. The bi-coloured marble facing of geometric intarsia is divided by elegant, fluted, Ionic lesenes.

Das Gebäude wurde 1467 fertiggestellt und präsentiert sich in rechteckiger Form mit einer kleinen Apsis. Die Gebäudeverkleidung aus zweifarbigen geometrischen Marmorintarsien wird durch elegante Lisenen bestimmt.

Achevé en 1467, le monument funéraire se présente sous la forme d'un rectangle complété d'une absidiole. Le revêtement de marbre bicolore à incrustations géométriques est scandé par de très élégants pilastres ioniques cannelés.

Acabado en 1467, se presenta en forma rectangular con un pequeño ábside. El revestimiento de mármol bicolor con incrustaciones geométricas se acentúa mediante elegantísimas lesenas.

Completato nel 1467, si presenta in forma rettangolare con una piccola abside. Il rivestimento in marmo bicolore con intarsi geometrici è scandito da elegantissime lesene.

Terminado em 1467, de forma retangular e com uma pequena abside. O revestimento em mármore bicolor, com entalhes geométricos, é delimitado por elegantíssimas pilastras.

Werd voltooid in 1467 en bestaat uit een rechthoekige vorm met een kleine apsis met vensters. De bekleding van tweekleurig marmer met geometrisch inlegwerk bevat elegante lisenen.

The restrained architecture of the portico with low arches on Ionic columns.

Le cloître du couvent se distingue par une galerie d'arcatures surbaissées sur colonnes ioniques.

Der Kreuzgang des Klosters ist von einem niedrig gewölbten Portikus aus ionischen Säulen geprägt.

El claustro del convento caracterizado por un porticado de arcos rebajados sobre columnas jónicas.

Il chiostro del convento che si distingue per la sobria architettura del portico ad archi ribassati su colonne ioniche.

O claustro do convento, que se distingue por um pórtico de arcos rebaixadas sobre colunas jónicas.

De kloostergang bestaat uit een galerij van verlaagde bogen op Ionische zuilen.

The library is divided into three naves by a double row of delicate arches.

La bibliothèque est partagée en trois nefs par une double rangée d'arcades légères.

La biblioteca è spartita in tre navate da una doppia fila di leggere arcate.

Die Bibliothek ist durch eine Doppelreihe leicht gewölbter Arkaden in drei Schiffe geteilt.

A biblioteca, repartida em três naves por uma fila dupla de arcadas leves.

La biblioteca, realizada en tres naves con una fila doble de arcadas finas.

De bibliotheek is opgedeeld in drie beuken door een dubbele rij van lichte bogen.

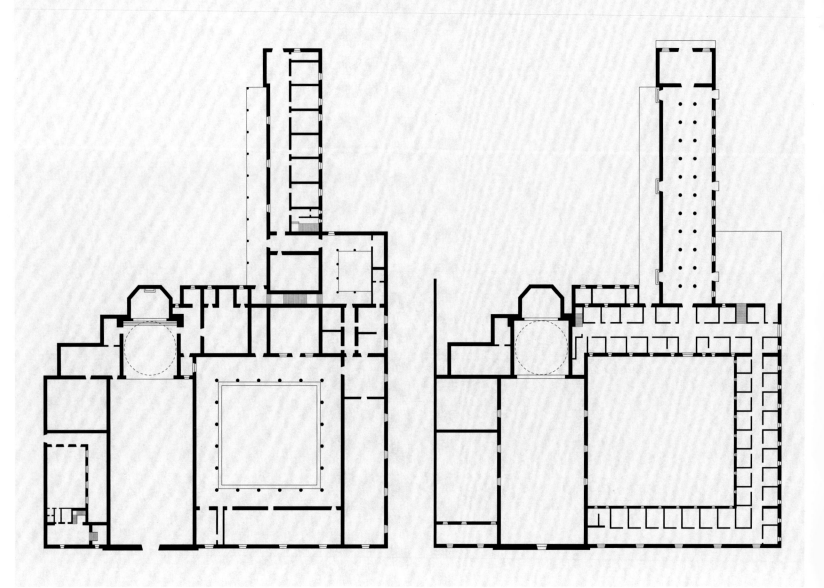

Plan of the ground floor and the first floor.

Plan du rez-de-chaussée et du premier étage.

Grundriss des Erdgeschosses und des ersten Obergeschosses.

Plano de la planta baja y de la primera planta.

Pianta del piano terra e del primo piano.

Planta do piso térreo e do primeiro andar.

Plattegrond van de begane grond en de eerste verdieping.

Beato Angelico

Annunciazione, 1435–1445.

Cappella de' Pazzi

Firenze
Filippo Brunelleschi, 1429–1459

Reminiscent of the Old Sacristy of San Lorenzo. Begun in 1429, it was not fully finished at the architect's death in 1446.

Souvenir de la Vieille Sacristie de San Lorenzo. Commencée en 1429, elle n'était pas totalement terminée à la mort de l'architecte, en 1446.

Erinnert an die Alte Sakristei von San Lorenzo. Der Bau wurde 1429 begonnen und war beim Tod des Architekten 1446 noch nicht ganz vollendet.

Recuerda a la Sacristía vieja de San Lorenzo. Su realización comenzó en 1429 y cuando falleció su autor, en 1446, no estaba completamente terminada.

Ricorda la Sagrestia Vecchia di San Lorenzo. Iniziata nel 1429, non era del tutto finita alla morte dell'architetto, 1446.

Recorda a Sacristia Velha de São Lourenço. Iniciada em 1429, ainda não estava terminada à morte do arquiteto, em 1446.

Doet denken aan de Oude Sacristie van San Lorenzo. De bouw begon in 1429 en was nog niet volledig voltooid toen de architect in 1446 overleed.

Details of the chapel interior.

Détails de l'intérieur de la chapelle.

Details im Innern der Kapelle.

Detalles del interior de la capilla.

Particolari dell'interno della cappella.

Pormenores do interior da capela.

Details aan de binnenkant van de kapel.

Spedale degli Innocenti

Firenze
Filippo Brunelleschi, 1420–1445

On a wide staircase, Brunelleschi raised a portico of nine round arches. The glazed terracotta sculptures in the roundels are by Andrea della Robbia.

Brunelleschi a élevé sur une série de degrés un portique de neuf arcatures en plein cintre. Les sculptures des médaillons en terre cuite vitrifiée sont l'œuvre de Andrea della Robbia.

Auf einem breiten Sockel erhebt sich der Portikus mit neun Rundbögen. Die Rundbilder aus glasiertem Terrakotta stammen von Andrea della Robbia.

Brunelleschi realizó un pórtico de nueve arcos redondos en esta amplia escalinata. Las esculturas de terracota vidriada de los medallones fueron realizadas por Andrea della Robbia.

Su un'ampia gradinata, Brunelleschi innalzò un portico di nove arcate a tutto sesto. Le sculture nei tondi in terracotta invetriata sono di Andrea della Robbia.

Nesta ampla escadaria, Brunelleschi ergueu um pórtico de nove arcos redondos. As esculturas de terracota vitrificada nos círculos são da autoria de Andrea della Robbia.

Brunelleschi bouwde op een brede trap een zuilengalerij met negen rondbogen. De ronde sculpturen van geglazuurd terracotta zijn van Andrea della Robbia.

Santa Maria del Fiore

Firenze
Filippo Brunelleschi, 1417

A compendium of Florentine architecture. To the left, the octagonal baptistery of St John; in the middle, Brunelleschi's dome; at right Giotto's bell tower.

Un des sommets de l'architecture florentine. À gauche, le baptistère octogonal de S. Giovanni; au centre, le dôme de Brunelleschi; à droite, le campanile de Giotto.

Ein Beispiel florentinischer Architektur. Links befindet sich das achteckige Baptisterium San Giovanni, in der Mitte die Kuppel von Brunelleschi und rechts der Glockenturm von Giotto.

Un compendio de arquitectura florentina. A la izquierda, el baptisterio de forma octagonal de S. Juan; en el centro, la cúpula de Brunelleschi, y a la derecha, el campanil de Giotto.

Una summa dell'architettura fiorentina. A sinistra il battistero ottagonale di San Giovanni, al centro la cupola di Brunelleschi, a destra il campanile di Giotto.

Uma síntese da arquitetura florentina. À esquerda, o batistério octogonal de S. João; ao centro, a cúpula de Brunelleschi; à direita, o campanário de Giotto.

Een overzicht van de Florentijnse architectuur. Links, de achthoekige San Giovanni-doopkapel, in het midden de koepel van Brunelleschi, rechts de klokkentoren van Giotto.

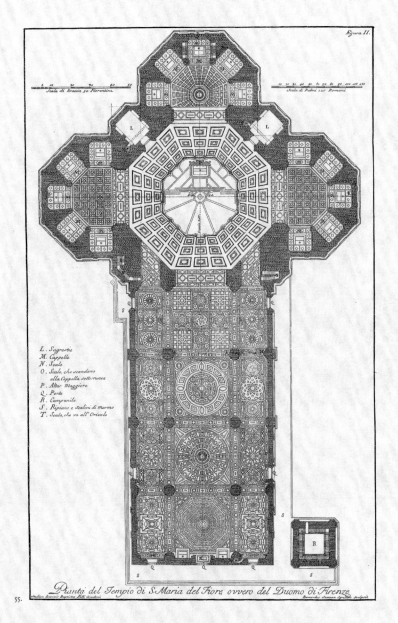

L . Sagrestie
M . Cappelle
N . Scale
O . Scale, che scendano
 alla Cappella sotterranea
P . Altar Maggiore
Q . Porte
R . Campanile
S . Ripiano e scalini di marmo
T . Scala, che va all' Orivolo

Pianta del Tempio di S. Maria del Fiore ovvero del Duomo di Firenze

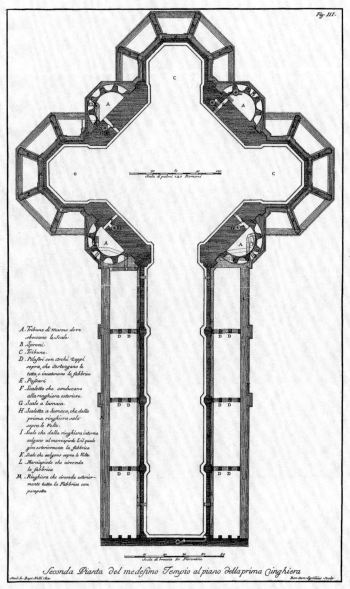

A . Tribune di marmo dove
 sboccano le Scale
B . Sproni
C . Tribune
D . Pilastri con archi e tappi
 sopra, che sostengano le
 tetta, e incatenano la fabbrica
E . Passari
F . Scalette che conducano
 alla ringhiera esteriore
G . Scale a lumaca
H . Scaletta a lumaca, che dalla
 prima ringhiera sale
 sopra le Volte
I . Scale che dalla ringhiera interna
 salgano al marciapiede Lil quale
 gira esteriormente la fabbrica
K . Scale che salgono sopra le Volte
L . Marciapiede che circonda
 la fabbrica
M . Ringhiera che circonda esterior-
 mente tutta la Fabbrica con
 parapetta

Seconda Pianta del medesimo Tempio al piano della prima Ringhiera

Fig. V.

Taglio del medesimo Tempio fatto sulla Linea IK della Figura II.

58. I.

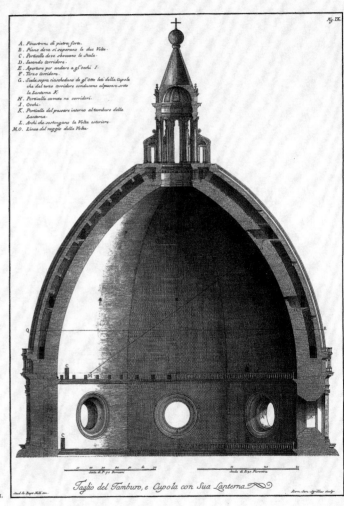

Fig. IX.

A . Finestroni di pietra forte.
B . Piano dove si separano le due Volte.
C . Porticella dove sboccano le Scale.
D . Secondo corridore.
E . Apertura per andare a gl'occhi I.
F . Terzo corridore.
G . Scala sopra ciascheduno de gl'Otto lati della Cupola
    che dal terzo corridore conducono al passare sotto
    la Lanterna K.
H . Porticella cavate ne' corridori.
I . Occhi.
K . Porticella del passare interno al tamburo della
    Lanterna.
L . Archi che sostengano la Volta esteriore.
M.O. Linea del raggio della Volta.

Taglio del Tamburo, e Cupola con Sua Lanterna

The dome of Santa Maria del Fiore was completed, with the exception of the lantern, in 1434 scrupulously following the design presented by Brunelleschi in 1417.

La coupole de Santa Maria del Fiore – à l'exception de la lanterne – a été terminée en 1434, en respectant scrupuleusement le projet soumis par Brunelleschi en 1417.

Mit Ausnahme der Laterne wurde die Kuppel von Santa Maria del Fiore 1434 fertiggestellt, wobei getreu nach Brunelleschis Entwurf von 1417 gearbeitet wurde.

La cúpula de Santa Maria del Fiore fue finalizada en 1434, excepto la linterna, respetando fielmente el proyecto que Brunelleschi presentó en 1417.

La cupola di Santa Maria del Fiore fu completata nel 1434 ad eccezione della lanterna, rispettando pienamente il progetto che Brunelleschi aveva eseguito nel 1417.

A cúpula de Santa Maria del Fiore, à exceção da lanterna, foi concluída em 1434, respeitando rigorosamente o projeto apresentado por Brunelleschi em 1417.

De koepel van de Santa Maria del Fiore werd, met uitzondering van de lantaarn, voltooid in 1434; precies volgens het ontwerp dat Brunelleschi in 1417 had voorgelegd.

The dome's marble lantern is in the form of a *tempietto*. Designed by Brunelleschi in 1436, it was completed in 1471 with the installation of the bronze globe by Andrea del Verrocchio.

La lanterne de marbre de la coupole est en forme de *tempietto*. Conçue par Brunelleschi en 1436, elle a été achevée en 1471 avec l'installation de la sphère de bronze, œuvre d'Andrea del Verrochio.

Die marmorne Laterne der Kuppel in Form eines *Tempietto*. Sie wurde nach einem Entwurf Brunelleschis 1436 erbaut und 1471 mit dem Aufsetzen der Bronzekugel von Andrea del Verrocchio vollendet.

La linterna de mármol de la cúpula con forma de templete. Realizada por Brunelleschi en 1436, fue finalizada en 1471 con la instalación del globo de bronce de Andrea del Verrocchio.

La lanterna marmorea della cupola è a forma di tempietto. Progettata da Brunelleschi nel 1436, fu ultimata nel 1471 con l'installazione del globo, opera in bronzo di Andrea del Verrocchio.

A lanterna de mármore da cúpula tem a forma de *tempietto*. Concebida por Brunelleschi em 1436, foi terminada em 1471 com a instalação do globo de bronze, obra de Andrea del Verrocchio.

De marmeren lantaarn van de koepel in de vorm van een tempeltje. Brunelleschi ontwierp hem in 1436 en in 1471 werd hij voltooid met de plaatsing van de bol, een bronzen werk van Andrea del Verrocchio.

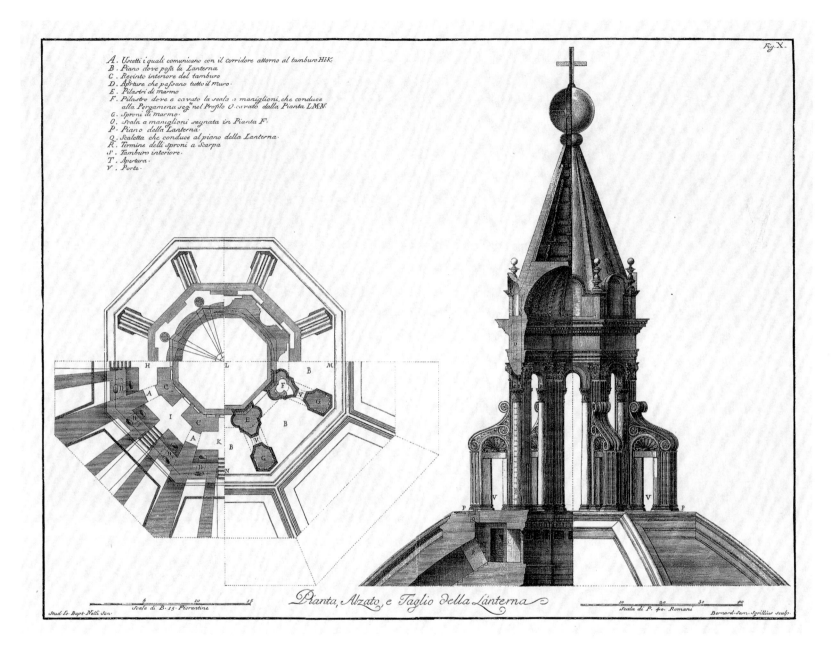

Fig. X.

A. *Urcetti i quali comunicano con il corridore attorno al tamburo HIK.*
B. *Piano dove posta la Lanterna.*
C. *Recinto interiore del tamburo.*
D. *Aperture che passano tutto il muro.*
E. *Pilastri di marmo.*
F. *Pilastro dove e cavato la scala a maniglioni, che conduce alla Pergamena seg:ta nel Profilo O cavato dalla Pianta LMN.*
G. *Sproni di marmo.*
O. *Scala a maniglioni segnata in Pianta F.*
P. *Piano della Lanterna.*
Q. *Scaletta che conduce al piano della Lanterna.*
R. *Termine delli sproni a Scarpa.*
S. *Tamburo interiore.*
T. *Apertura.*
V. *Porte.*

Pianta, Alzato, e Taglio della Lanterna

Scala di B. 15 Fiorentine

Stud.Io.Bapt.Nelli Sen.

Scala di P. 40 Romani

Bernard.Sans.Sgrilline sculp.

TOSCANA 231

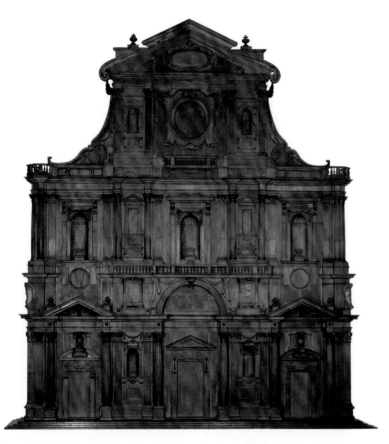

Bernardo Buontalenti

Wooden model of the façade.

Maquette en bois de la façade.

Holzmodell der Fassade.

Modelo de madera para la fachada.

Modello ligneo della facciata.

Modelo em madeira da fachada.

Houten model van de voorgevel.

Giovanni Antonio Dosio

Wooden model of the façade.

Maquette en bois de la façade.

Holzmodell der Fassade.

Modelo de madera para la fachada.

Modello ligneo della facciata.

Modelo em madeira da fachada.

Houten model van de voorgevel.

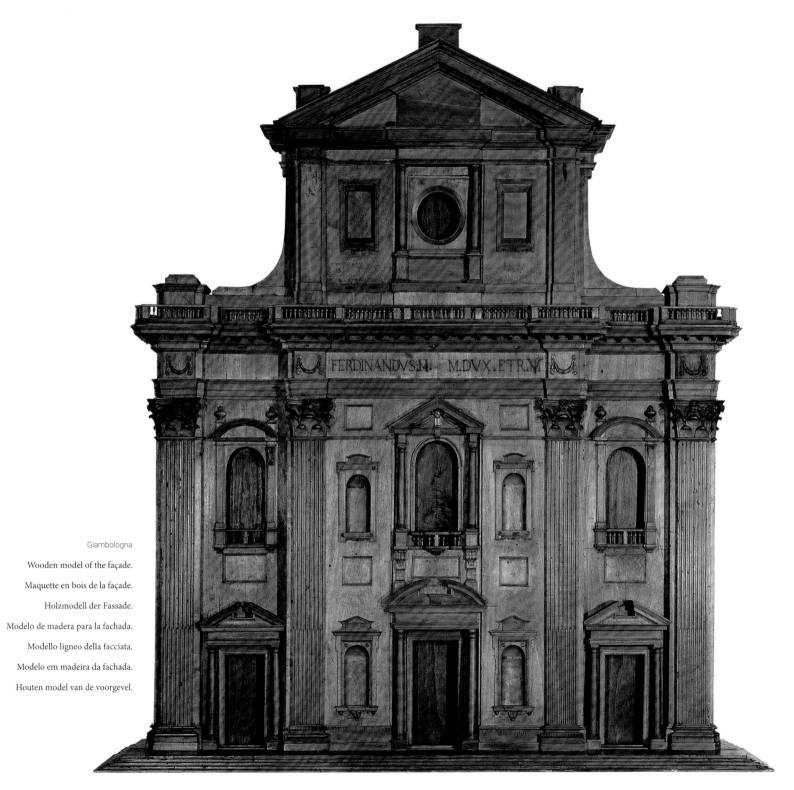

Giambologna

Wooden model of the façade.

Maquette en bois de la façade.

Holzmodell der Fassade.

Modelo de madera para la fachada.

Modello ligneo della facciata.

Modelo em madeira da fachada.

Houten model van de voorgevel.

Palazzo Rucellai

Firenze
Leon Battista Alberti, 1447–1451

LEON BATTISTA ALBERTI
BL 1

PALAZZO RUCELLAI FIRENZE
VIA DELLA VIGNA NUOVA

Partial facade of Palazzo Rucellai with
interior section.

Vue partielle du palais Rucellai et coupe intérieure.

Teilansicht des Palazzo Rucellai mit Innenbereich.

Fachada parcial del Palazzo Rucellai con la
parte interior.

Parziale prospetto di Palazzo Rucellai con
sezione interna.

Fachada parcial do Palazzo Rucellai com
secção interior.

Deel van de voorgevel van Palazzo Rucellai en kijkje
naar binnen.

Giorgio Vasari il Giovane.

Façade of Palazzo Rucellai.

Façade du palais Rucellai.

Fassade des Palazzo Rucellai.

Diseño de la fachada del Palacio Rucellai.

Disegno della facciata di Palazzo Rucellai.

Desenho da fachada do Palazzo Rucellai.

Voorgevel van Palazzo Rucellai.

Palazzo Strozzi

Firenze
Giuliano da Sangallo, Benedetto da Maiano, Simone del Pollaiolo, 1489–1530

Giuliano da Sangallo

Wooden model of Palazzo Strozzi.

Maquette en bois du palais Strozzi.

Holzmodell des Palazzo Strozzi.

Modelo de madera del Palacio Strozzi.

Modello ligneo di Palazzo Strozzi.

Modelo em madeira do Palazzo Strozzi.

Houten model van Palazzo Strozzi.

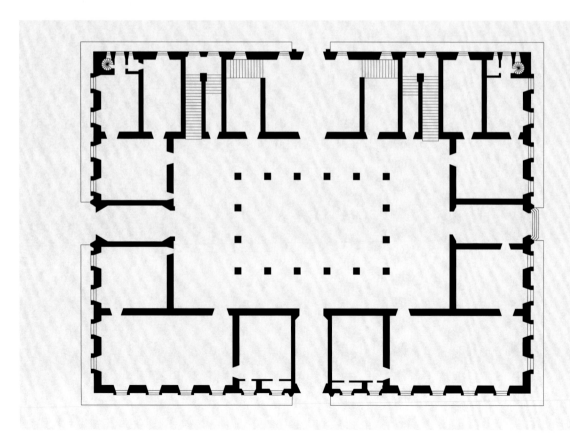

Plan of the palazzo.

Plan du palais.

Grundriss des Palastes.

Planta del palacio.

Pianta del palazzo.

Planta do palácio.

Plattegrond van het palazzo.

Giorgio Vasari il Giovane

Half elevation of Palazzo Strozzi, circa 1600.

Demi-élévation du palais Strozzi, vers 1600.

Teilansicht des Palazzo Strozzi, ca. 1600.

Semi-alzado del Palacio Strozzi, ca 1600.

Metà alzato di Palazzo Strozzi, 1600 ca.

Meio-alçado do Palazzo Strozzi, cerca de 1600.

Vooraanzicht van Palazzo Strozzi, ca. 1600.

Basilica di San Lorenzo

Firenze

Filippo Brunelleschi, 1418–1419

The cloister with portico and upper loggia.

Le cloître avec son portique surmonté
d'une galerie.

Der Kreuzgang mit Portikus und der darüber
liegenden Loggia.

El claustro con el pórtico y una galería superior.

Il chiostro con portico e soprastante loggiato.

O claustro com pórtico e arcos superiores.

De kloostergang met galerij en loggia daarboven.

Interior of the Basilica of San Lorenzo, 1418.

Intérieur de la basilique de San Lorenzo, 1418.

Das Innere der Basilika San Lorenzo, 1418.

El interior de la Basílica de San Lorenzo, 1418.

L'interno della Basilica di San Lorenzo, 1418.

O interior da basílica de São Lourenço, 1418.

Interieur van de San Lorenzo-basiliek, 1418.

Giuliano da Sangallo

Design for the façade of San Lorenzo, 1516.

Projet pour la façade de San Lorenzo, 1516.

Entwurf für die Fassade von San Lorenzo, 1516.

Proyecto para la fachada de S. Lorenzo, 1516.

Progetto per la facciata di San Lorenzo, 1516.

Projeto para a fachada de São Lourenço, 1516.

Ontwerp voor de voorgevel van de San Lorenzo, 1516.

Copy of a design
attributed to Raphael
for the façade of
San Lorenzo, 1504–1508.

Copie du projet atttribué
à Raphaël pour la
façade de San Lorenzo,
1504–1508.

Kopie eines Raffaello
zugeschriebenen
Entwurfs für die
Fassade von San
Lorenzo, 1504–1508.

Copia del proyecto
atribuido a Rafael,
1504–1508.

Copia del progetto
attribuito a Raffaello
per la facciata di
San Lorenzo, 1504–1508.

Cópia do projeto
atribuído a Raffaello
para a fachada de San
Lorenzo, 1504–1508.

Kopie van het ontwerp
voor de voorgevel
van de San Lorenzo,
dat aan Rafaël wordt
toegeschreven,
1504–1508.

Between 1428 and 1429 Brunelleschi built the Sacristy, a "manifesto" of Renaissance Architecture.

Entre 1428 et 1429, Brunelleschi a édifié la Sacristie, véritable « manifeste » architectural de la Renaissance.

Zwischen 1428 und 1429 errichtete Brunelleschi die Sakristei, ein Manifest der Renaissance-Architektur.

Entre 1428 y 1429, Brunelleschi realizó la Sacristía, "manifesto" de la arquitectura del Renacimiento.

Fra il 1428 e il 1429 Brunelleschi edificò la Sagrestia, "manifesto" del Rinascimento in architettura.

Entre 1428 e 1429, Brunelleschi edificou a Sacristia, verdadeiro "manifesto" do Renascimento em arquitetura.

Brunelleschi bouwde de Sacristie, 'manifest' van de renaissance-architectuur, tussen 1428 en 1429.

Interior of the dome of the Old Sacristy.

Intérieur de la coupole de l'Ancienne Sacristie.

Innenansicht der Kuppel der Alten Sakristei.

El interior de la cúpula de la Sacristía vieja.

L'interno della cupola della Sagrestia Vecchia.

O interior da cúpula da Sacristia Velha.

Binnenkant van de koepel van de Oude Sacristie.

Interior of the New Sacristy commissioned from Michelangelo in 1521 by Cardinal Giulio de' Medici and Pope Leo X.

Intérieur de la Nouvelle Sacristie, commandée à Michel-Ange en 1521 par le cardinal Jules de Médicis et le pape Léon X.

Die Innenarbeiten an der Neuen Sakristei übernahm Michelangelo 1521 im Auftrag von Kardinal Giulio de' Medici und Papst Leo X.

El interior de la Sacristía nueva encargada a Miguel Ángel en 1521 por el cardenal Julio de Médici y el papa León X.

L'interno della Sagrestia Nuova, commissionata a Michelangelo nel 1521 dal cardinale Giulio de' Medici e il papa Leone X.

O interior da Sacristia Nova, encomendada a Michelangelo em 1521 pelo cardeal Júlio de Médici e o papa Leão X.

Interieur van de Nieuwe Sacristie, waarvoor Michelangelo in 1521 de opdracht kreeg van kardinaal Giulio de' Medici en van paus Leo X.

New Sacristy, Michelangelo Buonarroti. To the left, funerary monument to Lorenzo de' Medici. To the right, that of Giuliano de' Medici.

La Nouvelle Sacristie, de Michel-Ange. À gauche, le monument funèbre de Laurent de Médicis ; à droite, celui de Julien de Médicis.

Neue Sakristei, Michelangelo Buonarroti. Links das Grabmal von Lorenzo de' Medici. Rechts das Grabmal von Giuliano de' Medici.

Sacristía nueva, Miguel Ángel Buonarroti. A la izquierda, el monumento fúnebre a Lorenzo de Médici. A la derecha, el de Juliano de Médici.

Sagrestia Nuova, Michelangelo Buonarroti. A sinistra, il monumento funebre a Lorenzo de' Medici. A destra, quello di Giuliano de' Medici.

A Sacristia Nova, Michelangelo Buonarroti. À esquerda, o monumento fúnebre a Lourenço de Médici; à direita, o de Juliano de Médici.

Nieuwe Sacristie, Michelangelo Buonarroti. Links het grafmonument van Lorenzo de' Medici. Rechts, dat van Giuliano de' Medici.

Biblioteca Laurenziana

Firenze
Michelangelo Buonarroti, 1524

Begun by Michelangelo in 1524 and finished
around 1570 by Vasari and Ammannati following
the master's drawings.

Commencée en 1524 par Michel-Ange et achevée
vers 1570 par Vasari et Ammannati, sur les plans
du Maître.

1524 begann Michelangelo mit dem Bau, der um
1570 von Vasari und Ammannati nach den Plänen
des Maestro fertiggestellt wurde.

Su construcción comenzó en 1524 de la mano de
Miguel Ángel y fue finalizada alrededor de 1570
por Vasari y Ammannati siguiendo los diseños
del Maestro.

Iniziata nel 1524 da Michelangelo e conclusa
attorno al 1570 dal Vasari e dall'Ammannati sui
disegni del Maestro.

Iniciada por Michelangelo em 1524 e concluída por
volta de 1570 por Vasari e Ammannati com base
nos projetos do Mestre.

Michelangelo begon met de bouw in 1524 en rond
1570 voltooiden Vasari en Ammannati die aan de
hand van tekeningen van de Meester.

Chiesa di Santo Spirito

Firenze
Filippo Brunelleschi, 1444
Giuliano da Sangallo, c. 1490

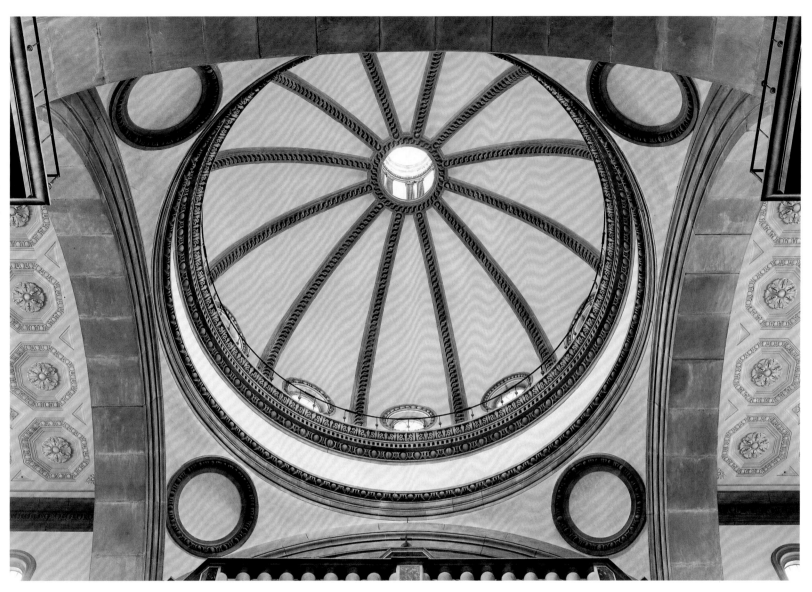

Interior of the presbytery's dome.

Sacristie, intérieur de la coupole.

Das Innere der Kuppel des Presbyteriums.

El interior de la cúpula del presbiterio.

L'interno della cupola del presbiterio.

O interior da cúpula do presbitério.

Binnenkant van de koepel boven het priesterkoor.

The church interior towards the main altar.

L'intérieur de l'église, en direction du chœur.

Das Innere der Kirche mit Blick auf den Hochaltar.

El interior de la iglesia hacia el altar pincipal.

L'interno della chiesa verso l'altare maggiore.

O interior da igreja, na direção do altar-mor.

Het interieur van de kerk richting het hoofdaltaar.

Palazzo Pitti

Firenze
Luca Fancelli, 1458
Bartolomeo Ammannati, 1549

Pietro da Cortona

Study for the façade of Pitti Palace. The Palazzo was begun in 1458 by the architect Luca Fancelli and was expanded by Bartolomeo Ammannati a century later, when it was purchased by Eleanor of Toledo, in 1549, for the new ducal palace.

Étude pour la façade du palais Pitti. Commencé en 1458 par l'architecte Luca Fancelli, le palais a été agrandi un siècle plus tard par Bartolomeo Ammannati lors de son acquisition par Éléonore de Tolède pour en faire le nouveau palais ducal (1549).

Entwurf für die Fassade des Palazzo Pitti. Die Bauarbeiten begannen 1458 unter der Leitung des Architekten Luca Fancelli und wurden ein Jahrhundert später von Bartolomeo Ammannati erweitert, als der Palast 1549 an Eleonora von Toledo verkauft und zum neuen Herzogspalast wurde.

Estudio de la fachada del palacio. La construcción del palacio comenzó en 1458, a las órdenes del arquitecto Luca Fancelli para ser posteriormente ampliado por Bartolomeo Ammannati un siglo más tarde, tras ser adquirido por Leonor de Toledo, en 1549, para alojar el nuevo palacio ducal.

Studio per la facciata del palazzo. Il palazzo fu iniziato nel 1458 dall'architetto Luca Fancelli per essere ulteriormente ampliato da Bartolomeo Ammannati un secolo più tardi, quando fu acquistato da Eleonora di Toledo, nel 1549, per farne la nuova reggia ducale.

Estudo para a fachada do palácio. Iniciado em 1458 pelo arquiteto Luca Fancelli, o palácio foi ampliado por Bartolomeu Ammannati um século mais tarde, quando foi adquirido por Leonor de Toledo, em 1549, para fazer dele o novo paço ducal.

Ontwerp voor de voorgevel van Palazzo Pitti. Architect Luca Fancelli begon in 1458 met de bouw van het palazzo. Een eeuw later, toen Eleonora van Toledo het aankocht, in 1549, breidde Bartolomeo Ammannati het uit tot het nieuwe hertogelijk paleis.

Glimpse of the courtyard portico. The whole palazzo is clad in rusticated ashlar.

Vue de la cour intérieure à portique. L'ensemble du palais est revêtu de bossages rustiques.

Blick auf den Säulengang. Der ganze Palast ist mit einem rustikalen Bossenwerk verkleidet.

Vista del patio porticado. Todo el palacio está revestido en paramento rústico.

Scorcio del cortile porticato. Tutto il palazzo è rivestito in bugnato rustico.

Perspectiva do pátio interior com arcos. Todo o palácio é revestido em bossagem rústica.

Gedeelte van de binnenplaats met zuilengalerij. Het palazzo is geheel bedekt met rustieke bossages.

Silver Museum. Frescoes by Giovanni da
San Giovanni, executed between 1635 and 1638.

Musée de l'Argenterie. Fresques par Giovanni da
San Giovanni exécutées entre 1635 et 1638.

Silbermuseum. Fresken von Giovanni da
San Giovanni aus den Jahren 1635 bis 1638.

Museo de la Plata. Los frescos fueron realizados
por Giovanni da San Giovanni entre 1635 y 1638.

Sala degli Argenti. Affreschi di Giovanni da
San Giovanni eseguiti tra il 1635 e il 1638.

Museu da Prata. Afrescos por Giovanni da
San Giovanni executados entre 1635 e 1638.

Zilvermuseum. Fresco's van Giovanni da
San Giovanni gemaakt tussen 1635 en 1638.

End of the grand staircase to the Palatine Gallery.

Extrémité du grand escalier de la Galerie Palatine.

Das obere Ende der Freitreppe der
Galleria Palatina.

La parte final de la escalinata de la
Galería Palatina.

La parte conclusiva dello scalone della
Galleria Palatina.

Topo da escadaria da Galeria Palatina.

Het laatste gedeelte van de trap van de
Galleria Palatina.

Bartolomeo Ammannati

Courtyard opening onto the Boboli Gardens.

La cour intérieure, avec son ouverture vers les jardins de Boboli.

Hof mit Öffnung zum Boboli-Garten.

El patio con la abertura hacia el jardín de Boboli.

Il cortile con l'apertura verso il Giardino di Boboli.

O pátio interior com abertura para o Jardim de Boboli.

De binnenplaats, met een doorgang naar de Boboli-tuinen.

Giusto Utens

Pitti Palace and the Forte del Belvedere, 1599.

Le palais Pitti et le fort du Belvedere, 1599.

Palazzo Pitti und das Forte del Belvedere, 1599.

Palazzo Pitti y el Forte del Belvedere, 1599.

Palazzo Pitti e il Forte del Belvedere, 1599.

Palazzo Pitti e o Forte del Belvedere, 1599.

Palazzo Pitti en Fort Belvedere, 1599.

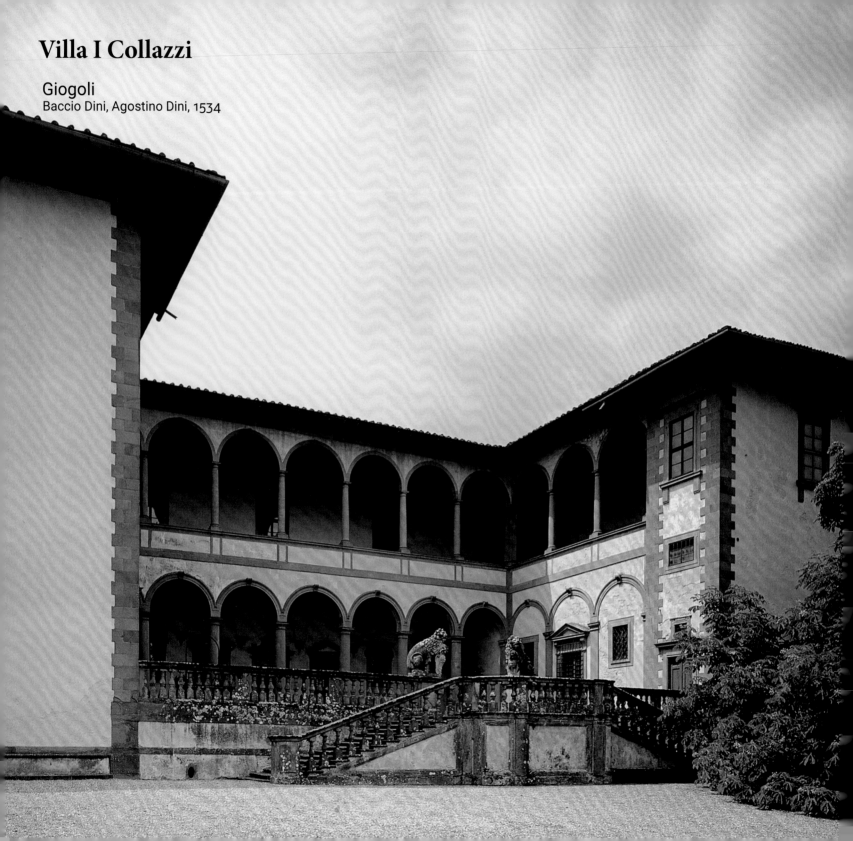

Villa I Collazzi

Giogoli
Baccio Dini, Agostino Dini, 1534

It would be the owners themselves, Baccio and Agostino Dini, who transformed the existing mansion into a villa in 1534.

Die Besitzer selbst, Baccio und Agostino Dini, nahmen 1534 den Umbau eines bestehenden Herrenhauses in eine Villa vor.

En 1534, Baccio et Agostino Dini, propriétaires, ont eux-mêmes transformé en villa un logis seigneurial préexistant.

Los mismos propietarios, Baccio y Agostino Dini, transformaron una casa señorial existente en una villa en 1534.

Furono gli stessi proprietari Baccio e Agostino Dini a trasformare in villa, nel 1534, una preesistente casa signorile.

Foram os próprios proprietários, Baccio e Agostino Dini, que transformaram em villa uma pré-existente casa senhorial em 1534.

Het waren de eigenaren Baccio en Agostino Dini zelf die in 1534 een bestaand herenhuis transformeerden tot deze villa.

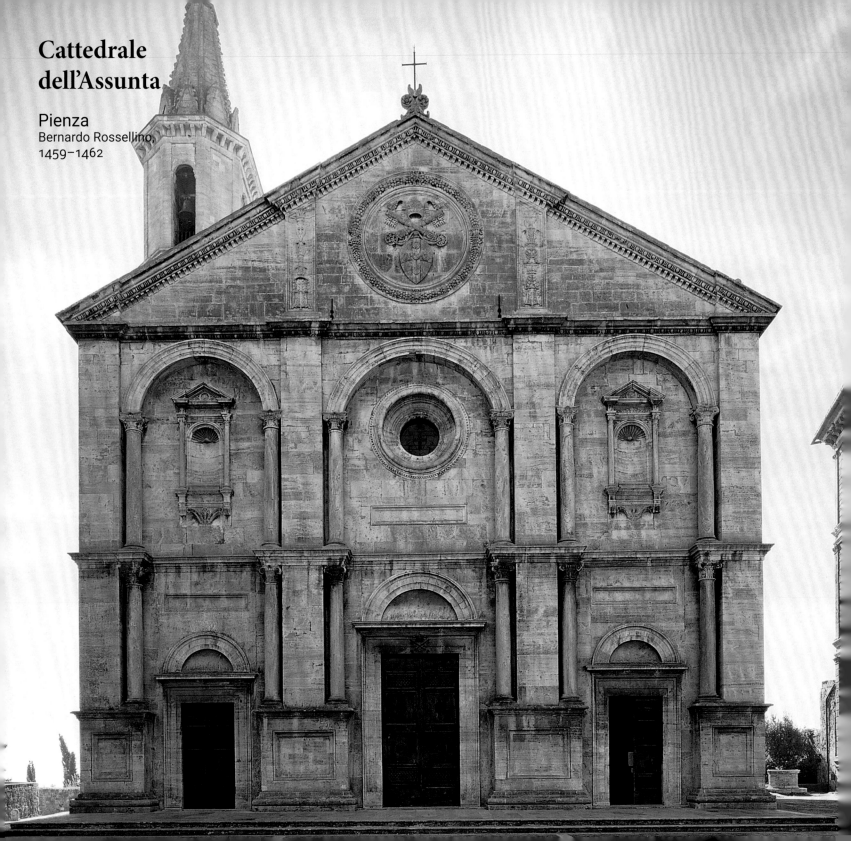

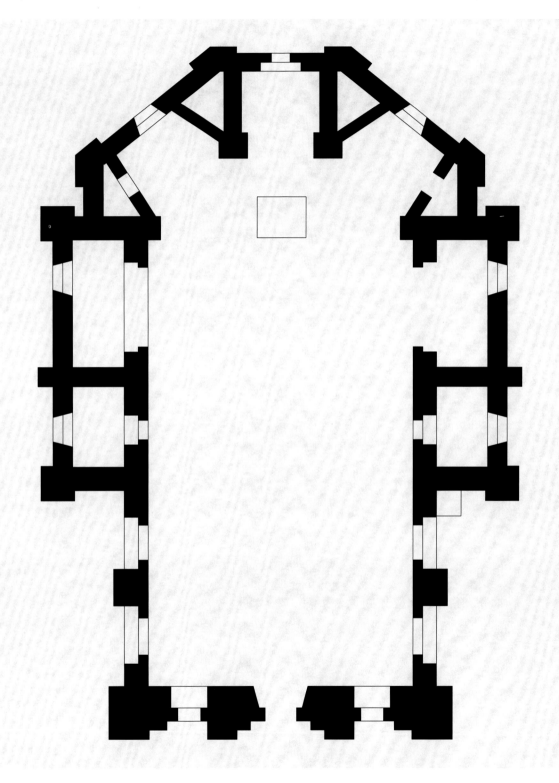

Commissioned from the Florentine architect, student and collaborator of Leon Battista Alberti, by Pope Pius II.

L'édifice a été commandé par le pape Pie II à l'architecte florentin, élève et collaborateur de Leon Battista Alberti.

Im Auftrag von Papst Pius II. übernahm der Florentiner Architekt, Schüler und Mitarbeiter von Leon Battista Alberti, die Bauarbeiten.

El papa Pío II encargó la obra al arquitecto florentino, alumno y colaborador de Leon Battista Alberti.

Fu commissionata all'architetto fiorentino, allievo e collaboratore di Leon Battista Alberti, da papa Pio II.

Foi encomendada pelo papa Pio II ao arquiteto florentino, discípulo e colaborador de Leon Battista Alberti.

De Florentijnse architect, leerling en medewerker van Leon Battista Alberti, kreeg deze opdracht van paus Pius II.

Palazzo Piccolomini

Pienza
Bernardo Rossellino, 1459

The magnificent three order loggia that offers a splendid view of the Val d'Orcia.

La grandiose galerie à trois étages, d'où l'on jouit du panorama splendide sur le val d'Orcia.

Die grandiose Loggia mit drei Säulenordnungen und einem atemberaubenden Blick auf das Valle dell'Orcia.

La gran galería de tres órdenes desde donde se puede disfrutar del magnífico panorama de la Valle de Orcia.

La grandiosa loggia a tre ordini da cui si gode lo splendido panorama della Val d'Orcia.

A grandiosa loggia a três ordens, de onde se aprecia o esplêndido panorama do Vale de Orcia.

De schitterende loggia van drie lagen, waarvandaan je een prachtig uitzicht hebt op Val d'Orcia.

Enea Silvio Piccolomini, known as Pope Pius II, on the advice of Leon Battista Alberti, entrusted the architect Bernardo Rossellino with a prodigious renovation project, that in a few years would transform his birthplace, the medieval town of Corsignano, into the ideal Renaissance city: Pienza the city of Pius.

Enea Silvio Piccolomini, bekannt als Papst Pius II., beauftragte den Architekten Bernardo Rossellino auf Empfehlung von Leon Battista Alberti, die Umgestaltung seines Geburtsortes Corsignano vorzunehmen. Dieser verwandelte sich in nur wenigen Jahren zu einer idealen Renaissancestadt: Pienza, die Stadt von Pius.

Enea Silvio Piccolomini, alias pape Pie II, confie à l'architecte Bernardo Rossellino, dont le maître fut Leon Battista Alberti, la réalisation d'un programme de rénovation urbanistique pour transformer le village médiéval de Corsignano (sa ville natale) en une ville Renaissance idéale : Pienza, la « ville de Pie ».

Enea Silvio Piccolomini, conocido como papa Pío II, aconsejado por Leon Battista Alberti, encargó al arquitecto Bernardo Rossellino un amplio plan de renovación que transformó en pocos años su pueblo natal, Corsignano, de estilo medieval, en la ciudad ideal del Renacimiento: Pienza, la ciudad de Pío.

Enea Silvio Piccolomini, conosciuto come Papa Pio II, affida all'architetto Bernardo Rossellino un programma di rinnovamento urbanistico che trastorma il paese medievale di Corsignano, suo luogo natale, nella città ideale del Rinascimento: Pienza, la città di Pio.

Enea Silvio Piccolomini, conhecido como papa Pio II, a conselho de Leon Battista Alberti entrega ao arquiteto Bernardo Rossellino um vasto programa de renovação, que em poucos anos transforma o povoado medieval de Corsignano, sua terra natal, na cidade ideal do Renascimento: Pienza, "a cidade de Pio".

Enea Silvio Piccolomini, bekend als paus Pius II, liet op advies van Leon Battista Alberti, de architect Bernardo Rossellino een hele reeks vernieuwingen doorvoeren. Hierdoor werd zijn geboorteplaats, het middeleeuwse dorpje Corsignano, in een paar jaar tijd veranderd in de perfecte renaissancestad: Pienza, de stad van Pius.

The interior courtyard.

La cour intérieure.

Der Innenhof.

El patio.

Il cortile interno.

O claustro interior.

De binnenplaats.

The travertine well designed by Rossellino, in 1462.

Le puits en travertin, dessiné par Rossellino en 1462.

Der Travertin-Brunnen wurde 1462 von Rossellino entworfen.

El pozo en travertino diseñado por Rossellino en 1462.

Il pozzo in travertino disegnato dal Rossellino nel 1462.

O poço em travertino, projetado por Rossellino em 1462.

De travertijnen put is in 1462 ontworpen door Rossellino.

Chiesa di San Biagio

Montepulciano
Antonio da Sangallo il Vecchio, 1518

An exceptional document of Renaissance religious architecture; it has a Greek cross plan with a central dome resting on a traditional drum.

Cet exceptionnel monument de l'architecture religieuse Renaissance présente un plan en croix grecque, avec une coupole centrale posée sur un tambour classique.

Ein außergewöhnliches Zeugnis religiöser Architektur der Renaissance. Der Grundriss zeigt ein griechisches Kreuz mit Zentralkuppel, die auf einem klassischen Tambour ruht.

Un documento excepcional de la arquitectura religiosa del Renacimiento; tiene un plano de cruz griego con una cúpula central que descansa en un tambor tradicional.

È un eccezionale documento di architettura rinascimentale religiosa. Presenta un impianto a croce greca con cupola centrale poggiata su un tamburo classico.

Um documento excepcional da arquitetura religiosa da Renascença; que tem uma planta em cruz grega, com uma cúpula central apoiada num tambor tradicional.

Dit is een uitstekend voorbeeld van religieuze renaissance-architectuur. De plattegrond bestaat uit een Grieks kruis met koepel in het midden, die rust op een klassieke tamboer.

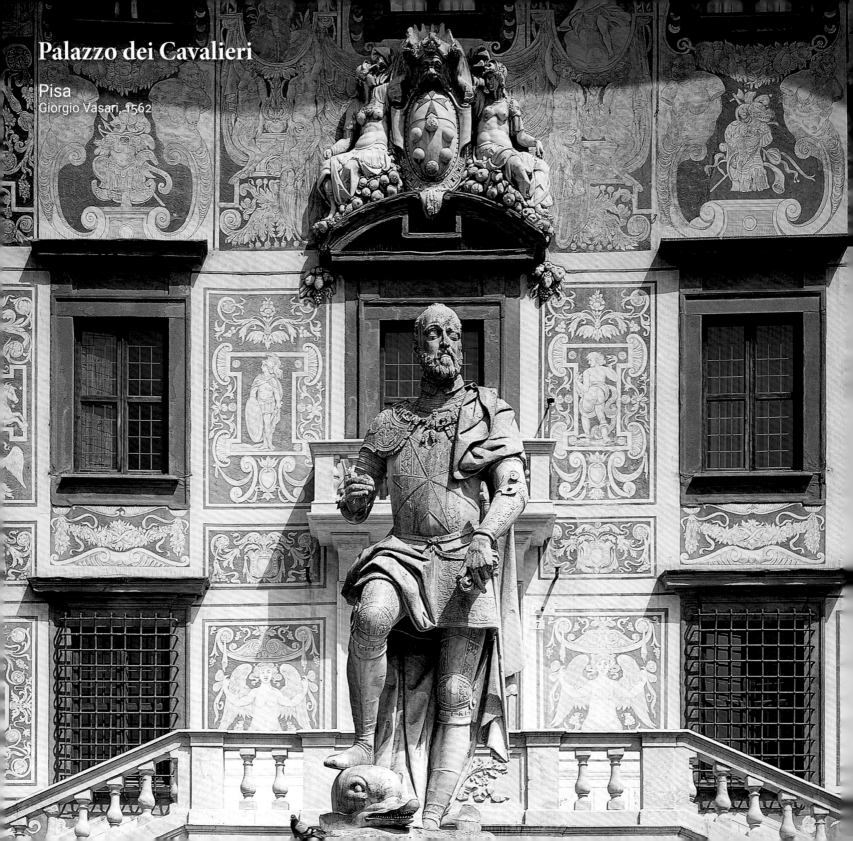

Palazzo dei Cavalieri

Pisa
Giorgio Vasari, 1562

This building results from a radical restructuring of the Palazzo degli Anziani (13th–14th centuries) begun in 1562 and designed by Giorgio Vasari for Cosimo I, commemorated in the statue in front of the building.

Das Gebäude ist das Ergebnis eines radikalen Umbaus des Palazzo degli Anziani (13.–14. Jh.). Die Arbeiten begannen 1562 unter der Leitung von Giogio Vasari, im Auftrag von Cosimo I., dessen Statue vor dem Palast prangt.

L'édifice résulte d'une restructuration radicale du palais des Anciens (XIIIᵉ–XIVᵉ siècles), commencée en 1562 sur les plans de Giorgio Vasari, pour le compte de Côme Iᵉʳ que glorifie la statue érigée devant le palais.

L'edificio è il risultato di una radicale ristrutturazione del Palazzo degli Anziani (secoli XIII–XIV) iniziata nel 1562 su progetto di Giorgio Vasari per desiderio di Cosimo I, celebrato nella statua davanti al palazzo.

Este edificio es el resultado de una remodelación radical del Palacio de los Ancianos (siglos XIII–XIV) que comenzó en 1562 siguiendo un proyecto de Giorgio Vasari por deseo de Cosme I, cuya estatua se encuentra enfrente del palacio.

O edifício é o resultado de uma renovação radical do Palazzo degli Anziani (séculos XIII–XIV), iniciada em 1562 com um projeto de Giorgio Vasari para de Cosme I, que é celebrado na estátua defronte ao palácio.

Het gebouw is het resultaat van een ingrijpende restauratie van het Palazzo degli Anziani (13e–14e eeuw), die in 1562 startte volgens het ontwerp van Giorgio Vasari in opdracht van Cosimo I, die wordt afgebeeld in het standbeeld voor het paleis.

The Palazzo dei Cavalieri, also called Palazzo della Carovana, and the church of Santo Stefano dei Cavalieri.

Le Palazzo dei Cavalieri, dit aussi Palazzo della Carovana, et l'église Santo Stefano dei Cavalieri.

Der Palazzo dei Cavalieri, auch Palazzo della Carovana genannt, und die Kirche Santo Stefano dei Cavalieri.

El Palazzo dei Cavalieri, denominado también el Palazzo della Carovana, y la iglesia de Santo Stefano dei Cavalieri.

Il Palazzo dei Cavalieri, detto anche Palazzo della Carovana, e la chiesa di Santo Stefano dei Cavalieri.

O Palazzo dei Cavalieri, também chamado Palazzo della Carovana, e a igreja de Santo Stefano dei Cavalieri.

Het Palazzo dei Cavalieri, ook wel Palazzo della Carovana genoemd, en de kerk van Santo Stefano dei Cavalieri.

Palazzo Ducale

Urbino
Luciano Laurana, 1466–1472
Francesco di Giorgio Martini, 1475–1482
Girolamo Genga, 1536

One of the highest expressions of Renaissance architecture commissioned by Duke Federico da Montefeltro, brilliant leader and refined humanist. Designed in 1466 by the architect Luciano Laurana, to whom we owe the splendid façade compressed between two slender, soaring towers.

Le palais ducal est une des plus grandes expressions de l'architecture Renaissance, commanditée par le duc Frédéric de Montefeltro, condottiere brillant mais aussi humaniste raffiné. Il a été conçu en 1466 par l'architecte Luciano Laurana à qui l'on doit la magnifique façade enserrée entre deux tours jumelles élancées.

Das Gebäude ist der erhabenste Ausdruck der Renaissance-Architektur. Es ist eine Auftragsarbeit des Herzogen Federico da Montefeltro, einem brillanten Feldherrn und feinsinnigen Humanisten. Der Palast wurde 1466 vom Architekten Luciano Laurana erbaut, dem auch die großartige, von zwei schmalen Türmen flankierte Fassade zu verdanken ist.

Es una de las máximas expresiones de la arquitectura del Renacimiento, por voluntad del duque Federico da Montefeltro, que fue un líder de éxito además de un refinado humanista. El palacio fue diseñado en 1466 por el arquitecto Luciano Laurana, a quien se debe la extraordinaria fachada respaldada por dos estrechas y altas torres.

È una delle massime espressioni dell'architettura del Rinascimento, voluto dal duca Federico da Montefeltro, brillante condottiero ma anche raffinato umanista. Fu progettato nel 1466 dall'architetto Luciano Laurana, cui si deve la splendida facciata stretta tra due sottili e slanciati torrioni.

É uma das expressões máximas da arquitetura do Renascimento, concebido a instâncias do duque Federico da Montefeltro, um comandante brilhante mas também um requintado humanista. O Palácio foi projetado em 1466 pelo arquiteto Luciano Laurana, a quem se deve a esplêndida fachada estreita entre dois esguios e subtis torreões.

Dit palazzo, een van de beste voorbeelden van de renaissance-architectuur, werd gebouwd voor hertog Federico da Montefeltro, een briljante condottiere en tevens een verfijnde humanist. Het werd in 1466 ontworpen door architect Luciano Laurana, aan wie de prachtige gevel te danken is tussen twee smalle, hoge torens.

The courtyard.

La cour.

Der Innenhof.

El patio.

Il cortile.

O pátio.

De binnenplaats.

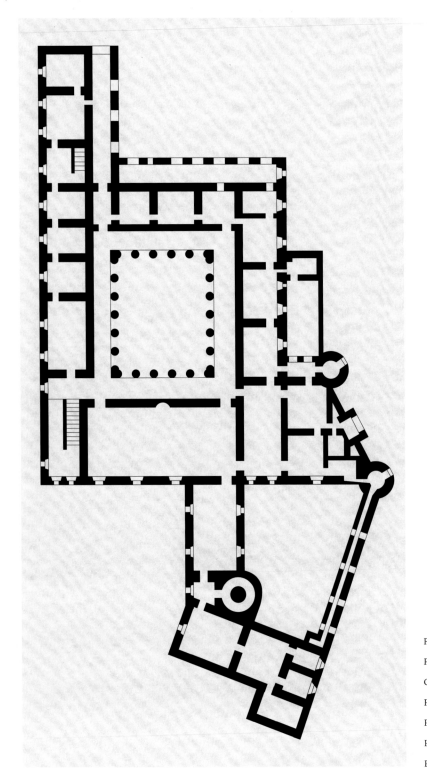

Plan of the vast ducal palace.

Plan du vaste palais ducal.

Grundriss des mächtigen Herzogspalasts.

Planta del gran palacio ducal.

Pianta della vasta reggia ducale.

Planta do extenso palácio ducal.

Plattegrond van het uitgestrekte hertogelijk paleis.

Intarsia in a door of the Sala degli Angeli.

Marqueterie d'une porte de la salle des Anges.

Intarsien in einer Tür der Sala degli Angeli.

Marquetería en una puerta de la Sala de los ángeles.

Porta intarsiata della Sala degli Angeli.

Porta marchetada da Sala dos Anjos.

Intarsia in een deur van de Zaal van de Engelen.

Laurana left Urbino in 1472 leaving the palace incomplete. Its construction was resumed after 1472 by Francesco di Giorgio Martini who left his signature in the decorative portals and in the windows of the "winged façade".

Laurana quitte Urbino en 1472, en laissant inachevé le palais ducal. La construction est alors reprise par Francesco di Giorgio Martini qui impose sa marque dans les portails et les fenêtres de la « façade à ailes ».

Laurana verließ Urbino im Jahr 1472 und hinterließ den unvollendeten Palast. Die Arbeiten wurden 1472 von Francesco di Giorgio Martini wieder aufgenommen. Er entwarf die Portale und die dekorativen Fenster der „Flügelfassade".

Laurana se marchó de Urbino en 1472 y dejó el palacio sin completar. Francesco di Giorgio Martini continuó las obras después de 1472 y dejó su "huella" en los portales y en las ventanas decorativas de la "fachada de alas".

Laurana si allontanò da Urbino nel 1472, lasciando incompiuta la reggia. La sua costruzione fu ripresa dopo il 1472 da Francesco di Giorgio Martini, che lasciò la sua firma nella grandiosità dei portali e nelle finestre della "facciata ad ali".

Laurana abandonou Urbino em 1472, deixando incompleto o paço ducal. A sua construção foi retomada após 1472 por Francesco di Giorgio Martini, que deixou a sua assinatura nos pórticos e nas janelas decorativas da "fachada de asas".

Laurana verliet Urbino in 1472 zonder het paleis te voltooien. Na 1472 werd de bouw hervat door Francesco di Giorgio Martini, die zijn stempel drukte op de portalen en de vensters van de 'gevleugelde gevel'.

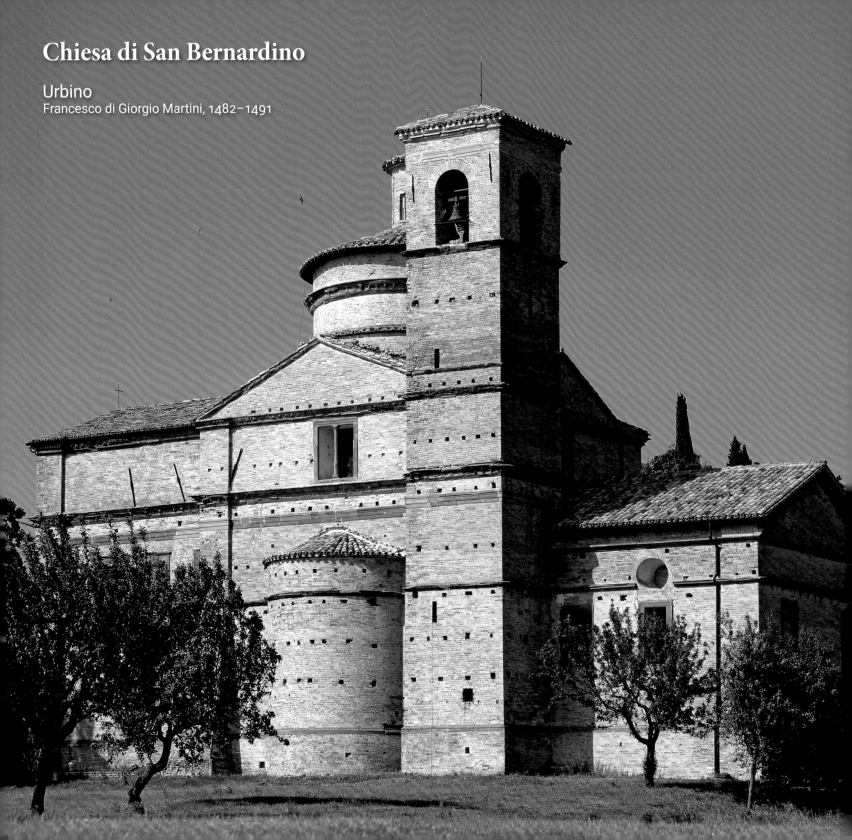

Chiesa di San Bernardino

Urbino
Francesco di Giorgio Martini, 1482–1491

The church has Latin cross architecture, with a barrel vault and a dome. Until 1810, Piero della Francesca's famous *Montefeltro Altarpiece,* now in Milan's Pinacoteca di Brera, was located here.

L'église offre une architecture claire : plan de croix latine, voûte en berceaux et coupole. La célèbre *Conversation sacrée* de Piero della Francesca est restée là jusqu'en 1810. Elle est aujourd'hui à la pinacothèque de Brera à Milan.

Die Kirche in Form eines lateinischen Kreuzes zeigt eine klare Architektur mit Tonnengewölbe und Kuppel. Bis 1810 beherbergte sie das berühmte Altarbild *Pala Montefeltro* von Piero della Francesca, das sich heute in der Pinacoteca di Brera in Mailand befindet.

La iglesia presenta una clara arquitectura de cruz latina, con techo abovedado y cúpula. Hasta 1810 estuvo colocada la famosa *Sacra Conversación* de Piero della Francesca que en la actualidad se encuentra en la Pinacoteca de Brera, Milán.

La chiesa presenta una architettura a croce latina, con volta a botte e cupola. Fino al 1810 vi era collocata la famosa *Pala Montefeltro* di Piero della Francesca, ora alla Pinacoteca di Brera a Milano.

A igreja apresenta uma pura arquitetura em cruz latina, com abóbada de berço e cúpula. Até 1810 ali se encontrou a famosa *Pala Montefeltro* de Piero della Francesca, atualmente parte da Pinacoteca de Brera em Milão.

De kerk heeft de vorm van een Latijns kruis, met tongewelf en koepel. Tot aan 1810 bevond zich hier de beroemde *Heilige Conversatie* van Piero della Francesca; tegenwoordig hangt hij in de Pinacoteca di Brera in Milaan.

Anonimo urbinate

Interior view of the church of San Bernardino.

Vue intérieure de l'église San Bernardino.

Innenansicht der Kirche San Bernardino.

Vista del interior de la iglesia de San Bernardino.

Veduta dell'interno della chiesa di San Bernardino.

Vista do interior da Igreja de São Bernardino.

De San Bernardino-kerk vanbinnen gezien.

Piero della Francesca

The famous *Montefeltro Altarpiece*, 1472–1474.

La célèbre *Conversation sacrée*, 1472–1474.

Die berühmte *Pala Montefeltro*, 1472–1474.

La famosa *Sacra Conversación*, 1472–1474.

La celebre *Pala Montefeltro*, 1472–1474.

A famosa *Pala Montefeltro*, 1472–1474.

De beroemde *Heilige Conversatie*, 1472–1474.

Rocca Roveresca

Mondavio
Francesco di Giorgio Martini, 1482–1492

Francesco di Giorgio Martini, the century's most famous designer of military fortifications, was commissioned by Giovanni della Rovere to build the towering structure.

Le cardinal Giovanni della Rovere chargea Francesco di Giorgio Martini, le plus illustre architecte militaire de son temps, de construire cette puissante place-forte.

Francesco di Giorgio Martini, der berühmteste Architekt militärischer Befestigungsanlagen seiner Zeit, erhielt von Giovanni della Rovere den Auftrag für den Bau dieser gewaltigen Festung.

Francesco di Giorgio Martini, el proyectista de fortificaciones militares más célebre del siglo, recibió el encargo de construir la poderosa estructura de Giovanni della Rovere.

Francesco di Giorgio Martini, il più famoso progettista di fortificazioni militari del secolo, ricevette l'incarico di costruire la poderosa struttura da Giovanni della Rovere.

Francesco di Giorgio Martini, ao mais famoso projetista de fortificações militares do século, é confiada, por Giovanni della Rovere, a tarefa de construir a poderosa estrutura.

Francesco di Giorgio Martini, de toentertijd beroemdste ontwerper van militaire vestingwerken, kreeg van Giovanni della Rovere opdracht de enorme vesting te bouwen.

Rocca Roveresca

Senigallia
Baccio Pontelli, c. 1490

Built on the orders of Cardinal Giovanni della Rovere.

Forteresse construite sur ordre du cardinal Giovanni della Rovere.

Auftragsarbeit von Kardinal Giovanni della Rovere.

Realizada por orden del cardenal Giovanni della Rovere.

Edificata per ordine del cardinale Giovanni della Rovere.

Edificada por ordem do cardeal Giovanni della Rovere.

Het fort werd gebouwd in opdracht van kardinaal Giovanni della Rovere.

Chiesa di Santa Maria
della Consolazione

Todi
Donato Bramante (attr.), 1508

Palazzo Farnese

Roma
Antonio da Sangallo il Giovane, 1516
Michelangelo, 1546-1549
Jacopo Barozzi (Vignola), 1569-1573
Giacomo Della Porta, 1589

The imposing façade of Palazzo Farnese overlooking the homonymous piazza.

Die imposante Fassade von Palazzo Farnese schließt die gleichnamige Piazza ab.

L'imposante façade du palais Farnèse, sur la place du même nom.

La imponente fachada del Palacio Farnese que domina la plaza homónima.

L'imponente facciata di Palazzo Farnese prospiciente l'omonima piazza.

A imponente fachada do Palazzo Farnese com vista para a praça homónima.

De indrukwekkende gevel van Palazzo Farnese kijkt uit over het gelijknamige plein.

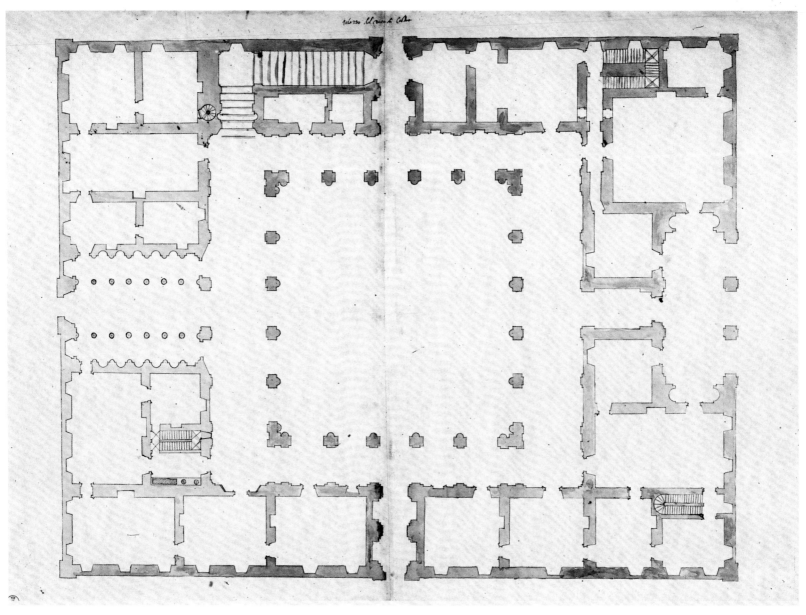

Antonio da Sangallo il Giovane

Study for the Palazzo Farnese, plan, circa 1541.

Étude pour le palais Farnèse, plan, vers 1541.

Entwurf des Palazzo Farnese, Grundriss, ca. 1541.

Estudio del proyecto del Palacio Farnese, planta, ca 1541.

Studio del progetto di Palazzo Farnese, pianta, 1541 ca.

Estudo para o Palazzo Farnese, planta, cerca de 1541

Ontwerptekening van Palazzo Farnese, plattegrond, ca. 1541.

The rear façade of the palazzo facing the Tiber.

La façade arrière du palais, du côté du Tibre.

Die dem Tiber zugewandte Rückfassade des Palastes.

La fachada posterior del palacio hacia el Tíber.

Loggia posteriore del palazzo, affacciata sul Tevere.

A fachada posterior do palácio virada para o Tibre.

De achtergevel van het palazzo met uitzicht op de Tiber.

Anonymous, project for the completion of Palazzo
Farnese, 1546.

Anonyme, projet pour l'achèvement du palais
Farnèse, 1546.

Anonym, Entwurf zur Fertigstellung des Palazzo
Farnese, 1546.

Anónimo. Proyecto para la finalización del Palacio
Farnese, 1546.

Anonimo. Progetto per il completamento di
Palazzo Farnese, 1546.

Anónimo. Projeto para a conclusão do Palazzo
Farnese, 1546.

Anoniem, ontwerp voor de voltooiing van het
Palazzo Farnese, 1546.

Designed by Antonio da Sangallo the Younger in 1516 for Cardinal Alessandro Farnese, future Pope Paul III, it was expanded by Michelangelo (1546–1549), by Vignola (1569–1573) and completed by Giacomo della Porta, 1589.

Commencé par Antonio da Sangallo le Jeune en 1516 pour le cardinal Alexandre Farnèse, futur pape Paul III, le palais fut agrandi par Michel-Ange (1546–1549) et par Vignole (1569–1573), puis terminé par Giacomo della Porta (1589).

Von Antonio da Sangallo dem Jüngeren im Jahr 1516 für den Kardinal Alessandro Farnese entworfen, dem späteren Papst Paul III. Eine Erweiterung erfolgte 1546–1549 durch Michelangelo und 1569–1573 durch Vignola. Fertiggestellt wurde er im Jahr 1589 von Giacomo della Porta.

Diseñado por Antonio da Sangallo el Joven en 1516 para el cardenal Alessandro Farnese, futuro papa Paulo III, fue ampliado por Miguel Ángel (1546–1549) y por Vignola (1569–1573) y finalizado por Giacomo della Porta (1589).

Progettato da Antonio da Sangallo il Giovane nel 1516 per il cardinale Alessandro Farnese, futuro papa Paolo III, fu ampliato da Michelangelo (1546–1549) e dal Vignola (1569–1573) e concluso da Giacomo della Porta (1589).

Projetado em 1516 por Antonio da Sangallo, o Jovem, para o cardeal Alessandro Farnese, futuro papa Paulo III, foi ampliado por Michelangelo (1546–1549) e por Vignola (1569–1573) e terminado por Giacomo della Porta (1589).

In 1516 ontworpen door Antonio da Sangallo de Jongere voor kardinaal Alessandro Farnese, later paus Paulus III; uitgebreid door Michelangelo (1546–1549) en door Vignola (1569–1573), en voltooid door Giacomo della Porta (1589).

Palazzo Fernese

' *Orazione detta la Morte, 3. Arco, che passa su la Strada Giulia, 4. Palazzo della Religione Teutonica, 5. Palazzo Mandosi.*

Complesso del Campidoglio
Palazzo Senatorio

Roma
Michelangelo, 1546–1554
Giacomo Della Porta, 1582–1602

CAPITOLII·SCIOGRAPHIA·EX·IPSO·EXEMPLARI·MICHAELIS·ANGELI·BONAROTI·A·STEPHANO·DVPERAC·PARISIENSI·ACCVRATE·DELINEATA·ET·IN·LVCEM·AEDITA·ROMAE·ANNO·SALVTIS·∞DLXIX

Étienne Dupérac

The renovation of the Palazzo Senatorio (an old, 13th century, medieval fortification with merlons) was entrusted to Michelangelo at the end of 1546. The work was finished by his collaborator Mario Maccarone in 1554.

La refonte du Palais des Sénateurs (ancien fortin crénelé du XIIIᵉ siècle) fut confiée à Michel-Ange à la fin de 1546. Les travaux furent achevés par son collaborateur Mario Maccarone en 1554.

Die Neugestaltung des Palazzo Senatorio (eine mittelalterliche Festung mit Zinnen aus dem 13. Jh.) wurde Michelangelo Ende 1546 anvertraut. Die Arbeiten wurden 1554 vom Mitarbeiter Mario Maccarone vollendet.

Miguel Ángel fue el encargado de renovar el Palazzo Senatorio (una fortificación medieval del siglo XIII con almenas) a finales de 1546. La obra fue finalizada en 1554 por su colaborador Mario Maccarone.

Il rinnovamento del Palazzo Senatorio (un vecchio fortilizio medievale merlato del XIII sec.) fu affidato a Michelangelo alla fine del 1546. I lavori furono conclusi dal collaboratore Mario Maccarone nel 1554.

A renovação do Palazzo Senatorio (antigo forte medieval ameado do século XIII) foi confiada a Michelangelo no final de 1546. Os trabalhos foram terminados por Mario Maccarone, seu colaborador, em 1554.

De renovatie van Palazzo Senatorio (een oud, gekanteeld middeleeuws fort uit de 13e eeuw) werd aan het einde van 1546 toevertrouwd aan Michelangelo. De werkzaamheden werden in 1554 voltooid door zijn medewerker Mario Maccarone.

Piazza del Campidoglio according to Michelangelo's design, 1569.

Place du Capitole selon le projet de Michel-Ange, 1569.

Der Kapitolsplatz nach einem Entwurf von Michelangelo, 1569.

Plaza del Campidoglio según el proyecto de Miguel Ángel, 1569.

Piazza del Campidoglio secondo il progetto michelangiolesco, 1569.

Praça do Capitólio segundo o projeto de Michelangelo, 1569.

Het Piazza del Campidoglio naar het ontwerp van Michelangelo, 1569.

Complesso del Campidoglio
Palazzo dei Conservatori

Roma
Michelangelo, 1563
Giacomo della Porta, 1564–1568

G. Vasi dis. sc.

Palazzi di Campidoglio

1. Scalinata della Chiesa di Araceli, 2. Palazzo o Galleria di Statue, 3. Palaz. del Senatore, 4. Palaz. dei Conservatori, 5. Salita verso Roma, 6. Salite verso Campo Vaccino.

The design for the new façade, begun by Michelangelo in 1563, was continued by Giacomo della Porta in 1564.

Die Neugestaltung erfolgte durch Michelangelo in 1563 und wurde von Giacomo della Porta weitergeführt.

La nouvelle façade, commencée par Michel-Ange en 1563, fut reprise par Giacomo della Porta en 1564.

En 1565 Giacomo della Porta continuó la remodelación que inició Miguel Ángel en 1564.

Il progetto della nuova facciata, avviato da Michelangelo nel 1563, fu proseguito da Giacomo della Porta nel 1564.

A reconstrução iniciada por Michelangelo, em 1563, foi continuada por Giacomo della Porta em 1564.

De bouw van een nieuwe gevel werd begonnen door Michelangelo in 1563, en werd in 1564 voortgezet door Giacomo della Porta.

The façade, punctuated by eight massive lesenes, features a portico running its entire length, gabled windows and is crowned by a balustrade adorned with statues.

La réfection lancée par Michel-Ange fut achevée par Giacomo della Porta. La façade, rythmée par huit pilastres gigantesques, offre un portique sur toute la longueur et un attique continu orné de statues.

Die Fassade mit acht massiven Lisenen zeigt einen durchgehenden Portikus mit Ädikulenfenstern, der mit einer mit Statuen geschmückten Balustrade bekrönt ist.

La fachada, respaldada por ocho lesenas grandes, muestra un pórtico a lo largo de la misma, y ventanas con gablete y una balaustrada de coronación decorada con estatuas.

La facciata, scandita da otto lesene gigantesche, mostra un portico che la percorre in tutta la sua lunghezza e una balaustra di coronamento ornata di statue.

A fachada, marcada por oito pilastras gigantescas, apresenta um pórtico que a percorre a todo o comprimento e janelas de tímpano, sendo coroada por uma balaustrada ornamentada por estátuas.

De gevel, met zijn acht enorme lisenen, bevat een galerij over de gehele lengte, vensters met timpanen, en een kroonlijst met beelden.

The internal courtyard and the loggia, which is dominated by a massive, Trajan era, statue of the goddess Roma.

La cour intérieure avec la loggia que domine une statue gigantesque de la déesse Rome, de l'époque de Trajan.

Der Innenhof und die Loggia, die von der riesigen Statue der Göttin Roma aus der Epoche von Trajan dominiert werden.

El patio interior y la galería donde domina una gran estatua de la diosa Roma de la época de Trajano.

Il cortile interno e la loggia, nella quale domina una gigantesca statua della dea Roma, di epoca traianea.

O pátio interior e a loggia, na qual domina uma estátua gigantesca da deusa Roma, da época de Trajano.

De binnenplaats en de zuilengalerij met een enorm standbeeld van de godin Roma uit de tijd van Trajanus.

CLEMENS XI P. M.
ROMÆ DE DACIA TRIVMPHANTIS
CAPITOLIVM Q NVMIDARVM REGVM STATVAS
EX HORTIS CÆSIIS
AVDITO ÆGYPTIORVM SIGNORVM ORNATV
PORTICVQ A FVNDAMENTIS EXCITATA
AD AVGENDAM CAPITOLII MAIESTATEM
TRANSTVLIT
ANNO SALVT MDCCXX

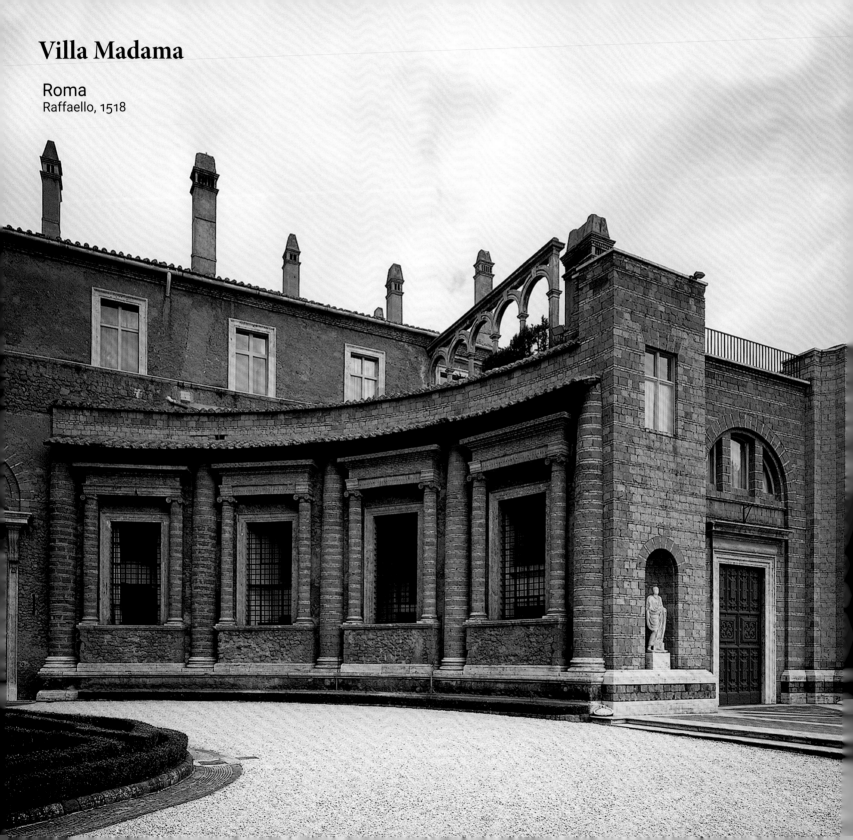

Villa Madama

Roma
Raffaello, 1518

The construction dates from the pontificate of Leo X (1513–1521) commissioned by his cousin, Cardinal Giulio de' Medici. According to Vasari, the drawings for the project were by Raphael (1518), while the construction, after the master's death, is by Giulio Romano. Others hold that the design was Antonio da Sangallo the Younger's.

Der Bau stammt aus der Zeit des Pontifikats von Leo X. (1513–1521) und wurde für seinen Cousin Kardinal Giulio de' Medici entworfen. Nach Vasari stammt der Entwurf von Raffael (1518), die Ausführung wurde nach seinem Tod von Giulio Romano übernommen. Andere Quellen schreiben das Projekt Antonio da Sangallo dem Jüngeren zu.

La construction remonte à l'époque du pontificat de Léon X (1513–1521), sur commande de son cousin, le cardinal Jules de Médicis. Selon Vasari, la conception est de Raphaël (1518), tandis que la construction – après la mort du maître – est l'œuvre de son élève Jules Romain. Pour d'autres, la conception serait d'Antonio Sangallo le Jeune.

La construcción data de la época del pontificado de León X (1513–1521) y fue encargada por su primo, el cardenal Julio de Médici. Según Vasari, los diseños originales son de Rafael (1518), mientras que la construcción, tras la muerte del Maestro, se debe a Giulio Romano. Para otras personas, en cambio, el proyecto perteneció a Antonio da Sangallo el Joven.

La costruzione risale al tempo del pontificato di Leone X (1513–1521) voluta dal cugino cardinale Giulio de' Medici. Secondo il Vasari, i disegni progettuali sono di Raffaello (1518), mentre la costruzione, dopo la morte del Maestro, si deve a Giulio Romano. Per altri il progetto sarebbe di Antonio da Sangallo il Giovane.

A construção remonta ao tempo do pontificado de Leão X (1513–1521), a pedido do seu primo, o cardeal Júlio de Médici. Segundo Vasari, o projeto é de Rafael (1518), devendo-se a construção a Giulio Romano, depois da morte do Mestre. Para outros, o projeto teria sido da autoria de Antonio da Sangallo, o Jovem.

De bouw dateert uit de periode van het pontificaat van Leo X (1513–1521) en was een opdracht van diens neef, kardinaal Giulio de' Medici. Volgens Vasari zijn de ontwerpen van Rafaël (1518), en is de bouw na de dood van de meester uitgevoerd door Giulio Romano. Volgens anderen zou het ontwerp van Antonio da Sangallo de Jongere zijn.

Interior of the loggia, said to be by Raphael, with frescoes by Giulio Romano.

L'intérieur de la loggia dite de Raphaël, avec les fresques de Jules Romain.

Das Innere der Loggia, die Raffael zugeschrieben wird, mit Fresken von Giulio Romano.

El interior de la galería, denominada de Rafael, con frescos de Giulio Romano.

L'interno della loggia, detta di Raffaello, con gli affreschi di Giulio Romano.

O interior da loggia, chamada de Rafael, com afrescos de Giulio Romano.

Binnenkant van de zuilengalerij, Loggia van Rafaël genoemd, met fresco's van Giulio Romano.

The labyrinth garden and the curious Elephant Fountain, work of Giovanni da Udine.

Le labyrinthe du jardin et la curieuse fontaine de l'Éléphant, œuvre de Giovanni da Udine.

Der labyrinthartige Garten und der kuriose Elefantenbrunnen von Giovanni da Udine.

El jardín con forma de laberinto y la curiosa Fuente del Elefante, obra de Giovanni da Udine.

Il giardino a labirinto e la curiosa Fontana dell'Elefante, opera di Giovanni da Udine.

O jardim em labirinto e a curiosa Fonte do Elefante, obra de Giovanni da Udine.

De doolhoftuin en de bijzondere Olifantfontein, een werk van Giovanni da Udine.

Villa Giulia

Roma
Giorgio Vasari, 1551–1555

The complex was built at the request of Julius III between 1551 and 1555 based on Giorgio Vasari's design with significant contributions by Bartolomeo Ammannati.

L'ensemble a été édifié pour Jules III, entre 1551 et 1555, sur les plans de Giorgio Vasari, avec des adjonctions importantes de Bartolomeo Ammannati.

El complejo fue construido entre 1551 y 1555 por encargo de Julio III sobre un diseño de Giorgio Vasari al que se le añadieron numerosas contribuciones de Bartolomeo Ammannati.

O complexo foi construído a pedido de Júlio III entre 1551 e 1555 com base no projeto de Giorgio Vasari, com contribuições significativas de Bartolomeo Ammannati.

Der Komplex wurde auf Anordnung von Julius III. zwischen 1551 und 1555 nach den Plänen von Giorgio Vasari, mit relevanten Beiträgen von Bartolomeo Ammannati, erbaut.

Il complesso viene edificato per volere di Giulio III tra, il 1551 e il 1555, su progetto di Giorgio Vasari e apporti rilevanti di Bartolomeo Ammannati.

Het complex werd tussen 1551 en 1555 gebouwd in opdracht van Julius III naar een ontwerp van Giorgio Vasari en flink wat ideeën van Bartolomeo Ammannati.

The semicircular portico with frescoed vault, the internal façade of which opens onto the courtyard.

Le portique avec sa voûte décorée de fresques, s'ouvre en hémicycle sur la cour intérieure.

Der Portikus mit den Gewölbefresken und der Innenfassade, der sich im Halbkreis zum Innenhof öffnet.

El pórtico semicircular con bóveda cuya fachada interna se asoma al patio.

Il porticato con la volta affrescata e la facciata interna che si apre a emiciclo sul cortile.

O pórtico semi-circular com abóbada afrescada, cuja fachada interior abre para o pátio.

De galerij met plafond met fresco's en de binnengevel die in een halve boog rond de binnenplaats loopt.

The dramatic nyphaeum designed by Bartolomeo Ammannati is articulated in two levels with loggias supported by herms.

Le nymphée spectaculaire, conçu par Bartolomeo Ammannati, se développe sur deux niveaux, avec des galeries soutenues par des hermès.

Das szenisch dargestellte Nymphäum stammt von Bartolomeo Ammannati und erstreckt sich über zwei Geschosse mit Loggien, die von Hermen gestützt werden.

El espectacular ninfeo diseñado por Bartolomeo Ammannati está articulado en dos niveles con galerías soportadas por hermas.

Lo scenografico ninfeo disegnato da Bartolomeo Ammannati si articola su due piani con logge sostenute da erme.

O fantástico ninfeu concebido por Bartolomeo Ammannati articula-se em dois níveis, com galerias suportadas por hermas.

Het spectaculaire nymfaeum ontworpen door Bartolomeo Ammannati heeft twee verdiepingen, ondersteund door hermen.

Palazzo Massimo alle Colonne

Roma
Baldassare Peruzzi, 1532

The last architectural project of Baldassare Peruzzi with the first nods to Mannerism evident in the portico.

Il représente le dernier projet architectural de Baldassare Peruzzi, dont le portique témoigne des premières manifestations du maniérisme.

Das letzte architektonische Werk von Baldassare Peruzzi, mit ersten Anzeichen manieristischer Architektur im Portikus.

Fue el último proyecto arquitectónico de Baldassare Peruzzi con las primeras notas del manierismo en el pórtico.

È l'ultimo progetto architettonico di Baldassare Peruzzi con i primi accenni del Manierismo nel portico.

Foi o último projeto arquitectónico de Baldassare Peruzzi, com os primeiros indícios do Maneirismo no pórtico.

Dit was het laatste architectonische ontwerp van Baldassare Peruzzi, met de eerste invloeden uit het maniërisme in de zuilengalerij.

G. Vasi dis. sc.

Palazzo Maßimi, detto delle Colonne

1. *Palazzo Santobono,* 2. *Chiesa di S. Pantaleo,* 3. *Palazzo della medesima Famiglia Maßimi, detto di Pirro,* 4. *Strada Papale verso il Palazzo Valle*

The palazzo in an engraving by Giuseppe Vasi, 1752.

Le palais, d'après une gravure de Giuseppe Vasi, 1752.

Stich des Palastes von Giuseppe Vasi, 1752.

El palacio en un grabado de Giuseppe Vasi, 1752.

Il palazzo nell'incisione di Giuseppe Vasi, 1752.

O palácio, em gravura de Giuseppe Vasi, 1752.

Het palazzo in een gravure van Giuseppe Vasi, 1752.

In the loggia facing the courtyard, elegant ionic columns support an entablature with fine stucco decorations.

Dans la galerie qui donne sur la cour, d'élégantes petites colonnes ioniques soutiennent un entablement finement décoré de stucs.

Loggia mit Blick auf den Innenhof mit eleganten ionischen Säulen, die das fein dekorierte Gebälk aus Stuck stützen.

En la galería que se asoma al patio, elegantes columnas jónicas soportan un entablamento finamente decorado en estuco.

Nella loggia che affaccia sul cortile, eleganti colonnine ioniche sostengono una trabeazione finamente decorata a stucco.

Na loggia virada para o pátio, elegantes colunas jónicas sustentam o entablamento, finamente decorado com estuque.

In de zuilengalerij die uitkijkt op de binnenplaats, ondersteunen elegante Ionische zuiltjes een hoofdgestel dat versierd is met fijn stucwerk.

Villa Medici

Roma
Nanni di Baccio Bigio, 1564
Bartolomeo Ammannati, 1576

Owned by the Crescenzi it was completely transformed by Nanni di Baccio Bigio in 1564 at the request of Cardinal Giovanni Ricci of Montepulciano. Upon the patron's death, his nephews sold the villa to Cardinal Ferdinando I de' Medici who wanted it even more luxurious and, to this end, entrusted it to Bartolomeo Ammannati in 1576.

Cette bâtisse des Crescenzi fut complètement transformée en 1564 par Nanni di Baccio Bigio, pour le compte du cardinal Giovanni Ricci di Montepulciano. À la mort du commanditaire, ses neveux vendent la villa au cardinal Ferdinand Ier de Médicis qui la veut encore plus luxueuse ; il en confie à cet effet le remaniement à Bartolomeo Ammannati, en 1576.

Das Gebäude der Crescenzi wurde im Auftrag vom Kardinal Giovanni Ricci aus Montepulciano, nach den Plänen von Nanni di Baccio Bigio in 1564 komplett umgebaut. Nach dem Tod des Auftraggebers verkauften seine Enkel die Villa an den Kardinal Ferdinand I. de' Medici. Dieser wollte sie noch luxuriöser gestalten und beauftragte 1576 Bartolomeo Ammannati für den Umbau.

Este edificio de los Crescenzi fue remodelado completamente por Nanni di Baccio Bigio (1564) por encargo del cardenal Giovanni Ricci di Montepulciano. Tras el fallecimiento del comitente, sus nietos vendieron la villa al cardenal Fernando I de Médici, quien encargó una decoración más lujosa a Bartolomeo Ammannati en 1576.

Un edificio dei Crescenzi fu completamente trasformato da Nanni di Baccio Bigio (1564) per incarico del cardinale Giovanni Ricci di Montepulciano. Alla morte del committente, i nipoti vendono la villa al cardinale Ferdinando I de' Medici, che la vuole ancora più lussuosa e per questo affida l'incarico a Bartolomeo Ammannati nel 1576.

Um edifício da família Crescenzi foi totalmente transformado por Nanni di Baccio Bigio (1564), por encomenda do cardeal Giovanni Ricci di Montepulciano. À morte do proprietário, os sobrinhos vendem a villa ao cardeal Fernando I de Médici, que a pretende ainda mais luxuosa e que, por isso, entrega a tarefa a Bartolomeo Ammannati em 1576.

Een gebouw van de Crescenzi's werd in 1564 volledig verbouwd door Nanni di Baccio Bigio in opdracht van kardinaal Giovanni Ricci di Montepulciano. Na de dood van de opdrachtgever verkochten de neven de villa aan kardinaal Ferdinando I de' Medici, die hem nog luxeuzer wil hebben en in 1576 hiervoor opdracht geeft aan Bartolomeo Ammannati.

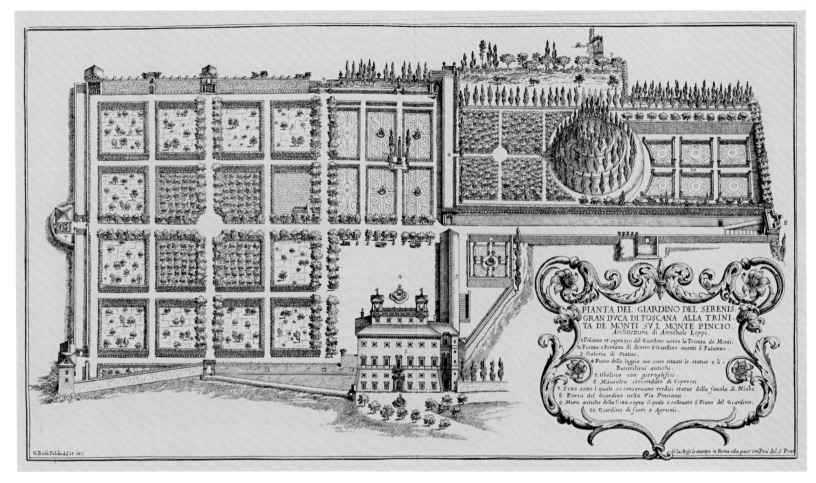

Giovan Battista Falda

Villa Medici, engraving, circa 1670.

La Villa Médicis, gravure, vers 1670.

Villa Medici, Stich, ca. 1670.

Villa Médici, grabado, ca 1670.

Villa Medici, incisione, 1670 ca.

Villa Médici, gravura, cerca de 1670

Villa Medici, gravure, ca. 1670.

View over the villa gardens from inside the loggia.

Vue sur les jardins de la villa, depuis l'intérieur de la galerie à serlienne.

Sicht auf den Garten der Villa vom Innern der Loggia.

Vista de los jardines de la villa desde el interior de la galería.

Veduta sui giardini della villa dall'interno della loggia.

Vista do jardim da villa desde o interior da loggia.

Uitzicht vanuit de loggia op de tuinen van de villa.

At one time the villa gardens held numerous nymphaeums and fountains such as this one, said to be Faustina portrayed as Venus.

Il y eut longtemps, dans les jardins de la villa, de nombreux nymphées et fontaines, comme cette fontaine de Faustine, représentée ici en Vénus.

Zahlreiche Nymphäen und Brunnen schmückten einst den Garten der Villa, wie hier der so genannte Brunnen der Faustina, die als Venus dargestellt wird.

Antiguamente, en el jardín de la villa existieron numerosos ninfeos y fuentes como esta, denominada de Faustina, representada como Venus.

Nel giardino della villa numerosi erano un tempo i ninfei e le fontane come questa detta di Faustina, rappresentata come Venere.

No jardim de villa existiam em tempos inúmeros ninfeus e fontes como esta, chamada da Faustina, representada como Vénus.

In de tuin van de villa stonden vroeger talloze nymfaea en fonteinen zoals deze, die de fontein van Faustina wordt genoemd, afgebeeld als Venus.

Palazzo Spada

Roma

Giulio Merisi,
Giulio Mazzoni,
1548–1550

Built by Cardinal Girolamo Capodiferro beginning in 1548, it was purchased in 1632 by Cardinal Bernardino Spada, to which it owes its extraordinary painting collection.

Construit à la demande du cardinal Girolamo Capodiferro à partir de 1548, il fut acquis en 1632 par le cardinal Bernardino Spada à qui l'on doit une extraordinaire collection de tableaux.

Der Palast wurde ab 1548 im Auftrag des Kardinals Girolamo Capodiferro errichtet und ging 1632 in den Besitz des Kardinals Bernardino Spada über, dem die einzigartige Gemäldegalerie geschuldet ist.

Este palacio fue diseñado por orden del cardenal Girolamo Capodiferro a partir de 1548 aunque en 1632 fue adquirido por el cardenal Bernardino Spada, a quien se debe la extraordinaria galería de cuadros.

Fatto edificare dal cardinale Girolamo Capodiferro a partire dal 1548, fu acquistato nel 1632 dal cardinale Bernardino Spada cui è legata la straordinaria quadreria.

Mandado edificar pelo cardeal Girolamo Capodiferro a partir de 1548, foi adquirido em 1632 pelo cardeal Bernardino Spada; a extraordinária colecção de pinturas foi por ele legada.

Vanaf 1548 gebouwd in opdracht van kardinaal Girolamo Capodiferro; in 1632 aangekocht door kardinaal Bernardino Spada, eigenaar van het opmerkelijke schilderijenkabinet.

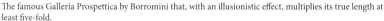

The famous Galleria Prospettica by Borromini that, with an illusionistic effect, multiplies its true length at least five-fold.

La célèbre Galleria Prospettica de Borromini, par son effet de trompe-l'œil, multiplie au moins par cinq la longueur réelle de cet espace.

La famosa Galleria Prospettica del Borromini che, con un effetto illusionistico, moltiplica di ben cinque volte l'effettiva lunghezza.

Der berühmte Galleria Prospettica von Borromini ist eine optische Täuschung und erzeugt die Vorstellung einer fünfmal längeren Galerie.

A famosa Galleria Prospettica de Borromini que, com um efeito de ilusão de óptica, multiplica por cinco o comprimento real.

La famosa Galleria Prospettica de Borromini que, con un efecto ilusorio, multiplica por cinco su longitud real.

De beroemde Galleria Prospettica van Borromini die, dankzij optische illusie, wel vijf keer zo lang lijkt.

Detail of the façade with splendid stucco decorations by Giulio Mazzoni.

Détail de la façade, avec la magnifique décoration en stuc de Giulio Mazzoni.

Details der Fassade mit prächtigen Verzierungen aus Stuck von Giulio Mazzoni.

Detalle de la fachada con la magnífica decoración en estuco de Giulio Mazzoni.

Particolare della facciata con la splendida decorazione in stucco di Giulio Mazzoni.

Detalhe da fachada, com uma esplêndida decoração em estuque de Giulio Mazzoni.

Detail van de voorgevel met prachtig stucwerk van Giulio Mazzoni.

Villa Borghese

Roma
Flaminio Ponzio, 1609–1613

VEDVTA E PROSPETTIVA DEL GIARDINO DELL' ECC.ᴹᴼ SIG.ᴿ PRENCIPE BORGHESE FVORI DI PORTA PINCIANA. *Architettura di Flaminio Pontico seguitata col Palazzo da GioüVansantio.*

1. Palazzo grande con le quattro facciate adornate di statue e bassirilievi.
2. Piazza auanti il Palazzo adornata di Statue e uasi.
3. Giardini secreti di Agrumi e di fiori.
4. Vccelliera.
5. Teatro auanti il Palazzo e facciata uerso leuante con la fontana di Narciso nel secondo recinto.
6. Portone che entra nel Parco e recinto.
7. Parco di lepri Capri daini Cerui &

Simon Felice del et inc.

G IacRossi le stampa in Roma alla pace con Priu del S. Pont.

Built between 1606 and 1613 from Flaminio Ponzio's design, the villa maintains intact its late 16th-century, mannerist character.

Construite entre 1600 et 1613 sur les plans de Flaminio Ponzio, la villa a gardé intact son caractère maniériste de la fin du XVIᵉ siècle.

Die Villa wurde unter der Leitung von Flaminio Ponzio zwischen 1606 und 1613 erbaut und spiegelt den manieristischen Stil gegen Ende des 16. Jahrhunderts wider.

Realizada entre 1606 y 1613 siguiendo el diseño de Flaminio Ponzio, la villa conserva intacto el estilo manierista de finales del siglo XVI.

Costruita tra il 1606 e il 1613 su progetto di Flaminio Ponzio, la villa mantiene intatti i caratteri manieristi di fine Cinquecento.

Construída entre 1606 e 1613 com projeto de Flaminio Ponzio, a villa mantém intactas as características maneiristas de finais do século XVI.

Deze villa, gebouwd tussen 1606 en 1613 naar ontwerp van Flaminio Ponzio, heeft haar maniëristische kenmerken uit het eind van de 16e eeuw behouden.

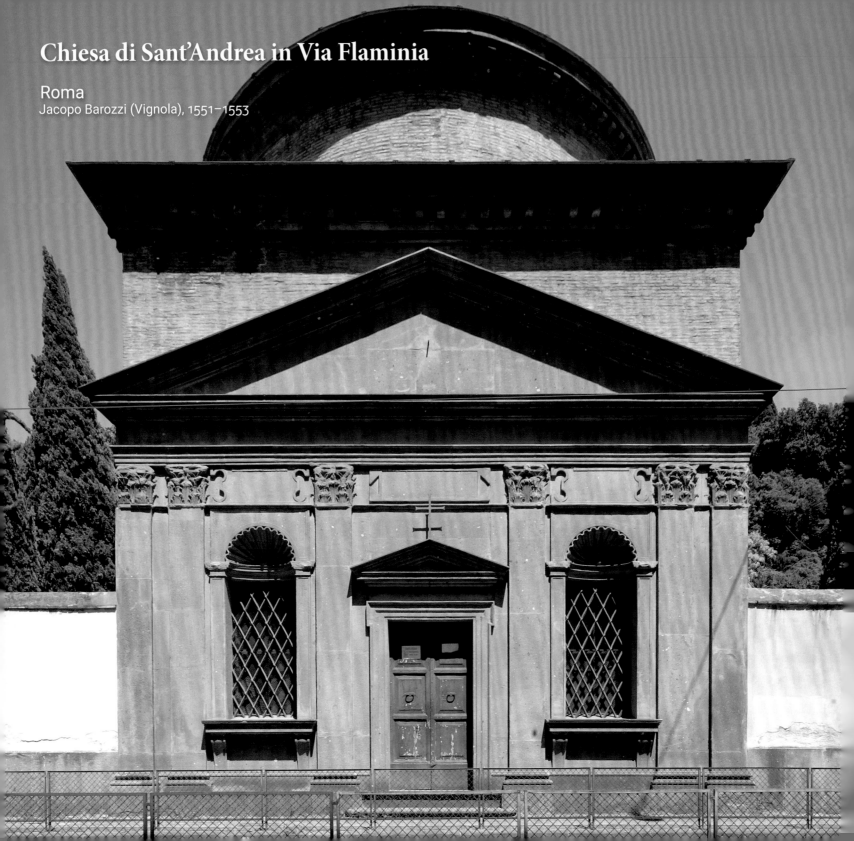

Chiesa di Sant'Andrea in Via Flaminia

Roma
Jacopo Barozzi (Vignola), 1551–1553

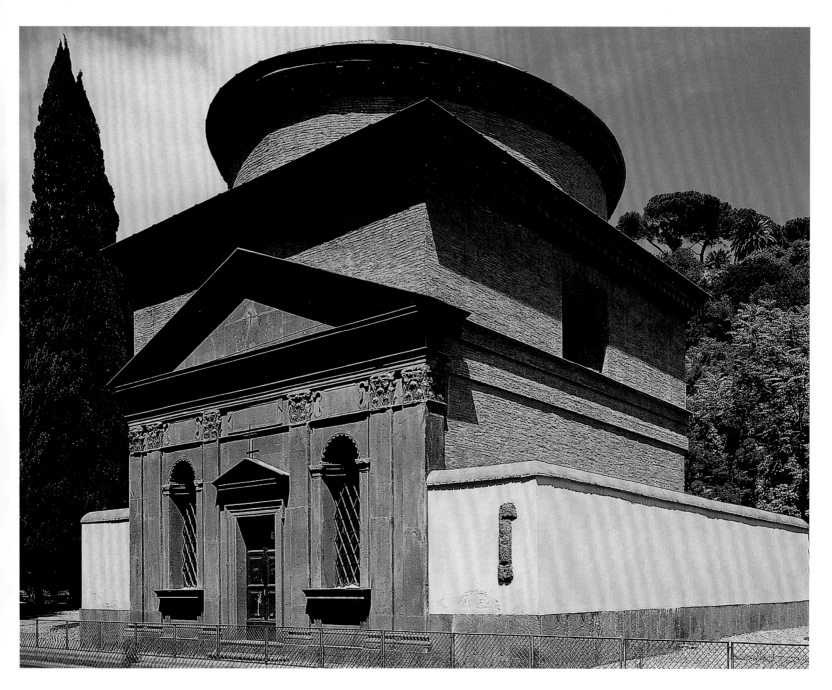

A simple rectangular hall forms the base for an oval dome, a new and characteristic element of Vignola's architecture.

Ein schlichter, rechteckiger Raum wird von einer ovalen Kuppel überspannt, einem neuen und charakteristischen Element in Vignolas Architektur.

Une simple pièce rectangulaire sert de base à la coupole ovale, élément nouveau et caractéristique de l'architecture de Vignole.

Una sencilla cámara rectangular conforma la base de la cúpula oval, elemento nuevo y característico de arquitectura vignolesca.

Una semplice aula rettangolare fà da base alla cupola ovale, elemento nuovo e caratterizzante dell'architettura vignolesca.

Uma simples sala retangular serve de base à cúpula oval, elemento novo e característico da arquitetura de Vignola.

Een eenvoudige, rechthoekige ruimte met daarbovenop een ovale koepel: een vernieuwend en kenmerkend element in de ontwerpen van Vignola.

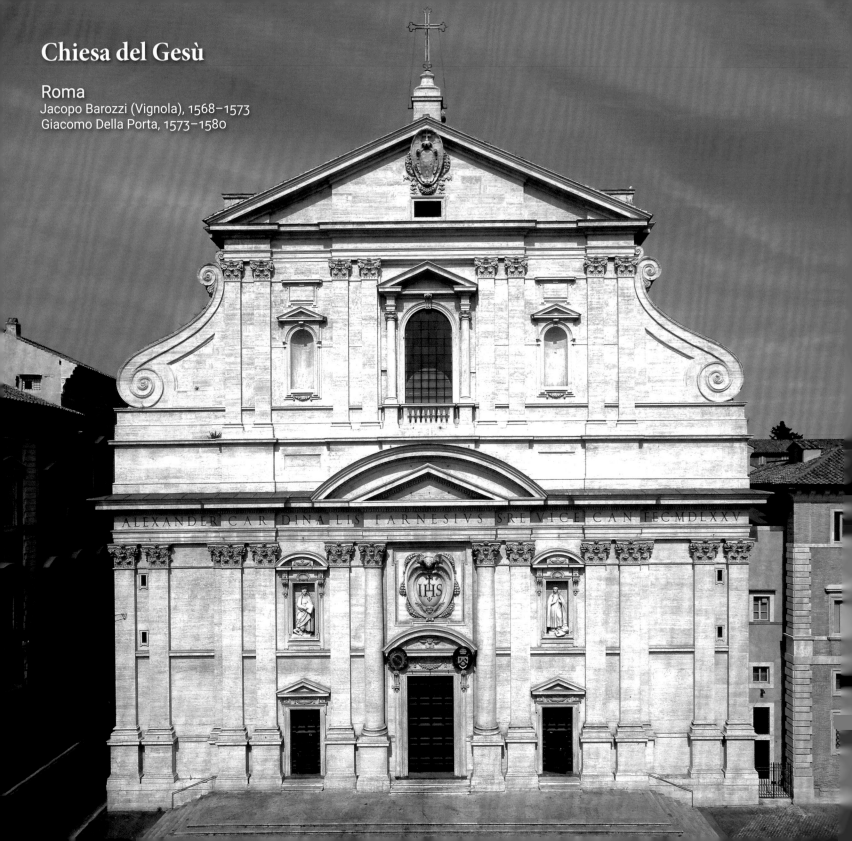

Chiesa del Gesù

Roma
Jacopo Barozzi (Vignola), 1568–1573
Giacomo Della Porta, 1573–1580

The façade is the work of Giacomo della Porta, 1571–1577, whose design was preferred to that of Vignola.

La façade est l'œuvre de Giacomo della Porta, 1571–1577, dont le projet a été préféré à celui de Vignola.

Die Fassade wurde nach dem Entwurf, der jenem von Vignola vorgezogen wurde, von Giacomo della Porta 1571–1577 angefertigt.

La fachada es obra de Giacomo della Porta, 1571–1577, cuyo diseño sobrepasó al de Vignola.

La facciata è opera di Giacomo della Porta, 1571–1577, il cui disegno fu preferito a quello di Vignola.

A fachada é de Giacomo della Porta (1571–1577) cujo projeto foi preferido ao de Vignola.

De voorgevel is het werk van Giacomo della Porta, 1571–1577, wiens ontwerp verkozen werd boven dat van Vignola.

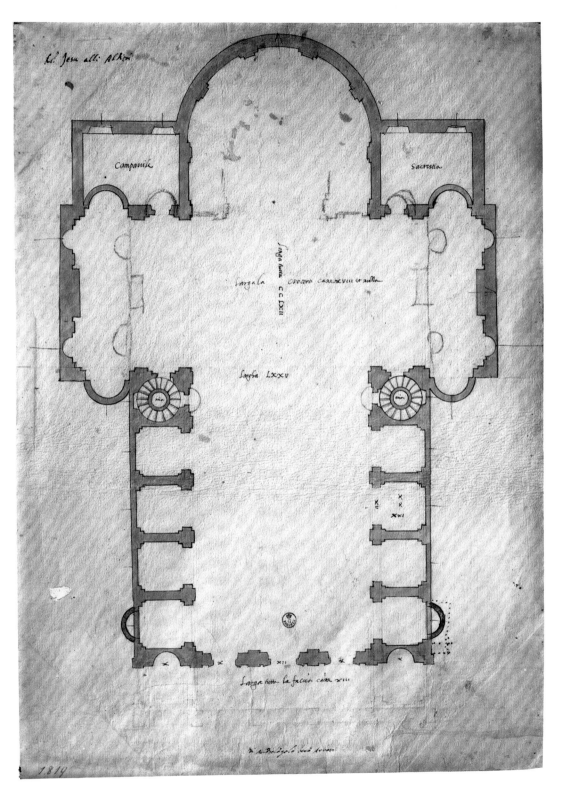

Plan of the Church of the Gesù in Rome, circa 1553.

Plan de l'église du Gesù à Rome, vers 1553.

Grundriss der Jesuskirche in Rom, ca. 1553.

Planta de la iglesia del Gesù en Roma, ca 1553.

Pianta della Chiesa del Gesù a Roma, 1553 ca.

Planta da Igreja de Jesus em Roma, cerca de 1553.

Plattegrond van de Gesù-kerk in Rome, ca. 1553.

The project called for a single nave extending into the presbytery and apse covered by a dome at the transept crossing.

Le plan comporte une nef unique prolongée par l'abside du presbyterium et couverte d'une coupole au croisement du transept.

Das einschiffige Langhaus schließt in seiner Verlängerung an den Chorraum und die Apsis an das Presbyterium und der Apsis an, die Vierung wird von einer Kuppel gekrönt.

El proyecto prevé una sola nave que se alarga hasta el presbiterio con ábside cubierto por una cúpula en el cruce con el transepto.

Il progetto del Vignola prevede un'unica navata che si prolunga nel presbiterio absidato, coperto da cupola all'incrocio con il transetto.

O projeto prevê uma única nave que se prolonga pela abside do presbitério, coberta por uma cúpula na intersecção com o transepto.

De kerk bestaat uit een enkel schip dat zich uitstrekt in het priesterkoor met apsis, en dat bedekt is met een koepel op de kruising met het transept.

Chiesa di Santa Maria del Popolo
Cappella Chigi

Roma
Raffaello, 1512

The interior of the dome decorated with gilded coffering and mosaics following the cartoons of Raphaël.

Das Innere der Kuppel ist mit einer goldenen Kassettendecke überzogen und mit Mosaiken auf Kartonvorlage von Raffael verziert.

L'intérieur de la coupole est décoré de caissons dorés et de mosaïques exécutées sur des cartons du même Raphaël.

L'interno della cupola ornata da cassettoni dorati, con mosaici eseguiti su cartoni dello stesso Raffaello.

El interior de la cúpula decorada con casetones dorados con mosaicos realizados sobre cartón de la mano del mismo Rafael.

O interior da cúpula decorada com caixotões dourados, com mosaicos seguidos de desenhos, também de Rafael.

De binnenzijde van de koepel is versierd met vergulde cassettes met mozaïeken op karton, gemaakt door Rafaël zelf.

Inside the church is the Chigi Chapel, commissioned by the banker Agostino Chigi from Raphael who designed it around a central plan, inspired by Bramante.

À l'intérieur de l'église se trouve la chapelle Chigi, commandée par le banquier Agostino Chigi à Raphaël qui a dessiné un édifice à plan central, en s'inspirant de Bramante.

Die Chigi-Kapelle im Innern der Kirche wurde im Auftrag des Bankiers Agostino Chigi nach Raffaels Entwurf errichtet, der sich für die Form des Zentralbaus von Bramante inspirieren ließ.

En el interior de la iglesia se encuentra la Capilla Chigi, encargada por el banquero Agostino Chigi a Rafael, que diseñó un ambiente de planta central inspirándose en Bramante.

All'interno della chiesa vi è la Cappella Chigi, commissionata dal banchiere Agostino Chigi a Raffaello, che disegnò un ambiente a pianta centrale ispirandosi a Bramante.

No interior da igreja encontra-se a Capela Chigi, encomendada pelo banqueiro Agostino Chigi a Rafael, que projetou um ambiente para a planta central inspirando-se em Bramante.

In de kerk bevindt zich de Chigi-kapel, een opdracht van de bankier Agostino Chigi aan Rafaël, die een op Bramante geïnspireerde centraal gebouwde ruimte ontwierp.

Chiesa di Santa Maria di Loreto

Roma
Antonio da Sangallo il Giovane, 1507
Jacopo del Duca, 1573–1576

The building is distinguished by two design phases: the cubic area of roman brick and travertine punctuated by double pilasters at the bottom; above, the 'Michelangelo-style' dome rests on an octagonal drum.

Das Kircheninnere wird von zwei verschiedenen Baustrukturen geprägt: der Kubus aus Ziegelstein und Travertin, der im unteren Teil mit zwei Pilastern verbunden ist, und der achteckige Kuppeltambour im Stil von Michelangelo im oberen Teil.

On distingue dans cet édifice les deux phases de la conception : un cube en briques et travertin, rythmé par des pilastres jumelés, dans sa partie inférieure ; une coupole « à la Michel-Ange » posée sur un tambour octogonal, dans sa partie supérieure.

En el edificio se distinguen las dos fases del proyecto: el área cúbica de ladrillo romano travertino caracterizado por pilastras dobles en la parte inferior y la cúpula del estilo de Miguel Ángel que se apoya sobre un tambor octagonal en la parte superior.

Nell'edificio si distinguono le due fasi progettuali: il cubo in laterizio e travertino, scandito da paraste binate nella parte inferiore, la "michelangiolesca" cupola poggiante su un tamburo ottagonale nella parte superiore.

No edifício podem distinguir-se as duas fases projetuais: o cubo em terracota e travertino, dividido por pilastras geminadas na parte inferior; a cúpula ao estilo de Michelangelo, apoiada num tambor octogonal na parte superior.

In het gebouw kunnen de twee projectfasen worden onderscheiden: de kubus in baksteen en travertijn met gepaarde pilasters in het onderste deel; en de koepel in de stijl van Michelangelo, die rust op een achthoekige tamboer, in het bovenste deel.

Basilica di San Pietro

Roma
Michelangelo Buonarroti, 1546
Giacomo Della Porta, 1572
Domenico Fontana, 1585

Michelangelo designed the dome and directed the construction from the foundations to the drum.

Michel-Ange a conçu la coupole et dirigé la construction de l'ensemble du soubassement, jusqu'au tambour.

Michelangelo entwarf die Kuppel und leitete den Kuppelbau vom Grundriss bis zum Tambour.

Miguel Ángel diseñó la cúpula y dirigió la construcción de toda la base hasta el tambor.

Michelangelo disegnò la cupola e diresse la costruzione di tutto il basamento fino al tamburo.

Michelângelo concebeu a cúpula e dirigiu a construção de todo o embasamento até ao tambor.

Michelangelo ontwierp de koepel en leidde de gehele bouw van het fundament tot aan de tamboer.

Antonio Labacco

Wooden model of St Peter's, after the design of Sangallo the Younger.

Maquette en bois de Saint-Pierre, selon le projet de Sangallo le Jeune.

Holzmodell des Petersdoms nach dem Entwurf von Sangallo dem Jüngeren.

Modelo de madera de San Pedro según el proyecto de Sangallo el Joven.

Modello ligneo di San Pietro, secondo il progetto di Sangallo il Giovane.

Modelo da Basílica de São Pedro, em madeira, conforme projeto de Sangallo, o Jovem.

Houten model van de Sint-Pieter, naar het ontwerp van Sangallo de Jongere.

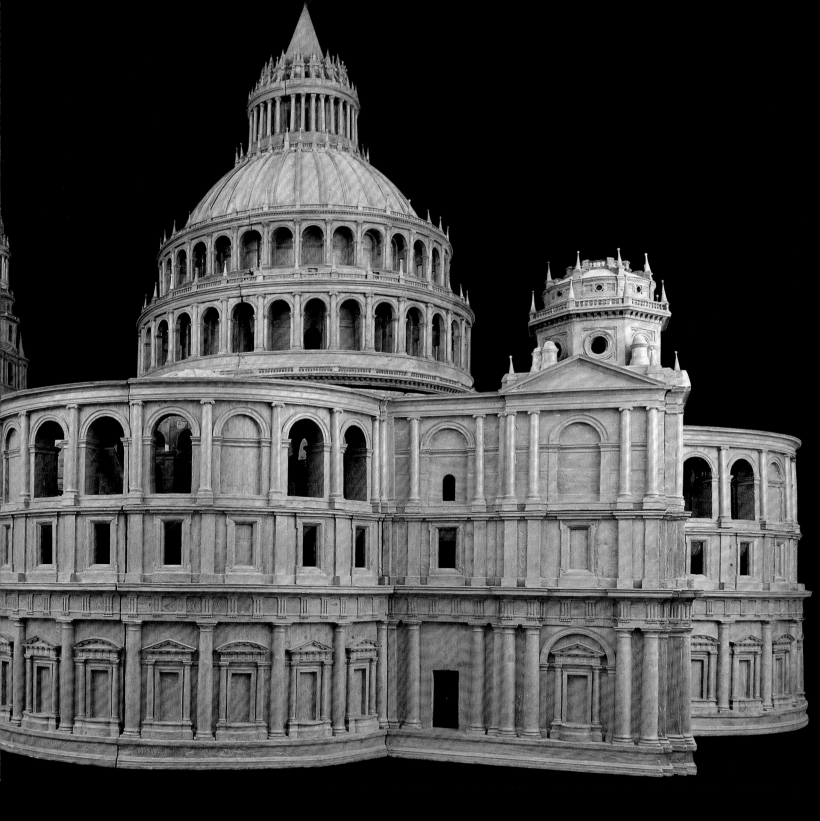

Antonio da Sangallo il Giovane

St Peter's, exterior elevation north, 1538.

Saint-Pierre, perspective extérieure septentrionale, 1538.

Nordansicht des Petersdoms, 1538.

San Pedro, perspectiva septentrional externa, 1538.

San Pietro, prospetto esterno settentrionale, 1538.

São Pedro, perspectiva exterior setentrional, 1538.

Sint-Pieter, zuidelijk buitenaanzicht, 1538.

Di fegno i fatto fitolate le fuer down nd fono
li quali p hedom pmoliqueti le bafe pofino
5 me liquoli & deliber pofano tfulpumi
mdto detum

259

1323.

IN HONOREM PRINCIP

The basilica's imposing façade created between 1607 and 1614 by Carlo Maderno.

L'imposante façade de la basilique, réalisée par Carlo Maderno entre 1607 et 1614.

Die imposante Fassade wurde zwischen 1607 und 1614 von Carlo Maderno vollendet.

La imponente fachada de la basílica realizada entre 1607 y 1614 por Carlo Maderno.

L'imponente facciata della basilica, realizzata tra il 1607 e il 1614 da Carlo Maderno.

A imponente fachada da basílica, realizada entre 1607 e 1614 por Carlo Maderno.

De imposante voorgevel van de basiliek werd tussen 1607 en 1614 gerealiseerd door Carlo Maderno.

Rocca di Ostia

Roma
Baccio Pontelli, ante 1490

Cardinal Giuliano della Rovere, later Pope Julius II, commissioned both its design and construction.

Le cardinal Giuliano della Rovere, futur pape Jules II, en a commandité la conception et la construction.

Kardinal Giuliano della Rovere, der spätere Papst Julius II., gab die Planung und den Bau in Auftrag.

El cardenal Giuliano della Rovere, posteriormente papa Julio II, encargó el proyecto y su construcción.

Il cardinale Giuliano della Rovere, in seguito papa Giulio II, ne commissionò il progetto e la costruzione.

O cardeal Giuliano della Rovere, futuro papa Júlio II, encomendou o seu projeto e a sua construção.

Kardinaal Giuliano della Rovere, later paus Julius II, gaf opdracht voor het ontwerp en de bouw.

Mura Leonine

Roma
Michelangelo, 1543–1548
Antonio da Sangallo il Giovane, 1543–1546

Built by Pope Leo IV in the mid 9th century, the Leonine Wall was extended and reinforced during the Renaissance under various pontificates: Nicholas V, Alexander VI, and Paul III. The best military architects of the time collaborated on the project.

Die Leoninische Mauer wurde Mitte des 9. Jahrhunderts unter Papst Leo IV errichtet und während der Renaissance unter verschiedenen Päpsten erweitert und verstärkt: Nikolaus V., Alexander VI. und Paul III. An den Arbeiten beteiligten sich die damals berühmtesten Militärarchitekten.

Construit sous le pontificat de Léon IV (847–855), le mur léonin a été agrandi et renforcé à la Renaissance sous divers pontifes : Nicolas V, Alexandre VI et Paul III. Les plus illustres architectes militaires de l'époque collaborèrent à ces travaux.

Costruite da papa Leone IV a metà del IX secolo, le Mura leonine furono ampliate e rafforzate in periodo rinascimentale sotto diversi pontefici: Niccolò V, Alessandro VI e Paolo III. Ai lavori collaborarono i più famosi architetti militari dell'epoca.

Realizada por encargo del papa León IV a mediados del siglo IX, la muralla Leonina fue ampliada y reforzada durante el Renacimiento bajo varios pontificados: Nicolás V, Alejandro VI y Paulo III. El proyecto contó con la colaboración de los mejores arquitectos militares de la época.

Edificada a pedido do papa Leão IV em meados do século IX, a Muralha Leonina foi ampliada e reforçada durante o Renascimento sob diversos pontificados: Nicolau V, Alexandre VI e Paulo III. O projeto contou com a colaboração dos melhores arquitetos militares da época.

De Leonische Muur was midden 9e eeuw gebouwd door paus Leo IV en tijdens de Renaissance uitgebreid en versterkt onder verschillende pausen: Nicolaas V, Alexander VI en Paulus III. De bekendste militaire architecten uit die tijd namen deel aan de werkzaamheden.

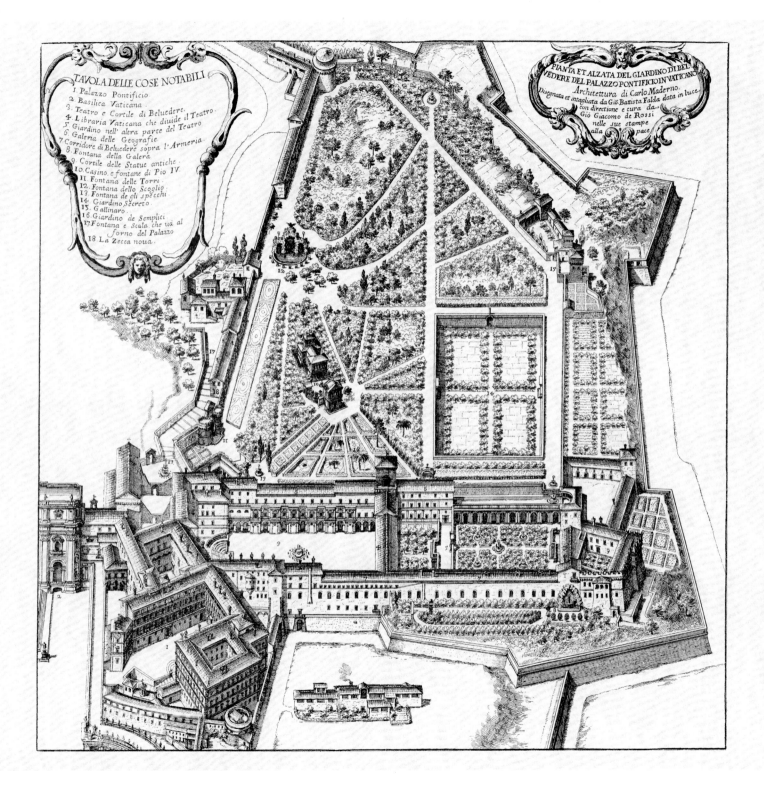

TAVOLA DELLE COSE NOTABILI

1. Palazzo Pontificio.
2. Basilica Vaticana.
3. Teatro e Cortile di Beluedere.
4. Libraria Vaticana che diuide il Teatro.
5. Giardino nell'altra parte del Teatro.
6. Galeria delle Geografie.
7. Corridore di Beluedere sopra l'Armeria.
8. Fontana della Galera.
9. Cortile delle Statue antiche.
10. Casino, e fontane di Pio IV.
11. Fontana delle Torri.
12. Fontana dello Scoglio.
13. Fontana de gli specchi.
14. Giardino Secreto.
15. Gallinaro.
16. Giardino de Semplici.
17. Fontana e Scala che uà al forno del Palazzo
18. La Zecca noua.

PIANTA ET ALZATA DEL GIARDINO DI BEL
VEDERE DEL PALAZZO PONTIFICIO IN VATICANO
Architettura di Carlo Maderno.
Disegnata et intagliata da Giò. Battista Falda data in luce,
con directione e cura da
Giò Giacomo de Rossi
nelle sue stampe
alla pace

Palazzo Farnese

Caprarola

Jacopo Barozzi (Vignola), 1559–1573

Built following Vignola's design, which transformed into a palazzo the pentagonal fortress—only partially begun—by Sangallo the Younger.

Der Bau wurde nach dem Entwurf Vignolas, der die fünfeckige Festung in einen Palast umwandelte, von Sangallo dem Jüngeren begonnen.

Édifice surélevé par Vignola qui transforme en palais une forteresse pentagonale commencée – en partie seulement – par Sangallo le Jeune.

Fue construido siguiendo el diseño de Vignola, que transformó en este palacio la fortaleza pentagonal que comenzó Sangallo el Joven.

Fu eretto dal Vignola trasformando in palazzo la fortezza pentagonale solo in parte iniziata da Sangallo il Giovane.

Foi erigido segundo projeto de Vignola, que assim transformava em palácio a fortaleza pentagonal, iniciada – apenas parcialmente – por Sangallo, o Jovem.

Het werd gebouwd naar ontwerp van Vignola, die de vijfhoekige vesting van Sangallo de Jongere – die slechts deels voltooid was – in een paleis veranderde.

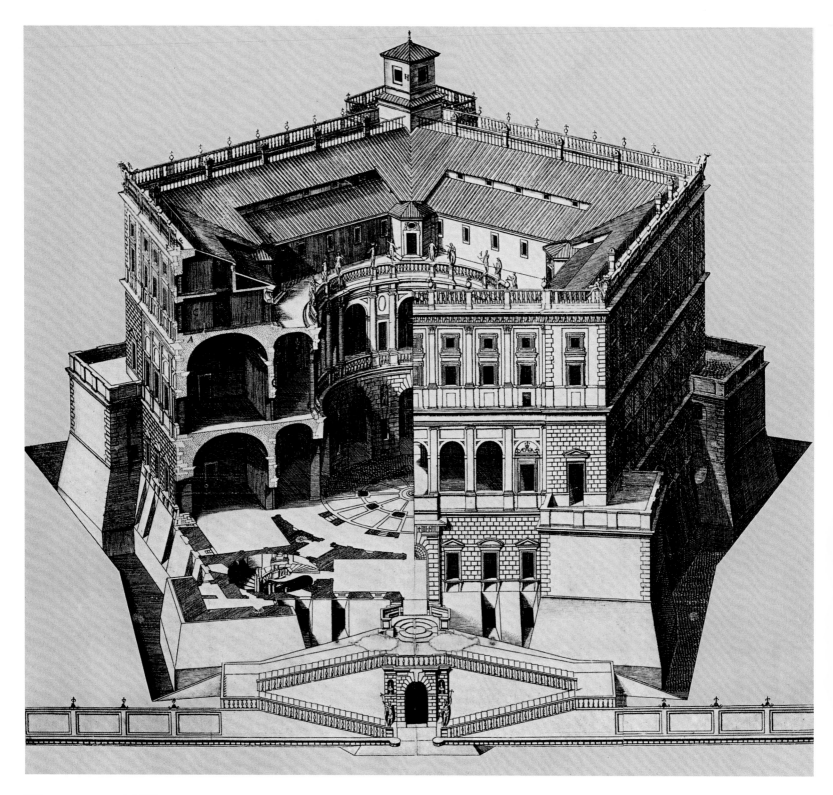

The round courtyard within the pentagon is an
ingenious invention of Vignola. The palazzo was begun
in 1559 and completed in 1575 by Giambattista Fornovo,
Vignola's collaborator.

La cour intérieure ronde inscrite dans le pentagone est une
invention géniale de Vignola. Le palais a été commencé en
1559 et achevé en 1575 par Giambattista Fornovo, collaborateur
de Vignola.

Der Rundhof im fünfeckigen Bau gehört zu den genialen
Erfindungen von Vignola. Die Arbeiten am Palast begannen
1559 und wurden 1575 von Giambattista Fornovo, einem
Mitarbeiter von Vignola, vollendet.

El patio de forma circular inmerso en el pentágono es un
magnífico invento de Vignola. La construcción del palacio
comenzó en 1559 y finalizó en 1575 de la mano de Giambattista
Fornovo, colaborador de Vignola.

Il cortile rotondo iscritto nel pentagono è una geniale
invenzione del Vignola. Il palazzo fu iniziato nel 1559 e concluso
nel 1575 da Giambattista Fornovo, collaboratore del Vignola.

O pátio interior circular inserido no pentágono é uma genial
invenção de Vignola. O palácio foi iniciado em 1559 e terminado
em 1575 por Giambattista Fornovo, colaborador de Vignola.

De ronde binnenplaats, ingevat in een vijfhoek, is een geniaal
idee van Vignola. De bouw van het palazzo begon in 1559 en
werd voltooid in 1575 door Giambattista Fornovo, medewerker
van Vignola.

The Scala Regia leading to the piano nobile.
Stylistically inspired by Bramante, Vignola created
an exquisitely harmonious spiral, punctuated by a
rhythmic sequence of paired Doric columns.

La Scala Regia menant à l'étage noble. En
s'inspirant d'une idée de Bramante, Vignola crée
une spirale d'une harmonie exquise, scandée par
une suite de colonnes doriques jumelées.

Die Scala Regia, die zur Beletage führt. Gestützt
auf eine Idee von Bramante entwarf Vignola
eine elegante Stufenspirale, die von gekuppelten
dorischen Säulenpaaren gestützt wird.

La Scala Regia que conduce al piano nobile.
Inspirado en una idea bramantesca, Vignola
creó una espiral de extraordinaria armonía
decorada por una secuencia rítmica de columnas
dóricas pareadas.

La Scala Regia che conduce al piano nobile.
Attingendo a un'idea bramantesca, Vignola creò
una spirale di squisita armonia, scandita dalla
sequenza ritmica di colonne doriche binate.

A Escadaria Real que conduz ao andar nobre.
Inspirado por uma ideia bramantesca, Vignola
criou uma espiral de requintada harmonia,
marcada pela sequência rítmica de colunas
dóricas geminadas.

De Scala Regia die naar de bel-etage leidt.
Vignola maakte, naar een idee van Bramante, een
uiterst harmonieuze spiraal met een ritmische
opeenvolging van gepaarde Dorische zuilen.

The entryway portal at the chapel.

Portail d'entrée de la chapelle.

Das Eingangsportal zur Kapelle.

El portal de acceso a la Capilla.

Portale dell'ingresso della cappella.

Portal de acesso à capela.

Het toegangsportaal van de kapel.

The Room of the Farnese Deeds, painted by Matteo Zuccari (1563–1565), is the most prestigious area of the palazzo, exalting the Farnese family. At the bottom, above the fireplace, a portrait of Henry II of France.

La salle des Fastes farnésiens représente l'espace le plus prestigieux du palais, avec l'éloge de la famille représenté par Matteo Zuccari (1563–1565). Dans le fond, au-dessus de la petite cheminée, le portrait d'Henri II de France.

La Sala dei Fasti Farnesiani representa el ambiente más prestigioso del palacio donde resalta un cuadro de la familia realizado por Matteo Zuccari (1563–1565). Al fondo, encima de la chimenea, el retrato de Enrique II de Francia.

A Sala dei Fasti Farnesiani representa o espaço de maior prestígio do palácio, com a glorificação da família, num quadro de Matteo Zuccari (1563–1565). Ao fundo, sobre a lareira, o retrato de Henrique II de França.

Die Sala dei Fasti Farnesiani ist der angesehenste Saal des Palastes und wurde von Matteo Zuccari mit der Familiengeschichte ausgemalt (1563–1565). Über dem Kamin thront das Porträt Heinrichs II. von Frankreich.

La Sala dei Fasti Farnesiani rappresenta l'ambiente di maggior prestigio del palazzo, con l'esaltazione della famiglia dipinta da Matteo Zuccari (1563–1565). Nel fondo, sopra il caminetto, il ritratto di Enrico II di Francia.

De Sala dei Fasti Farnesiani is het meest prestigieuze vertrek van het palazzo, met een schilderij van Matteo Zuccari (1563–1565) waarop de familie verheerlijkt wordt. Achterin, boven de haard, een portret van Hendrik II van Frankrijk

Vault of the Theatre Room in the winter apartment on the ground floor.

Voûte de la salle du Théâtre, dans les appartements d'hiver, au rez-de-chaussée.

Deckengewölbe des Theatersaals im Erdgeschoss der Winterwohnung.

Bóveda de la Sala del Teatro del apartamento de invierno de la planta baja.

Volta della Sala del Teatro nell'appartamento d'inverno, al piano terreno.

Abóbada da Sala do Teatro nos aposentos de inverno, no piso térreo.

Plafond van de Theaterzaal in het winterappartement op de begane grond.

Jupiter Room is the most sumptuous part in the Prelate's apartment on the ground floor. Decorated between 1560 and 1562: vaults by Taddeo Zuccari and walls by Vignola.

La Salle de Jupiter est l'espace le plus luxueux de l'appartement des Prélats, au rez-de-chaussée, décoré entre 1560 et 1562 par Taddeo Zuccari (pour la voûte) et par Vignola (pour les murs).

Der Jupitersaal ist der prächtigste Saal im Erdgeschoss der Prelati-Wohnung. Die Verzierungen am Deckengewölbe entstanden zwischen 1560 und 1562 von Taddeo Zuccari, die Wände sind von Vignola.

La Sala de Júpiter es el ambiente más fastuoso del apartamento de los Prelados de la planta baja. Bóveda decorada por Taddeo Zuccari y paredes por Vignola entre 1560 y 1562.

Sala di Giove: è il più fastoso ambiente dell'Appartamento dei Prelati, al piano terra. Decorato tra il 1560 e il 1562 da Taddeo Zuccari nella volta e da Vignola sulle pareti.

A Sala de Júpiter é o mais faustoso ambiente do Apartamento dos Prelados, no piso térreo. Decorado entre 1560 e 1562 por Taddeo Zuccari na abóbada e por Vignola nas paredes.

De Zaal van Jupiter is het weelderigste vertrek van het Appartement van de Prelaten op de begane grond. Het plafond is tussen 1560 en 1562 versierd door Taddeo Zuccari en de wanden door Vignola.

The second floor loggia of the round courtyard with arches flanked by Ionic columns and decorated on the inside with grotesques.

Galerie du deuxième étage de la cour intérieure ronde, avec ses arcades encadrées de colonnes ioniques et décorée de grotesques à l'intérieur.

Die Loggia im zweiten Obergeschoss des Rundhofs mit Arkaden, die von ionischen Säulen flankiert werden, und deren Innenwände mit Grotesken verziert sind.

La galería en el segundo piso del patio circular con arcadas con columnas jónicas y decoración grutesca en la parte interior.

La loggia al secondo piano del cortile rotondo, con arcate affiancate da colonne ioniche, è internamente decorata a grottesche.

A loggia do segundo andar do pátio interior circular, com arcos ladeados por colunas jónicas e decorada no interior com grotescos.

De loggia op de tweede verdieping van de ronde binnenplaats met bogen naast Ionische zuilen, is volledig versierd met grotesken.

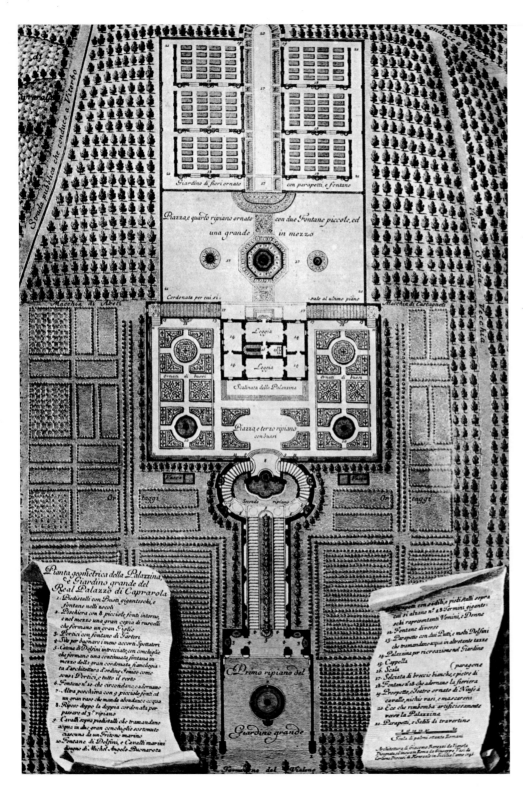

Giuseppe Vasi

Plan of the gardens.

Plan des jardins.

Grundriss der Gärten.

Planta de los jardines.

Pianta dei giardini.

Planta dos jardins.

Plattegrond van de tuin.

The view from the Lily Fountain towards the Palazzina del Piacere is enhanced by the Chain of Dolphins, a stream of water coursing in the opposite direction between two flanking staircases.

La perspective de la fontaine du Lys, dans la direction de la Palazzina del Piacere, met en valeur la « chaîne des Dauphins », un courant d'eau entre deux escaliers, qui coule en sens inverse du parcours du visiteur.

Der Lilienbrunnen und die Delphinkette, eine Wassertreppe mit Blick auf die Palazzina del Piacere, von dem ein Bächlein über eine Kaskade zwischen zwei Freitreppen hinabfließt.

La vista de la Fontana del Giglio hacia la Palazzina del Piacere resalta la Cadena de Delfines, un arroyo de agua entre dos escalinatas que fluye en sentido contrario al recorrido del visitante.

La prospettiva dalla Fontana del Giglio, verso la Palazzina del Piacere, valorizza la Catena dei Delfini, un ruscello d'acqua che scorre in senso contrario tra due scalinate affiancate.

Perspectiva da Fonte do Lírio em frente da Palazzina del Piacere, que valoriza a Cadeia de Golfinhos, um regato que corre no sentido inverso ao do visitante, ladeado por duas escadarias.

Het uitzicht vanaf de Fontein van de Lelie op het Palazzina del Piacere doet de Dolfijnketting goed uitkomen: een waterstroompje dat tussen twee naastgelegen trappen loopt.

Basilica di San Bernardino

L'Aquila
Cola dell'Amatrice, 1524–1540

Preceded by a short staircase, the Renaissance façade is of three superimposed orders: first Doric, then Ionic and Corinthian columns.

Précédée de quelques marches, la façade Renaissance superpose ses trois ordres marqués par des colonnes doriques, ioniques et corinthiennes.

Die Renaissance-Fassade ruht auf einem kurzen Treppenpodest und ist in drei Ordnungen mit dorischen, ionischen und korinthischen Säulen gegliedert.

Precedida por una pequeña escalinata, la fachada de estilo renacentista consta de tres órdenes superpuestos separados por columnas dóricas, jónicas y corintias.

Preceduta da una breve scalinata, la facciata rinascimentale è a tre ordini sovrapposti, partiti da colonne doriche, ioniche e corinzie.

Precedida por uma pequena escadaria, uma fachada renascentista de três ordens sobrepostas divididas por colunas dóricas, jónicas e coríntias.

De renaissancistische gevel, met ervoor een korte trap, bestaat uit drie lagen met Dorische, Ionische en Corinthische zuilen.

Palazzo Orsini di Gravina

Napoli
Gabriele D'Agnolo, 1513–1549

One of the most important civil buildings of the Neapolitan Renaissance. With a façade of rusticated ashlar on the ground floor and lesene-framed windows on the first floor.

C'est l'un des édifices civils les plus importants de la Renaissance napolitaine. Il se présente avec une façade en bossages rustiques au rez-de-chaussée et des fenêtres encadrées de pilastres à l'étage supérieur.

Das Gebäude ist eines der wichtigsten Bürgerhäuser der neapolitanischen Renaissance. Die Fassade besteht im Erdgeschoss aus einem rustikalen Bossenwerk und wird im Obergeschoss von Fenstern durchbrochen, die mit Lisenen umrahmt sind.

Es uno de los edificios civiles más importantes del Renacimiento napolitano. La fachada de la planta baja está revestida con paramento rústico y las ventanas del piso superior están enmarcadas por lesenas.

È uno dei più importanti edifici civili del rinascimento napoletano. Si presenta con una facciata in bugnato rustico al piano terreno e finestre incorniciate da lesene in quello superiore.

É um dos mais importantes edifícios civis do Renascimento napolitano. Apresenta uma fachada em bossagem rústica no piso térreo e janelas emolduradas por pilastras no piso superior.

Dit is een van de belangrijkste civiele bouwwerken uit de Napoletaanse renaissance. Het onderste deel van de voorgevel bevat een rustieke bossage; het bovenste deel wordt omlijst door lisenen.

Chiesa di Sant'Anna dei Lombardi
Cappella Tolosa

Napoli
Giuliano da Maiano, 1485–1490

The Capella Tolosa, in the Tuscan Renaissance style is reminiscent of San Lorenzo's Old Sacristy.

La chapelle de Tolosa, dans le goût de la Renaissance toscane, rappelle par exemple la Vieille Sacristie de San Lorenzo.

Die Tolosa-Kapelle im Stil der toskanischen Renaissance erinnert an die Alte Sakristei von San Lorenzo.

La Capilla Tolosa, de estilo renacentista toscano, recuerda a la Sacristía vieja de San Lorenzo.

La Cappella Tolosa, di gusto rinascimentale toscano, ricorda la Sagrestia Vecchia di San Lorenzo.

A Cappella Tolosa, ao gosto do Renascimento toscano, relembra a Sacristia Velha de São Lorenzo.

De Tolosa-kapel, in Toscaans renaissancistische stijl, doet denken aan de Oude Sacristie van San Lorenzo.

Chiesa del Gesù Nuovo

Napoli
Giuseppe Valeriano, 1584

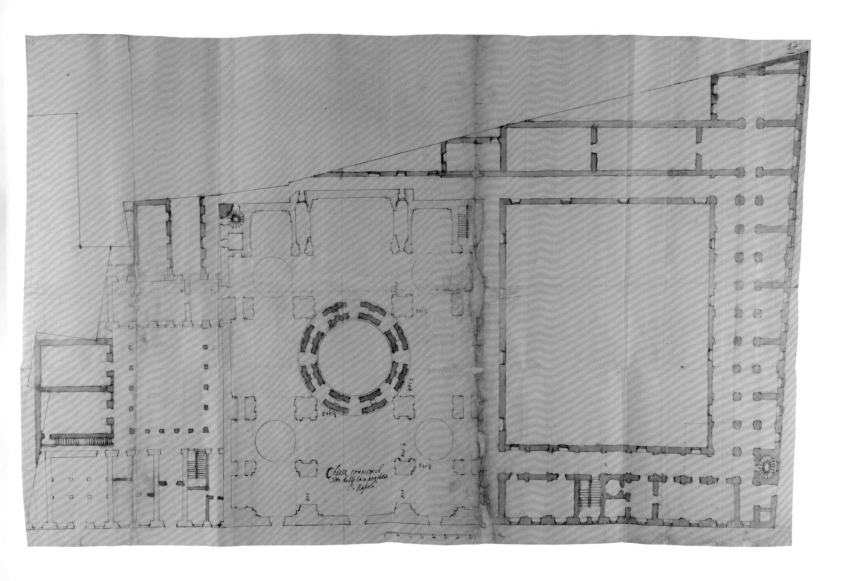

Created for the Society of Jesus, it features a beautiful, diamond-point ashlar façade.

Die Kirche wurde für den Jesuitenorden erbaut und ist mit einem Bossenwerk aus Diamantquadern verkleidet.

Réalisé pour la Compagnie de Jésus, il présente une belle façade en bossage en pointes de diamant.

Realizzata per la Compagnia di Gesù, presenta una bella facciata in bugnato a punta di diamante.

Realizada por la Compañía de Jesús, presenta una hermosa fachada labrada a punta de diamante.

Edificada para a Companhia de Jesus, apresenta uma bela fachada em bossagem a ponta de diamante.

Deze kerk, gebouwd in opdracht van de jezuïetenorde, heeft een mooie voorgevel met diamantreliëf.

Castel Nuovo

Napoli
Guillermo Sagrera, 1450

Alfonso I of Aragon entrusted the Spanish architect with the rebuilding of the Angevin fortress after the damage it suffered during the two decades of war for the kingdom's conquest. The monumental triumphal arch, amongst the supreme examples of the Renaissance in southern Italy, is from this period, 1453–1468.

Nach dem zwanzigjährigen Erbfolgekrieg beauftragte Alfons I. von Aragon den spanischen Architekten mit dem Wiederaufbau der zerstörten angevinischen Festung. Der zwischen 1453 und 1468 erschaffene monumentale Triumphbogen zählt zu den wichtigsten Werken der süditalienischen Renaissance.

Alphonse Iᵉʳ d'Aragon confia à cet architecte espagnol la reconstruction de la forteresse angevine du Château-Neuf, endommagée par vingt ans de guerre pour la conquête du royaume. De cette période, 1453–1468, date le monumental arc de triomphe qui est l'un des plus hauts témoignages de la Renaissance dans l'Italie méridionale.

Alfonso I de Aragón encargó al arquitecto español la reconstrucción de la fortaleza angevina tras la destrucción que sufrió durante los veinte años de guerra por la conquista del reino. El espectacular arco del triunfo data de aquella época, 1453–1468, testimonio importante del Renacimiento del sur de Italia.

Alfonso I di Aragona affidò all'architetto spagnolo la ricostruzione della fortezza angioina dopo le distruzioni subite nel corso di vent'anni di guerra per la conquista del regno. È di quel periodo, 1453–1468, il monumentale arco di trionfo, testimonianza tra le più alte del Rinascimento nell'Italia meridionale.

Afonso I de Aragão entregou ao arquiteto espanhol a reconstrução da fortaleza angevina, após a destruição sofrida no decurso de vinte anos de guerra pela conquista do reino. É daquele período, 1453–1468, o monumental arco do triunfo, um dos maiores testemunhos do Renascimento na Itália do Sul.

Alfons I van Aragón gaf de Spaanse architect opdracht het Anjoufort te herbouwen nadat het vernietigd was gedurende de twintig jaar aan oorlog om de verovering van het rijk. Uit deze tijd, 1453–1468, stamt de monumentale triomfboog, een van de belangrijkste getuigenissen van de Zuid-Italiaanse renaissance.

Palazzo Abatellis

Palermo
Matteo Carnilivari, 1490–1495

The façade and entryway portal in late Catalan-Gothic style with Renaissance features.

La façade et le portail d'entrée rappelant le gothique tardif catalan, présentent des traits caractéristiques de la Renaissance.

Die Fassade und das Eingangsportal im Stil der Katalanischen Spätgotik und mit Einflüssen der Renaissance.

La fachada y el portal de acceso son de estilo gótico tardío catalán con detalles renacentistas.

La facciata e il portale d'ingresso in forme tardogotiche catalane con soluzioni rinascimentali.

A fachada e o portal de entrada em linhas de gótico tardio çatalão, com elementos característicos do Renascimento.

De voorgevel en de toegangsdeur in Catalaanse laat-gotische stijl met renaissancistische kenmerken.

Fontana Pretoria

Palermo
Francesco Camilliani, 1554–1555

Dramatic and superb production form the mid-16th century, work of the
Florentine sculptor Francesco Camilliani.

Cette superbe et spectaculaire réalisation du milieu du XVIᵉ siècle est l'une des
plus remarquables œuvres du sculpteur florentin Francesco Camilliani.

Eindrucksvoller und prächtiger Bau aus der Mitte des 16. Jahrhunderts, ein Werk
des florentinischen Architekten Francesco Camilliani.

Magnífica y espectacular creación de mediados del siglo XVI, obra del escultor
florentino Francesco Camilliani.

Scenografica e superba realizzazione di metà Cinquecento, opera dello scultore
fiorentino Francesco Camilliani.

Realização grandiosa e sublime de meados do século XVI, uma das mais notáveis
da obra do escultor florentino Francesco Camilliani.

Indrukwekkend, schitterend werk uit midden 16e eeuw, gemaakt door de
Florentijnse beeldhouwer Francesco Camilliani.

Glossary

APSE
the semi-cylindrical terminal part of a basilica covered by a half-dome.

ACANTHUS
species of thistle with jagged leaves, which are used in the decoration of Corinthian capitals.

ACROTERION
decoration at the pediment's apex and corners.

ANDRONE (ENTRANCE HALL)
passage from the entryway to the courtyard.

ARCHITRAVE
load-bearing, horizontal architectural element supported by piers or columns.

ARCHIVOLT
decorative moulding that follows the arch's curve.

ASHLAR
squared/dressed block of stone.

ATRIUM
rectangular portico fronting the entrance of a church and sometimes a villa.

BALUSTRADE
parapet formed by small columns and pilasters united by a top moulding.

BAY
space between two successive load-bearing elements.

BINATE
term referring to an architectural element paired with another exactly the same.

BRACKETS
cantilevered structure made up of a small arch supported by corbels.

BUILDING STONE
worked block of stone, serving as an ornamental element or incorporated into a (masonry) wall.

BUTTRESS
architectural element that serves to reinforce a structure by acting against a vault's lateral thrust.

CAPITAL
element of a trilithic system that surmounts the column.

CARYATID
sculpted female figure, which serves as a vertical support.

CASE MOULDING
decoration of a space by way of horizontal and vertical cornices.

CENTRING
curved form or wooden structure used in the construction of arches, vaults and domes.

CHARTERHOUSE
type of monastery developed by the Carthusians, consisting of two cloisters, a church, and the monk's individual dwellings.

CLOISTER
colonnaded courtyard, the monastery's communal living area.

COFFER
sunken element within a flat or vaulted surface, it can coincide with the structural elements or serve a purely decorative function.

COMPOSITE
combination of the Ionic and Corinthian orders.

CORINTHIAN COLUMN
similar to the Ionic column, capital with acanthus leaves and volutes at the corners.

CORNICE
horizontal element projecting out from a wall.

COUNTER-FACADE
interior wall opposite the apse.

CROSSING
in a church, the intersection of nave and transept.

CRYPTOPORTICO
semi-subterranean portico.

DOME
architectural structure resulting from the rotation of an arc around a vertical axis.

DORIC COLUMN
without a base, fluted shaft and capital made up of simple geometric elements.

DRUM
cylindrical or polygonal connecting structure upon which a dome is built.

ENTABLATURE
complex of horizontal elements of the trilith, divided into architrave, frieze and cornice.

EXEDRA
semicircular colonnade or arcade.

EXTRADOS
external, convex surface of an arch.

FISHPOND
ornamental pond with fish.

FLUTING
rectilinear grooves, sometimes undulated, carved in the shaft of columns, piers, pilasters, or corbels.

FORNIX
opening of an arch or monumental door.

FRIEZE
architectural element positioned above the architrave, denotes a sculptural composition with a horizontal course.

GABLE
the summit of a building, terminal part of an architectural structure.

GAZEBO
kiosk in masonry or wrought iron.

GREEK CROSS
cross with arms of equal length.

INTERCOLUMNIATION
spacing between two columns, the diameter of which is used as a unit of measure.

INTRADOS
concave, internal surface of the arch.

IONIC COLUMN

with a base, fluted shaft and capital with lateral volutes.

LANCET ARCH

made up of two circular arches that meet at a peak.

LATIN CROSS

a cross that is formed by two different segments, the smaller segment about three-fourths the length of the larger.

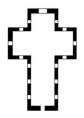

LANTERN

topmost part of the dome, usually in the shape of a small, circular temple.

LESENE

an engaged pilaster or column with a decorative function protruding from a façade.

LOGGIA

open-sided portico, usually with a vaulted roof, located inside or in front of a building.

LUNETTE

semi-circular surface, sometimes decorated, positioned above a rectangular opening.

MAUSOLEUM

monumental tomb.

MOULDING

a shaped strip with an ornamental function used to connect or protect architectural elements.

MULLIONED WINDOW

window made up of an opening divided into two equal parts by a vertical element.

NAVE

longitudinal portion of a church flanked by columns or piers.

OCULUS

small, circular aperture.

ORDER

a set of compositional rules and principles pertaining to individual elements in an architectural whole.

PEDIMENT

triangle formed by an entablature and the slope of a double-pitch roof.

PENDENTIVE

spherical, triangular shaped area formed by the connection between a dome placed atop a squared base.

PERISTYLE

colonnaded portico surrounding a building or a courtyard.

PILASTER

load bearing pier with a flat profile that projects slightly from the wall.

PORTAL

door of monumental or unusually large proportions.

PORTICO

part of a building that is open on one of its long sides the roof of which is supported by columns.

PRESBYTERY

part of the basilica reserved to the clergy, located at the back of the central nave and terminating in the apse.

PRONAOS

colonnaded atrium projecting from the façade.

ROUND ARCH

the simplest type of arch, consisting of a half-circle.

RIB

moulded masonry arch on which a vault rests.

ROSE WINDOW

large, circular window with richly patterned interiors made with architectural or decorative elements.

RUSTICATION

façade cladding made with rough convex stone blocks that taper in towards the edges with wide, concave joints.

SACRISTY

room attached to the church and communicating with the presbytery. During the Renaissance it often became a room of great beauty and refinement.

SOFFIT

underside of the arch, internal part of the arch.

SERLIAN

opening with three lights of which the central light is arched and the two lateral ones feature entablature.

SUBSTRUCTURES

structure partially or completely below ground designed to form the foundation for construction on sloping terrain.

TELAMON

sculpted male figure that serves as a vertical support.

TYMPANUM

triangular area within the pediment. It can take multiple forms: continuous, broken, curved.

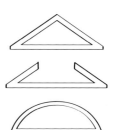

TRILITH

structural system divided into one horizontal element whose force is discharged to the two vertical elements.

TRANSEPT

perpendicular to the main body of the central nave, whereby the floor plan assumes the shape of a Latin cross.

VESTIBULE

enclosed esplanade fronting a Roman house, in the Renaissance it became an open area fronting the portico, androne, or antechamber.

VAULT

curved roof based on the principle of the arch. It can take on different forms: barrel vault, groin vault, rib vault or cloister vault.

VOLUTE

a spiral ornament, it also references the large S elements connecting the narrow upper part with the lower part of a church façade.

Glossaire

ABSIDE

extrémité semi-cylindrique d'une basilique, couverte par une voûte en cul-de-four.

ACANTHE

variété de chardon à feuilles dentelées, reproduite dans l'ornementation d'un chapiteau corinthien.

ACROTÈRE

ornementation plastique au sommet et aux angles d'un fronton.

ARC BRISÉ ou OGIVAL

constitué de deux arcs de cercle se joignant en pointe.

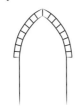

ARC EN PLEIN CINTRE

type d'arc le plus simple, constitué d'un demi-cercle.

ARCHITRAVE

élément architectonique portant, appuyé horizontalement sur des colonnes ou des piliers.

ARCHIVOLTE

bandeau ornementé qui épouse le profil d'un arc.

ATRIUM

porche rectangulaire placé devant une église ou (parfois) une villa.

BALUSTRADE

parapet formé de petits piliers et de colonnettes, unis par un bandeau plat au-dessus.

BOSSAGE

saillie ou protubérance laissée sur le parement d'une pierre taillée, dans un revêtement de façade.

CAISSON

élément en creux dans une surface plane ou voûtée, qui peut être intégré à la structure ou avoir une fonction exclusivement ornementale.

CANNELURES

rainures généralement rectilignes (parfois ondulées), ornant les fûts des colonnes et les montants des piliers et des pilastres (parfois les consoles).

CARYATIDE

figure féminine sculptée, employée comme soutien vertical.

CHAPITEAU

élément architectonique plus ou moins ornementé, qui surmonte une colonne, un pilastre ou un pilier.

CHARTREUSE

forme de monastère développée par l'Ordre des chartreux et consistant en deux clôtures, une pour l'église, une autre pour le logement des moines.

CINTRE

profil courbe d'un arc, ou échafaudage de charpente provisoire employé pour la construction d'arcs, de voûtes ou de coupoles.

CLAVEAU

bloc de pierre taillé en coin, utilisé dans la construction des linteaux, des voûtes et des corniches.

CLOÎTRE

cour intérieure entourée de galeries, qui est, dans un monastère, l'un des lieux de la vie communautaire.

COLONNE CORINTHIENNE

semblable à la colonne inonique, mais avec un chapiteau orné de feuilles d'acanthe.

COLONNE DORIQUE

colonne sans base, avec un fût cannelé à arêtes vives et un chapiteau composé d'éléments géométriques simples.

COLONNE IONIQUE

colonne sur base, avec un fût à cannelures parallèles et un chapiteau orné de volutes latérales.

COMPOSITE (ORDRE)

combinaison des ordres ionique et corinthien.

CONTRE-FAÇADE

revers de la façade d'une église, tourné vers le chœur.

CONTREFORT

élément architectonique disposé en renfort d'une structure murale de piédroit, pour contribuer les poussées horizontales des voûtes.

CORBEAU

structure saillante constitué d'un petit arc posant sur une console .

CORNICHE

élément horizontal en saillie par rapport à un mur.

COUPOLE

structure architecturale engendrée par la rotation d'un arc autour d'un axe vertical.

CROISÉE

croisement entre la nef et le transept d'une église.

CROIX GRECQUE

croix à branches égales

CROIX LATINE

croix formée de deux branches inégales, la plus petite étant située aux trois-quarts de la plus grande.

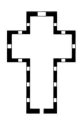

CRYPTOPORTIQUE

portique partiellement enterré.

ENTABLEMENT

structure de soutien horizontale qui se décompose en trois éléments, de bas en haut architrave, frise et corniche.

ENTRECOLONNEMENT

distance entre deux colonnes dont le diamètre sert d'unité de mesure.

EXÈDRE

hémicycle avec un portique ou une colonnade.

EXTRADOS

surface extérieure et convexe d'un arc ou d'un claveau.

FAÎTE

sommet d'un édifice, partie terminale d'un organisme architectural.

FENÊTRE BILOBÉE

fenêtre constituée d'une baie divisée en deux parties égales par un élément vertical.

FRISE

élément architectonique situé au-dessus de l'architrave et portant une ornementation sculptée à déroulement horizontal.

FRONTON

triangle vertical déterminé par un entablement horizontal et les rampants d'un toit à double pente.

GÉMINÉ

se dit d'un élément architectonique couplé à un autre de même nature.

INTRADOS

surface intérieure et concave d'un arc ou d'un claveau.

LANTERNE

couronnement d'une coupole, habituellement sous la forme d'un tempietto circulaire.

LÉSÈNE

pilastre de soutien à profil plat, légèrement en saillie d'un mur.

LOGGIA

galerie ouverte sur les côtés.

LUNETTE

surface en demi-cercle, parfois décorée, au-dessus de la percée rectangulaire d'une ouverture.

MAUSOLÉE

tombeau monumental.

MODÉNATURE

moulure de raccord ou de protection des éléments architectoniques, dont le galbe et la proportion déterminent les jeux d'ombre et de lumière.

NEF

structure d'une église dans le sens de la longueur, au moyen d'alignements de colonnes ou de pilastres.

NERVURE

moulure formant saillie sur la croisée d'ogives d'une voûte.

OCULUS

petite ouverture de forme circulaire.

ORDRE

ensemble de normes et de principes de composition régissant les éléments individuels d'une structure architecturale.

PAVILLON

kiosque en maçonnerie ou en fer.

PENDENTIF

triangle sphérique de maçonnerie (de pierre ou de brique), raccordant directement la base circulaire d'une coupole au plan carré de ses murs de soutien (à la différence du trompillon).

PÉRISTYLE

portique pourtournant à colonnade, entourant un édifice ou une cour intérieure .

PILASTRE

pilier engagé à fonction décorative, en saillie sur une façade.

PORCHE

passage du portail d'entrée à la cour intérieure.

PORTAIL

porte monumentale ou de dimensions supérieures à la moyennne.

PORTÉE

ouverture d'un arc ou d'une porte monumentale.

PORTIQUE

partie d'un édifice ouverte sur un des côtés, avec une couverture soutenue par des colonnes ou des piliers.

PRESBYTERIUM

partie d'un sanctuaire réservée au clergé et située derrière l'autel, dans l'abside.

PRONAOS

atrium à portique, en saillie sur une façade.

ROSACE

grande verrière circulaire généralement dotée d'un remplage de pierre et très souvent de vitraux.

SACRISTIE

local contigu à l'église, en communication avec le presbyuterium. Elle se transforme souvent, à la Renaissance, en une pièce d'une grande beauté décorée avec raffinement.

SERLIENNE

percée à triple baie, dont la plus haute (au centre) est couverte d'un arc en plein cintre, les deux autres d'un linteau à hauteur de l'imposte.

SUBSTRUCTION

structure architectonique, partiellement ou totalement souterraine, destinée à former le plan de pose d'une construction dans le cas d'un terrain en pente.

TAMBOUR

structure cylindrique ou polygonale de raccord, sur laquelle se dresse une coupole.

TÉLAMON

figure masculine sculptée, employée comme soutien vertical.

TRAVÉE

espace compris entre deux éléments de soutien successifs.

TYMPAN

surface triangulaire (ou arrondie) à l'intérieur d'un fronton. Il peut revêtir diverses formes continue, brisé, etc.

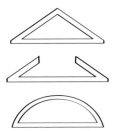

TRANSEPT

corps de fabrique perpendiculaire à la nef, dans une église, qui donne au plan la forme d'une croix latine.

TROMPE ou TROMPILLON

membre architectonique utilisé dans la construction des coupoles, pour passer du plan carré au plan octogonal, par un jeu de voûte et d'arc diagonal en encorbellement.

VESTIBULE

espace clos à l'entrée de la domus romaine, il devient à l'époque romaine un lieu ouvert devant un portique, un porche ou une antichambre.

VIVIER

bassin plus ou moins ornemental, avec des poissons.

VOLUTE

membre d'architecture enroulé en spirale et formé de plusieurs circonvolutions. Peut désigner aussi le grand élément en S raccordant la partie supérieure d'une façade d'église à sa partie inférieure, plus large.

VOUSSURE

partie intérieure d'un arc (rouleau).

VOÛTE

couverture maçonnée à l'aide de voussoirs en pierre ou en brique, et qui exploite sur le principe de l'arc. Elle peut prendre diverses formes : en berceau, à croisée d'arêtes, en arc de cloître, domicile, etc.

Glossar

AKANTHUS

distelartige Pflanze mit gezackten Blättern, wird für die Verzierung korinthischer Kapitelle verwendet.

AKROTERION

Verzierung zur Bekrönung des Giebelfirstes und an den Giebelecken.

ANDRON (Eingangshalle)

Durchgang vom Eingangsbereich zum Innenhof.

APSIS

halbkreisförmiger Raumteil am Ende einer Basilika, überdeckt von einer Halbkuppel.

ARCHITRAV

tragendes, horizontales architektonisches Element, das auf Pfeilern oder Säulen ruht.

ARCHIVOLTE

geschmückter Rund- oder Spitzbogen.

ATRIUM

rechteckige Säulengalerie im Eingangbereich einer Kirche oder einer Villa.

BALUSTRADE

Brüstung aus kleinen Säulen und Pfeilern, auf denen ein Querbalken liegt.

BOGENRÜCKEN

konvexe Außenseite eines Bogens.

CHORRAUM

für den Klerus bestimmter Teil einer Basilika, liegt am Ende des Mittelschiffs und endet in der Apsis.

DORISCHE SÄULE

ohne Basis, der Schaft ist mit Vertiefungen versehen, das Kapitell ist aus einfachen geometrischen Elementen aufgebaut.

EXEDRA

halbrunder Bogen- oder Säulengang.

FENSTERROSE

großes, kreisrundes Fenster mit Maßwerkfüllung aus architektonischen oder dekorativen Elementen.

FISCHTEICH

Zierteich mit Fischen.

FORNIX

Öffnung eines Bogens oder eines Tors.

FRIES

architektonisches Element über dem Architrav, besteht aus horizontalen plastischen Bauteilen.

GEBÄLK

Komplex aus horizontalen Elementen des Triliths, bestehend aus Architrav, Fries und Sims.

GEKUPPELT

Begriff, der angibt, dass ein architektonisches Element zweimal in exakt der gleichen Form vorkommt.

GEKUPPELTES FENSTER

Fenster, das aus zwei Fensteröffnungen besteht, die durch einen Mittelpfosten verbunden sind.

GESIMS
Verzierung mithilfe von horizontalen und vertikalen Leisten.

GEWÖLBE
gebogene Decke, basiert auf dem Prinzip des Bogens. Kann verschiedene Formen aufweisen: Tonnengewölbe, Kreuzgratgewölbe, Kreuzrippengewölbe oder Klostergewölbe.

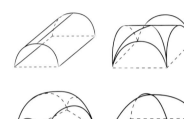

GIEBEL
die oberste Fläche eines Gebäudes, der abschließende Teil einer architektonischen Struktur.

GIEBELFELD
Dreieck aus einem Gebälk und zwei Dachschrägen.

GRIECHISCHES KREUZ
Kreuz, dessen Arme gleichlang sind.

INNERE WÖLBUNG
gebogene Innenseite eines Bogens.

INTERKOLUMNIUM
Abstand zwischen zwei Säulen, deren Durchmesser als Maßeinheit verwendet wird.

IONISCHE SÄULE
mit Basis, der Schaft ist mit Vertiefungen versehen, das Kapitell hat seitliche Voluten.

JOCH
Abstand zwischen zwei aufeinanderfolgenden tragenden Elementen.

KANNELIERUNG
senkrechte Furchen, manchmal wellenförmig, am Schaft von Säulen, Pfeilern oder Konsolen.

KAPITELL
Element eines Trilithen, das die Säule bekrönt.

KARTAUSE
Form eines Klosterbaus, der auf die Kartäuser zurückgeht; besteht aus zwei Kreuzgängen, einer Kirche und den Einsiedeleien der Mönche.

KARYATIDE
Skulptur einer weiblichen Figur mit tragender Funktion.

KASSETTE
vertieftes Element einer flachen oder gewölbten Oberfläche, kann sowohl ein strukturelles Element als auch ein reines Zierelement sein.

KIRCHENSCHIFF
Längsraum einer Kirche, der von Säulen oder Pfeilern flankiert wird.

KOMPOSITE SÄULE
zusammengesetzt aus ionischen und korinthischen Elementen.

KORINTHISCHE SÄULE
ähnelt der ionischen Säule, Kapitell mit Akanthusblättern und Voluten.

KRAGBOGEN
freitragende Struktur aus einem kleinen Bogen, der auf Kragsteinen ruht.

KREUZGANG
Säulengalerie um einen Innenhof, gemeinschaftlicher Aufenthaltsraum eines Klosters.

KRYPTOPORTIKUS
teilweise unterirdisch gelegener Gewölbegang.

KUPPEL
architektonische Struktur mit einem Bogen, der um eine vertikale Achse verläuft.

LAIBUNG
Unterseite des Bogens, Innenseite des Bogens.

LATEINISCHES KREUZ
ein Kreuz aus zwei unterschiedlich langen Balken, von denen der kürzere Dreiviertel von der Länge des längeren beträgt.

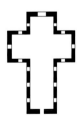

LATERNE
oberster Teil der Kuppel, meist in Form eines kleinen, runden Tempels.

LISENE
eine hervortretende vertikale Verstärkung der Wand mit dekorativer Funktion.

LOGGIA
offene Säulenhalle, meist mit gewölbtem Dach, innerhalb eines Gebäudes oder vor einem Gebäude.

LUNETTE
halkreisförmiges Wandfeld, häufig mit Schmuck versehen, über einer rechteckigen Öffnung.

MAUSOLEUM
monumentales Grabmal.

OCULUS
runde Öffnung.

ORDNUNG
ein System von kompositorischen Regeln und Prinzpien bezüglich einzelner Elemente in einem architektonischen Ganzen.

PENDENTIF
dreieckiges Bauelement, das den Übergang zwischen dem kreisförmigen Grundriss einer Kuppel und dem quadratischen Grundriss ihrer Unterlage führt,

PERISTYL
Säulenhallen, die ein Gebäude oder einen Hof umgeben.

PILASTER
tragender Pfeiler mit flachem Profil, der etwas aus der Wand herausragt.

PORTAL
Eingang von monumentaler oder überdurchschnittlicher Größe.

PORTIKUS
Teil eines Gebäudes, der auf einer seiner Längsseiten offen ist und dessen Dach von Säulen getragen wird.

QUADERSTEIN

quaderförmiger/behauener Steinblock.

QUERSCHIFF

rechtwinklig zum Langhaus verlaufend,
bildet im Grundriss ein lateinisches Kreuz.

RIPPE

bogenförmiges Bauteil, das ein Gewölbe
trägt.

RUNDBOGEN

einfachste Ausführung eines Bogens, besteht
aus einem Halbrund.

RUSTIKA

Mauerwerk aus Steinquadern, deren
Stirnseite nur grob behauen ist und die sich
zum Rand hin mit breiten konkaven Fugen
verjüngen.

SAKRISTEI

Nebenraum einer Kirche, grenzt an den
Chorraum. In der Renaissance handelte
es sich häufig um einen wunderschön
gestalteten Raum.

SALETTL

Gartenhaus aus Stein oder Metall.

SCHALUNG

gebogene Form oder Holzstruktur, mit der
man Bögen, Gewölbe und Kuppeln herstellt.

SERLIANA

dreiteilige Öffnung, über dem Mittelteil
befindet sich ein Bogen, die beiden
Seitenteile weisen ein Gebälk auf.

SIMS

horizontales Element, das aus einer Wand
hervorragt.

SPITZBOGEN

aus zwei Kreisen konstruiert, die an der
Spitze zusammentreffen.

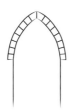

STREBEWERK

architektonisches Element, dient dazu, den
Gewölbeschub und die Windlast aus dem
Mittelschiff einer Basilka und dem Hochchor
abzuleiten.

TAMBOUR

rundes oder vieleckiges Verbindungsstück,
das die Kuppel trägt.

TELAMON

Skulptur einer männlichen Figur mit
tragender Funktion.

TRILITH

Strukturelles System, bestehend aus einem
horizontalen Element, dessen Last auf zwei
vertikale Elemente verteilt wird.

TYMPANON

dreieckiger Bereich an der Basis. Kann
verschiedene Formen aufweisen:
durchgehend, gebrochen, gebogen.

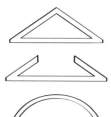

UNTERBAU

zum Teil oder vollständig unteriridische
Struktur, die in einer Schräge das Fundament
für ein Gebäude bildet.

VESTIBÜL

umschlossener Raum vor einer römischen
Wohnung; in der Renaissance ein offener
Raum vor einem Säulengang, einer Halle
oder einem Vorzimmer.

VIERUNG

das Zusammentreffen des Haupt- und
Querschiffs einer Kirche.

VOLUTE

ein schneckenförmiges Ornament, auch
die großen S-förmigen Elemente, die den
schmalen Obergaden mit dem breiten
unteren Fassadenstück einer Kirche
verbinden.

VORHALLE

Säulenhalle, die aus der Fassade hervorragt.

WERKSTEIN

bearbeiteter Steinblock, dient als Zierelement
oder Teil eines Mauerwerks.

WESTWAND

Innenwand gegenüber der Apsis.

ZIERLEISTE

ein gestalteter Streifen mit Zierfunktion, wird
verwendet, um architektonische Elemente.zu
verbinden oder zu schützen

Glosario

ÁBSIDE

parte semicircular de la iglesia situada en la
cabecera por una semicúpula.

ACANALADURA

surcos verticales rectilíneos, a veces
ondulados, sobre los fustes de columnas o
pilastras, en los parástades o en las ménsulas.

ACANTO

tipo de cardo de hoja irregular con el que se
decora el capitel corintio.

ACROTERA

decoración dispuesta en el vértice o sobre las
esquinas de un frontón.

AJIMEZ

ventana dividida en dos partes iguales
mediante un elemento vertical.

ARQUITRABE

elemento arquitectónico portante que
apoya de forma horizontal sobre pilastras o
columnas.

ARQUIVOLTA

moldura decorada que sigue la curva del
arco.

ARCO DE MEDIO PUNTO

tipo de arco más simple con forma de
semicírculo.

ARCO OJIVAL

formado por dos tramos de arco que forman una cúspide.

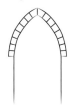

ATLANTE (telamón)

estatua masculina empleada como soporte vertical.

ATRIO

porticado rectangular situado al principio de la iglesia o de la villa.

BALAUSTRADA

parapeto formado por columnas y pilastras pequeñas unidas por una moldura superior.

BÓVEDA DE CAÑÓN (arco)

abertura de un arco o una puerta monumental.

BÓVEDA

cubierta curva resultante de la forma del arco. Existen diferentes tipos: de cañón, de crucería, baída y esquifada.

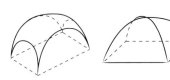

CAPITEL

elemento del sistema de estructuras de trilito que se dispone en el extremo superior de la columna.

CARTELA

estructura saliente compuesta por un arco pequeño que se apoya sobre ménsulas.

CARIÁTIDE

estatua femenina empleada como soporte vertical.

CASETÓN

elemento hueco sobre una superficie plana o abovedada. Puede servir como elemento estructural o tener una función simplemente decorativa.

CERCHA

estructura curva o de madera empleada para la construcción de arcos, bóvedas y cúpulas.

CARTUJA

tipo de monasterio creado por los Certosinos compuesto por dos claustros, la iglesia y las habitaciones individuales de los monjes.

CLAUSTRO

patio porticado que en el monasterio representa el espacio de la vida comunitaria.

COLUMNA DÓRICA

sin basa, con fuste acanalado y capitel compuesto por elementos geométricos simples.

COLUMNA JÓNICA

con basa, fuste acanalado y capitel con volutas laterales.

COLUMNA CORINTIA

parecida a la columna jónica, con capitel con hojas de acanto y volutas en las esquinas.

COMPUESTO

combinación de los órdenes jónico y corintio.

CONTRAFUERTE

elemento de arquitectura usado para reforzar una estructura con el fin de contrarrestar los empujes horizontales de las bóvedas.

CONTRAFACHADA

pared interna en frente del ábside.

CORNISA

elemento horizontal saliente en relación con la pared.

CRIPTOPÓRTICO

pórtico semisubterráneo.

CRUZ GRIEGA

cruz con brazos de igual medida.

CRUZ LATINA

cruz formada por dos segmentos diferentes donde el segmento menor está a una proporción de tres cuartos respecto al mayor.

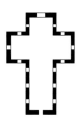

CRUCERÍA

cruce entre la nave de una iglesia y el transepto.

CÚPULA

elemento arquitectónico originado por la rotación de un arco alrededor de un eje vertical.

DINTEL

parte inferior e interior del arco.

ENTABLAMENTO

conjunto de elementos horizontales del trilito que se divide en tres secciones: arquitrabe, friso y cornisa.

ESTANQUE

bañera decorativa con peces.

EXEDRA

hemiciclo con columnata o porticado.

FASTIGIO

parte más alta de un edificio, parte final de un elemento de arquitectura.

FRISO

elemento de arquitectura situado sobre el arquitrabe caracterizado por esculturas sobre una franja horizontal.

FRONTÓN

triángulo formado por un entablamento y cornisas del techo de doble capa.

GAZEBO

quiosco de piedra o de hierro.

INTERCOLUMNIO

espacio entre dos columnas cuyo diámetro se usa como unidad de medida.

INTRADÓS

superficie interior y cóncava del arco.

LINTERNA

parte superior de la cúpula normalmente con forma de templete circular.

LESENA

pilar o columna decorativa adosada a una pared.

LOGIA

pórtico con laterales abiertos, normalmente cubierto por una bóveda, ubicado en el interior o en la parte delantera del edificio.

LUNETA

superficie semicircular, a veces decorada, encima del vano rectangular de una abertura.

MAUSOLEO

tumba monumental.

MOLDURA

elemento decorativo saliente que une o protege los elementos arquitectónicos.

MUESTRA

decoración de un compartimento mediante cornisas horizontales y verticales.

NAVE

espacio longitudinal de la iglesia situado entre filas de columnas o pilastras.

NERVADURA

nervios de una bóveda.

ÓCULO

pequeña abertura circular.

ORDEN

sistema arquitectónico de normas y principios de composición de cada elemento.

PARAMENTO

revestimiento de la fachada realizado con sillares salientes y juntas incrustadas en las aristas.

PARÁSTADE

pilastra de soporte de perfil plano ligeramente saliente respecto a la pared.

PAREADO

término que hace referencia a un elemento arquitectónico acoplado con otro igual.

PERISTILO

pórtico de columnas que rodea un edificio o un patio.

PINÁCULO

unión en forma de triángulo esférico entre una cúpula y su base cuadrada.

PORCHE

paso desde el portal de entrada al patio.

PORTAL

puerta de un tamaño mucho mayor de lo normal.

PÓRTICO

espacio cubierto de un edificio y con un lateral abierto sostenido por columnas.

PRESBITERIO

parte de la basílica reservada al clero que une la nave central con el ábside.

PRONAO

atrio con columnas delante de la fachada.

ROSETÓN

ventana circular calada con elementos arquitectónicos o decorativos.

SACRISTÍA

cuarto adyacente a la iglesia comunicado con el presbiterio. A menudo en el Renacimiento se convirtió en un local refinado de gran belleza.

SERLIANA

apertura triple cuya parte central tiene forma de arco y las otras dos con entablamento.

SILLAR

bloque de piedra cuadrado.

SILLAR ALMOHADILLADO

piedra labrada que se emplea como elemento de decoración o que forma parte de la misma construcción.

SUBSTRUCCIÓN

estructura parcial o completamente subterránea que forma el plano de apoyo de una construcción en los casos con el terreno sobre una pendiente.

TAMBOR

estructura cilíndrica o poligonal sobre la base de una cúpula a modo de prolongación.

TÍMPANO

superficie triangular dentro del frontón. Puede ser de diferentes tipos: continua, partido o circular.

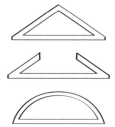

TRILITO

estructura caracterizada por un elemento horizontal que descarga la fuerza sobre dos elementos verticales.

TRANSEPTO

nave transversal a la nave central gracias a la cual la planta tiene forma de cruz latina.

TRASDÓS

superficie externa y convexa del arco.

VANO

espacio comprendido entre dos elementos de soporte sucesivos.

VESTÍBULO

espacio cercado delante de las casas romanas. En el Renacimiento se convirtió en un espacio abierto delante del pórtico, entrada o antesala.

VOLUTA

decoración con forma de espiral. También representa el gran elemento con forma de S que une la parte superior más estrecha de una iglesia a la inferior de la fachada.

Glossario

ABSIDE
parte terminale della basilica semicilindrica coperta da una semicupola.

ACANTO
specie di cardo con foglie frastagliate, che trovano impiego nella decorazione del capitello corinzio.

ACROTERIO
decorazione al vertice e agli angoli del frontone.

ANDRONE
passaggio dal portale d'ingresso al cortile.

ARCHITRAVE
elemento architettonico portante appoggiato orizzontalmente su pilastri o colonne.

ARCHIVOLTO
fascia decorata che segue la curva dell'arco.

ARCO A TUTTO SESTO
tipologia di arco più semplice, costituito da metà circonferenza.

ARCO ACUTO
costituito da due archi di cerchio che si incontrano a cuspide.

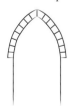

ATRIO
porticato rettangolare anteposto alla chiesa e talvolta alla villa.

BALAUSTRATA
parapetto formato da colonnine e pilastrini uniti da una fascia superiore.

BECCATELLO
struttura a sbalzo costituita da un piccolo arco poggiante su mensole.

BIFORA
finestra costituita da un vano diviso in due parti uguali da un elemento verticale.

BINATO
termine riferito a un elemento architettonico accoppiato a un altro uguale.

BOZZA
blocco squadrato di pietra.

BUGNATO
rivestimento di facciata realizzato con conci sporgenti e giunti incavati sugli spigoli.

CAMPATA
spazio compreso fra due successivi elementi di sostegno.

CAPITELLO
elemento del sistema trilitico che conclude la colonna.

CARIATIDE
figura femminile scolpita, impiegata come sostegno verticale.

CASSETTONE
elemento incavato entro una superficie piana o voltata, può coincidere con gli elementi strutturali oppure avere funzione esclusivamente decorativa.

CENTINATURA
sagomatura curva o struttura lignea impiegata per la costruzione di archi, volte, cupole.

CERTOSA
forma di monastero sviluppata dai Certosini, consistente in due chiostri, la chiesa e singole abitazioni dei monaci.

CHIOSTRO
cortile porticato, nel monastero è il luogo della vita comunitaria.

COLONNA DORICA
priva di base, fusto scanalato e capitello costituito da elementi geometrici semplici.

COLONNA IONICA
con base, fusto scanalato e capitello con volute laterali.

COLONNA CORINZIA
simile alla colonna ionica, capitello con foglie di acanto e volute agli angoli.

COMPOSITO
combinazione degli ordini ionico e corinzio.

CONCIO
blocco di pietra lavorato, funge da elemento ornamentale o costitutivo di una muratura.

CONTRAFFORTE
elemento architettonico posto a rinforzo di una struttura per contrastare le spinte orizzontali delle volte.

CONTROFACCIATA
parete interna antistante l'abside.

CORNICE
elemento orizzontale aggettante rispetto alla parete.

COSTOLONE
nervatura di una volta.

CRIPTOPORTICO
portico in parte sotterraneo.

CROCE GRECA
croce con bracci uguali.

CROCE LATINA
croce formata da due segmenti diversi, il segmento minore è circa a tre quarti di quello maggiore.

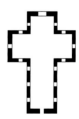

CROCIERA
incrocio tra la navata di una chiesa e il transetto.

401

CUPOLA

struttura architettonica derivante dalla rotazione di un arco intorno ad un asse verticale.

ESEDRA

emiciclo colonnato o porticato.

ESTRADOSSO

superficie esterna e convessa dell'arco.

FASTIGIO

sommità di un edificio, parte terminale di un organismo architettonico.

FORNICE

apertura di un arco o di una porta monumentale.

FREGIO

elemento architettonico situato sopra l'architrave, indica una composizione scultorea con andamento orizzontale.

FRONTONE

triangolo formato da una trabeazione e dagli spioventi del tetto a doppia falda.

GAZEBO

chiosco in muratura o in ferro.

GHIERA

sottarco, parte interna dell'arco.

INTERCOLUMNIO

distanza fra due colonne, il cui diametro è adoperato come unità di misura.

INTRADOSSO

superficie interna e concava dell'arco.

LANTERNA

parte superiore della cupola, solitamente in forma di tempietto circolare.

LESENA

semipilastro o semicolonna con funzione decorativa, sporgente da una facciata.

LOGGIA

portico aperto sui lati, solitamente coperto a volta, situato all'interno o antistante l'edificio.

LUNETTA

superficie semicircolare, talvolta decorata, al di sopra del vano rettangolare di un'apertura.

MAUSOLEO

tomba monumentale.

MODANATURA

membratura sagomata con funzione ornamentale, di raccordo o protezione di elementi architettonici.

MOSTRA

decorazione di un vano mediante cornici orizzontali e verticali.

NAVATA

ripartizione della chiesa in senso longitudinale, tramite file di colonne o pilastri.

OCULO

piccola apertura di forma circolare.

ORDINE

complesso di norme e principi compositivi riguardanti i singoli elementi di un insieme architettonico.

PARASTA

pilastro di sostegno a profilo piatto leggermente sporgente alla parete.

PENNACCHIO

raccordo a forma di triangolo sferico tra una cupola e la sua base quadrata.

PERISTILIO

portico colonnato che avvolge un edificio o un cortile.

PESCHIERA

vasca ornamentale con pesci.

PORTALE

porta di monumentalità o dimensioni maggiori del normale.

PORTICO

parte di edificio aperta su uno dei lati lunghi con copertura sorretta da colonne.

PRESBITERIO

parte della basilica riservata al clero, situato sul fondo della navata centrale e concluso dall'abside.

PRONAO

atrio porticato sporgente dal filo di facciata.

ROSONE

finestrone circolare dalla ricca trama interna a elementi architettonici o decorativi.

SACRESTIA

locale attiguo alla chiesa, in comunicazione con il presbiterio. Spesso nel Rinascimento si trasformò in locale di grande bellezza e raffinatezza.

SCANALATURA

incavo rettilineo, talvolta ondulato, nei fusti di colonne e pilastri, nelle paraste, nelle mensole.

SERLIANA

apertura a tre luci di cui la centrale ad arco e le due laterali con trabeazione.

SOSTRUZIONE

struttura parzialmente o completamente sotterranea destinata a formare il piano di posa di una costruzione nel caso di terreno in pendenza.

TAMBURO

struttura cilindrica o poligonale di raccordo sulla quale si imposta la cupola.

TELAMONE

figura maschile scolpita, impiegata come sostegno verticale.

TIMPANO

superficie triangolare compresa entro il frontone. Può assumere diverse forme: continuo, spezzato, curvo.

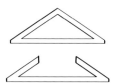

TRABEAZIONE

complesso degli elementi orizzontali del trilite, si articola in architrave, fregio e cornice.

TRILITE

sistema strutturale articolato in un elemento orizzontale che scarica gli sforzi su due elementi verticali.

TRANSETTO

corpo di fabbrica perpendicolare alla navata centrale, mediante il quale la pianta assume la forma di una croce latina.

VESTIBOLO

spianata recintata dinanzi alla domus romana, nel Rinascimento diventa un luogo aperto davanti al portico, androne o anticamera.

VOLTA

copertura curva che sfrutta il principio dell'arco. Può assumere diverse forme: a botte, a crociera, a vela, a padiglione.

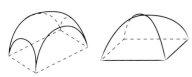

VOLUTA

forma ornamentale avvolta a spirale, indica anche il grande elemento a S che raccorda la parte superiore più stretta e quella inferiore della facciata di una chiesa.

Glossário

ABÓBADA

cobertura curva que utiliza o princípio do arco. Pose assumir diversas formas: de berço, de aresta, de vela, de claustro, etc.

ABSIDE

parede semicircular que fecha a nave principal da igreja, com remate superior em semi-cúpula.

ACANTO

espécie de cardo de folhas recortadas, muito utilizada na decoração do capitel coríntio.

ACROTÉRIO

decoração nos vértices central e laterais do frontão.

ALICERCE

estrutura, parcial ou totalmente subterrânea, destinada a formar o plano de fundação de uma construção nos casos de terrenos com declive.

ARCO AGUDO

formado por dois arcos circulares que se cruzam formando uma cúspide.

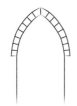

ARCO DE OGIVA

→ *Arco agudo*

ARCO DE VOLTA PERFEITA

o tipo mais simples de arco, formado por um semicírculo.

ARQUITRAVE

elemento arquitectónico portante, apoiado horizontalmente em pilares ou colunas.

ARQUIVOLTA

faixa decorada que acompanha a curva do arco.

ATLANTE

figura masculina esculpida, utilizada como sustentação vertical.

ÁTRIO

pórtico rectangular que antecede as igrejas e, por vezes, as villa.

BALAUSTRADA

parapeito formado por pequenas colunas ou pilares unidos por uma faixa superior.

BOSSAGEM

revestimento de fachada feito com pedras de cunha salientes e com juntas côncavas nos cantos.

CAIXOTÃO

elemento estriado numa superfície plana ou abobadada, que pode coincidir com os elementos estruturais ou ter função exclusivamente decorativa.

CAMBOTA

contorno curvo ou estrutura de madeira utilizada para a construção de arcos, abóbadas e cúpulas.

CAPITEL

elemento do sistema trílito que termina a coluna.

CARIÁTIDE

figura feminina esculpida, utilizada como sustentação vertical.

CARTUXA

forma de mosteiro desenvolvida pela ordem dos Cartuxos, que consiste em dois claustros, a igreja e as residências particulares dos monges.

CLAUSTRO

pátrio interior que, nos mosteiros, é o palco da vida comunitária.

COLUNA CORÍNTIA

semelhante à coluna jónica, capitel com folhas de acanto e volutas menores nos cantos.

COLUNA DÓRICA

desprovida de base, com fuste canelado e capitel constituído por elementos geométricos simples.

COLUNA JÓNICA
com base, fuste canelado e capitel com volutas laterais.

CONTRA-FACHADA
parede interior em frente da abside.

CONTRAFORTE
elemento arquitectónico que reforça uma estrutura para sustentar a pressão horizontal das abóbadas.

CORETO
pequeno pavilhão em alvenaria ou ferro.

CORNIJA
elemento horizontal que sobressai da parede.

CRIPTOPÓRTICO
galeria abobadada semi-subterrânea.

CRUZ CRISTÃ
→ *Cruz latina*

CRUZ GREGA
cruz com braços do mesmo tamanho.

CRUZ LATINA
cruz formada por dois segmentos, o menor com um comprimento de cerca de três quartos do maior.

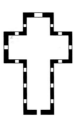

CRUZEIRO
numa igreja, o espaço de intersecção da nave central com o transepto.

CÚPULA
estrutura arquitectónica resultante da rotação de um arco em torno de um eixo vertical.

ENTABLAMENTO
conjunto dos elementos horizontais do trílito, constituído por arquitrave, friso e cornija.

ESTRIA
entalhe rectilíneo, por vezes ondulado, nos fustes das colunas e pilares, nas pilastras e nas mísulas.

ÊXEDRA
hemiciclo de colunas ou pórtico.

EXPOSIÇÃO
decoração de um vão com cornijas horizontais e verticais.

EXTRADORSO
superfície exterior e convexa do arco.

FORNICE
abertura de um arco ou porta monumental.

FRISO
elemento arquitectónico situado acima da arquitrave, que indica uma composição decorativa com orientação horizontal.

FRONTÃO
triângulo formado por uma cimalha e duas empenas de telhado a duas águas.

GALERIA
→ *Loggia*

GEMINADO
termo que se refere a dois elementos arquitectónicos iguais acoplados.

HALL DE ENTRADA
passagem entre o pórtico de entrada e o pátio interior.

INTERCOLÚNIO
espaço entro duas colunas, cujo diâmetro é utilizado como unidade de medida.

INTRADORSO
superfície interior e côncava do arco.

JANELA MAINELADA
janela constituída por um vão dividido em duas partes iguais por um elemento vertical.

LANTERNA
parte superior da cúpula, geralmente em forma de pequeno templo circular.

LESENA
semi-pilar ou semi-coluna com funções decorativas, saliente de uma fachada.

LOGGIA
pórtico aberto de ambos os lados, geralmente coberto, situado no interior ou na parte anterior do edifício.

LUNETA
superfície semi-circular, por vezes decorada, na parte superior do vão rectangular de uma abertura.

MATACÃES
estruturas em relevo, formadas por um pequeno arco apoiado em mísulas.

MAUSOLÉU
Jazigo monumental.

MODINATURA
conjunto de molduras com funções ornamentais, de ligação ou de remate de elementos arquitectónicos.

NAVE
divisão longitudinal da igreja através de fileiras de colunas ou pilares.

NERVURA
segmento de arco numa abóbada.

ÓCULO
pequena abertura de forma circular.

ORDEM
conjunto de designações e princípios constitutivos respeitantes aos elementos específicos de um sistema arquitectónico.

ORDEM COMPÓSITA
combinação das ordens jónica e coríntia.

PEDRA DE ALVENARIA
bloco de pedra trabalhado, com função de elemento decorativo ou como parte de um trabalho de alvenaria.

PENACHO
ligação triangular esférica de uma cúpula com a sua base quadrangular.

PERISTILO
pórtico com colunas que envolve um edifício ou um pátio interior.

PILASTRA
pilar de suporte de perfil plano, ligeiramente saliente da parede.

PINÁCULO
ponto mais alto de um edifício, parte terminal de um organismo arquitectónico.

PORTAL
porta monumental ou de dimensões superiores às normais.

PÓRTICO
parte de um edifício, aberta de um dos lados (em comprimento) com uma cobertura apoiada em colunas.

PRESBITÉRIO
parte da basílica reservada ao clero, situa-se ao fundo da nave central e termina na abside.

PRONAU
átrio com arcadas, saliente da linha da fachada principal.

ROSÁCEA
grande janela circular, com uma rica tessitura interior de elementos arquitectónicos ou decorativos.

SACRISTIA
local contíguo à igreja, comunicante com o presbitério. No Renascimento, transformou-se frequentemente em local de grande beleza e requinte.

SERLIANA
abertura a três vãos, sendo o central em arco de volta perfeita e os dois laterais com entablamento.

SILHAR
bloco esquadriado de pedra.

TAMBOR
estrutura cilíndrica ou poligonal de ligação, sobre a qual assenta a cúpula.

TÍMPANO
superfície triangular limitada pelos lados do frontão. Pose assumir diversas formas: contínuo, quebrado ou curvo.

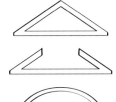

TRAMO
espaço compreendido entre dois elementos de apoio consecutivos.

TRANSEPTO
corpo do edifício, perpendicular à nave central, e pela qual a planta assume a forma de uma cruz latina.

TRÍLITO
sistema estrutural articulado, composto por um elemento horizontal cujo peso é suportado por dois elementos verticais.

VESTÍBULO
átrio fechado defronte às casas romanas, durante o Renascimento torna-se um local aberto fronteiro ao pórtico, hall de entrada ou antessala.

VIVEIRO
tanque decorativo com peixes.

VOLUTA
elemento decorativo espiralado, remete ainda para o grande elemento em S que liga a parte superior mais estreita e a parte inferior da fachada de uma igreja.

Woordenlijst

ACANTHUS
een distelsoort met gekartelde bladeren, die in de decoratie van Corinthische kapitelen verwerkt zit.

ACROTERIUM
versiering aan de top en de hoeken van een fronton.

APSIS
halfrond uiteinde van een basiliek, bedekt met een halfkoepel.

ARCHITRAAF
dragend architectonisch element dat horizontaal op pilaren of zuilen rust.

ARCHIVOLT
versierde strook op de welving van een boog.

ATRIUM
rechthoekige zuilengalerij die zich aan de voorzijde van een kerk of villa bevindt.

BALUSTRADE
muurtje bestaande uit zuiltjes of korte pilaren met een balk erbovenop.

BELIJSTING
horizontaal en verticaal lijstwerk ter decoratie van een vertrek.

BIFORA
raam dat in twee gelijke delen gesplitst wordt door een verticaal element.

BOOGRUG
convexe buitenkant van een boog.

BOSSAGE
gevelbedekking met holtes en uitstulpingen.

BOUWSTEEN
bewerkt blok steen, wordt gebruikt ter decoratie of als onderdeel van metselwerk.

BOZZA
vierkant blok steen.

CANELLURE
verticale, soms golvende, groeven in zuilen, pilasters, lisenen en kraagstenen.

CASSETTE
uitgediept element in een plat of gewelfd vlak, kan van pas komen in een constructie of een puur decoratieve functie hebben.

CERTOSA
kloostertype bedacht door Certosini, bestaande uit twee kloostergangen, een kerkgebouw en aparte onderkomens voor de monniken.

COMPOSIETZUIL
zuil met combinatie van Ionische en Corinthische elementen.

CONTRAFAÇADE
binnenwand voorafgaand aan de apsis.

CORINTHISCHE ZUIL
lijkt op een Ionische zuil, kapiteel bevat rondom acanthusbladeren en voluten.

CRYPTOPORTICUS
deels ondergrondse zuilengang.

DORISCHE ZUIL

zonder voetstuk, met groeven en een kapiteel met eenvoudige geometrische elementen.

EXEDRA

halve cirkelvorm van zuilen.

FORMEEL

gebogen vorm of houten structuur waarmee men bogen, gewelven en koepels maakt.

FORNIX

opening van een boog of monumentale deur.

FRIES

architectonisch element boven op een architraaf, bestaat uit een horizontaal gebeeldhouwde compositie.

FRONTON

driehoek gevormd door een hoofdgestel en twee dakhellingen.

GALERIJ

bouwwerk dat aan een van de lange zijden open is, met een overdekking die ondersteund wordt door zuilen.

GEPAARD

term om aan te geven dat een architectonisch element een tweetal vormt.

GEVELSPITS

hoogste punt van een gebouw, laatste deel van een architectonisch werk.

GEWELF

boogvormige bedekking. Is er in verschillende vormen: ton, kruis, koepel, paviljoen.

GRIEKS KRUIS

kruis met gelijke delen.

HAL

gang tussen toegangsdeur en binnenplaats.

HOOFDGESTEL

geheel van horizontale delen van een triliet, bestaande uit architraaf, fries en kroonlijst.

INTERCOLUMNIUM

afstand tussen twee zuilen, van middelpunt to middelpunt.

INTRADOS

binnenste, gebogen deel van een boog.

IONISCHE ZUIL

met voetstuk, groeven en een kapiteel met voluten aan de zijkant.

KAPITEEL

kopstuk van een zuil bij een trilietstructuur.

KARIATIDE

gebeeldhouwd vrouwenfiguur, gebruikt als verticale ondersteuning.

KLOOSTERGANG

zuilengalerij rond een binnenplaats, gemeenschappelijke ruimte in een klooster.

KOEPEL

architectonische structuur met een boog die rondom een verticale as loopt.

KROONLIJST

horizontaal element dat uitspringt ten opzichte van de muur.

KRUIS

kruising van het schip van een kerk met het transept.

LANTAARN

bovenste deel van een koepel, heeft gewoonlijk de vorm van een rond tempeltje.

LATIJNS KRUIS

kruis met twee ongelijke delen: het kleinste deel is ca. drie kwart van het grootste deel.

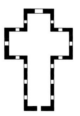

LISEEN

halfzuil met een decoratieve functie, springt uit een gevel.

LOGGIA

galerij die open is aan de zijkanten, meestal bedekt is met een gewelf, en gelegen is in of voor een gebouw.

LUNET

halfcirkelvormig oppervlak, soms versierd, boven een rechthoekige opening.

MAUSOLEUM

monumentale tombe.

MEZEKOUW

onregelmatige constructie bestaande uit een kleine boog over kraagstenen.

OCULUS

kleine, cirkelvormige opening.

ONDERBOUW

deels of geheel ondergrondse structuur, bedoeld als ondergrond voor een gebouw op hellend terrein.

ORDE

geheel aan bouwkundige normen en regels voor de afzonderlijke elementen van een architectonisch bouwwerk.

OVERSPANNING

ruimte tussen twee opeenvolgende steunende elementen.

PENDENTIEF

boldriehoek die de koepel met de vierkante onderbouw verbindt.

PERISTYLIUM

zuilengalerij rond een gebouw of een binnenplaats.

PILASTER

platte steunpilaar die iets uit de muur steekt.

POORT

monumentale deur, van grotere afmetingen dan normaal.

PRIEEL

gemetseld of metalen tuinhuisje.

PRIESTERKOOR

voor de clerus bestemd deel van een basiliek, gelegen aan het eind van het middenschip en afgesloten door de apsis.

PROFIEL

gefreesd lijstwerk met een decoratieve functie, of voor het samenvoegen of afschermen van architectonische elementen.

RIBBEN

geraamte van een gewelf.

RONDBOOG

eenvoudigste boogsoort, halfcirkelvormig.

ROOSVENSTER

cirkelvormig venster, rijkversierd met architectonische of decoratieve elementen..

SACRISTIE

ruimte naast de kerk, staat in verbinding met het priesterkoor. Tijdens de Renaissance was dit vaak een zeer mooi en verfijnd vertrek.

SCHIP

langgerekte ruimte in een kerk met zuilen of pilaren erlangs.

SERLIANA

drie-delige opening: boven het middelste deel loopt een boog; boven de twee delen opzij een hoofdgestel.

SPITSBOOG

bestaat uit twee cirkelbogen die samenkomen aan de top.

STEUNBEER

architectonisch element ter versterking van een structuur, vangt de horizontale druk van gewelven op.

TAMBOER

cirkelvormig of veelhoekig verbindingsstuk waar de koepel op rust.

TELAMON

gebeeldhouwd mannenfiguur, gebruikt als verticale ondersteuning.

TIMPAAN

driehoekig oppervlak in een fronton. Is er in verschillende vormen: doorlopend, onderbroken, gebogen.

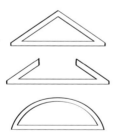

TRANSEPT

ruimte loodrecht op het middenschip, waardoor de plattegrond de vorm van een Latijns kruis krijgt.

TRILIET

structuur bestaande uit twee verticale elementen die een horizontaal element ondersteunen.

VESTIBULE

omsloten ruimte voorafgaand aan een Romeinse woning; tijdens de Renaissance een open ruimte voorafgaand aan een zuilengang, hal of antichambre.

VISVIJVER

siervijver met vissen.

VOLUUT

spiraalvormige versiering, tevens het S-vormige element dat het bovenste, smalste deel van een kerk verbindt met het gevelwerk eronder.

VOORHOF

bezuilde hal die uitsteekt ten opzichte van de gevel.

Photographic credits

Alfio Garozzo: p. 391

Archivio di Stato di Modena: pp. 306–307.

Archivio Magnus: pp. 1, 17, 30–32, 34, 36–39, 45, 54–55, 58–60, 62, 64, 67, 69–71, 74–75, 77, 79, 81, 83, 86–97, 99–105, 107–113, 116, 118, 120–121, 124, 126–141, 143–147, 150–151, 153, 155–161, 169–171, 186–187, 189, 200, 205–206, 212–216, 220–227, 236, 240, 244–245, 248–254, 258, 260–261, 268, 273, 281, 290, 297, 303, 308–309, 313, 328, 332, 339, 341, 346, 349–352, 354–355, 358–359, 363, 366–367, 370, 376

Archivio Storico Civico Biblioteca Trivulziana, Comune di Milano: p. 47

Biblioteca Civica di Trieste: p. 85

Biblioteca Estense Universitaria, Modena: p. 385

Cameraphoto Arte: pp. 56–57, 63, 66, 68, 74, 76, 82

Civica Raccolta delle Stampe Achille Bertarelli, Castello Sforzesco, Milano: p. 311

Civico Museo Storico di Palmanova (UD): pp. 162–163

Comune di Todi, Museo Pinacoteca e Parco Culturale della Città di Todi, Biblioteca Comunale, Archivio Storico: p. 301

Fondazione Casa Buonarroti, Firenze: p. 12

Fondazione Musei Civici Venezia: pp. 61, 84

Guido Baviera: pp. 17, 300

Luciano Pedicini: pp. 380, 384, 386

Marco Ravenna: pp. 168, 262–263

Mario De Biasi: pp. 35, 44

Massimo Listri: pp. 16, 20, 23, 25–27, 29, 40–43, 178–185, 188, 190–199, 201–203, 208–209, 217–219, 234–235, 238, 256–257, 265–267, 270–271, 274–277, 282–285, 302, 305, 314, 316–325, 327, 329–331, 333–338, 387

Musei Civici, Vicenza: p. 14

Museo dell'Opera di Santa Maria del Fiore, Firenze: p. 230

Museo della Basilica di San Petronio, Bologna: p. 170 top

Nicolò Orsi Battaglini: pp. 228–229, 232–233, 269

Paolo Marton: p. 98

Photoservice Electa: pp. 18–19, 21–22, 24, 46, 48–51, 148–149, 164–167, 172–177, 204, 207, 210–211, 242, 255, 272, 278, 280, 286–289, 292–295, 298–299, 310, 312, 315, 326, 340, 342, 344–345, 347–348, 353, 360–362, 364–365, 368–369, 371–375, 377–379, 381–383, 388–390

Pino Guidolotti: pp. 52–53, 72–73, 76–78, 80–81, 106, 114–117, 119, 122–123, 125, 142, 145, 152

Scala Archives: p. 259

Soprintendenza per il Patrimonio Storico, Artistico ed Etnoantropologico di Mantova: p. 28

Soprintendenza Speciale per il Patrimonio Storico, Artistico ed Etnoantropologico e per il Polo Museale della Città di Firenze, Gabinetto Fotografico: pp. 2, 4–5, 8, 10, 237, 241, 246–247, 264, 296, 304, 343, 356–357

Stiftung Museum Kunstpalast Düsseldorf: p. 20

Studio Böhm Venezia: p. 65

Su concessione del Ministero per i Beni e le Attività Culturali – Soprintendenza per i Beni Storici Artistici e etnoantropologici delle Marche: p. 291

Vincenzo Silvestri: p. 243